RETHINKING THE FUTURE

Original contributions from:

Warren Bennis

Stephen Covey

Eli Goldratt

Gary Hamel

Michael Hammer

Charles Handy

Kevin Kelly

Philip Kotler

John Kotter

John Naisbitt

Michael Porter

CK Prahalad

Al Ries

Peter Senge

Lester Thurow

Jack Trout

Edited by Rowan Gibson

RETHINKING THE FUTURE

Rethinking business, principles,
competition, control & complexity,
leadership, markets and the world

NICHOLAS BREALEY
PUBLISHING

LONDON

First published in the UK and the USA by
Nicholas Brealey Publishing Limited in 1997

36 John Street
London
WC1N 2AT, UK
Tel: +44 (0)171 430 0224
Fax: +44 (0)171 404 8311

18900 Olive Avenue
Sonoma
California 95476, USA
Tel: (707) 939 7570
Fax: (707) 938 3515

Reprinted 1997 (with corrections)

ISBN 1-85788-103-6

Library of Congress Cataloging-in-Publication Data
Gibson, Rowan.
    Rethinking the future : rethinking business, principles, competition,
control, leadership, markets and the world / Rowan Gibson.
        p.   cm.
    Includes index.
    ISBN 1-85788-103-6
    1. Organizational change.   2. Organizational effectiveness.
3. Strategic planning.   4. Competition.   I. Title.
HD58.8.G53   1997
658.4—dc20   96-25422
                                                                    CIP

British Library Cataloguing in Publication Data
A catalogue record for this book is available from the British Library.

Printed in Great Britain by Biddles Ltd.

To my wife, Anke

*and to all the great minds
who made this book possible*

CONTENTS

FOREWORD

NOT SINCE THE dawn of the Industrial Revolution have managers had more to learn (and unlearn) about the art of business leadership. And seldom have they been offered so much diverse and confusing advice. The reason for the current upheaval in management thinking is the arrival on the world scene of a revolutionary new 'system for creating wealth'. Historians can slice the past into countless slivers. But in terms of transformational change, there have been only a few true turning points in history, each associated with the emergence of a different system for wealth creation.

The invention of agriculture provided the human race with a new way to convert the earth's resources into wealth, and almost everywhere launched a 'First Wave' of change in civilization that gave rise to peasant-centered economies and eventually supplanted hunting and foraging as the primary means of human subsistence.

Similarly, the Industrial Revolution triggered a 'Second Wave' of change that gave us a factory-based system for wealth creation. In turn, this led to mass production, the drive for larger and larger markets, and the need for bigger, ever more bureaucratic business organizations. Until very recently, most of what was taught in management texts and in schools of business reflected 'Second Wave' thinking.

Based on assumptions of linearity and equilibrium, and heavily quantified, the dominant management paradigm paralleled the mechanistic assumptions of western economics, which, in turn, attempted to parallel Newtonian physics. This multileveled parallelism—the belief that management 'science' fitted perfectly with economic 'science' and that both were compatible with what was known about physics—made the industrial management paradigm enormously persuasive.

Indeed, all three of these disciplinary 'layers' formed parts of an even larger set of epistemological and philosophical ideas which has elsewhere been described as 'indust-reality'—reality as perceived through the eyes of people reared in an industrial culture. In short, the dominant business paradigm of the Second Wave era was part of a much larger architecture of thought.

In 1970, we publicly attacked the prevailing paradigm for the first time in our book *Future Shock*, and suggested that businesses were going to restructure themselves repeatedly and move 'beyond bureaucracy'; that they would have to reduce hierarchy and take on the character of what we termed 'ad-hocracy'. At the time, all this sounded sensationalist to many readers. We had a similar experience in 1972, when we delivered a consulting report to AT&T, then the world's largest privately held corporation, saying that it would have to break itself up. For years, that report was literally kept hidden from the very managers who needed to prepare the firm for the break-up which, in fact, came 12 years later—the biggest and most excruciating corporate break-up in history. And when in 1980, in our book *The Third Wave*, we coined the term 'de-massification' to describe the coming move beyond mass production, mass distribution, mass media and socioeconomic homogeneity, we again were thought by some to be too visionary.

We suspect that many of the contributors to this volume have faced comparable skepticism. The reason is simple: anyone who attacks a dominant paradigm too early can expect to be regarded with suspicion by the reigning intellectual and academic establishment. But paradigms—including management paradigms—are not permanent. And the industrial era management model, especially in the US, is now blowing its bolts and rivets.

Today's knowledge revolution, having launched a gigantic 'Third Wave' of economic, technical and social change, is forcing businesses to operate in radically new, continually shifting ways that stand Second Wave notions on their head. The industrial faith in such things as vertical integration, synergy, economies of scale and hierarchical, command-and-control organization is giving way to a fresh appreciation of outsourcing, minimization of scale, profit centers, networks and other diverse forms of organization. Every shred of industrial-era thinking is now being rescrutinized and brilliantly reformulated.

It is precisely when an old paradigm crumbles and the new one is not yet fixed in place that we get great bursts of creative thinking. This is such a moment, and some of today's most innovative thinking about management is reflected in these pages.

Of course, as in any collection, some contributions are better than others, some fresher and more pioneering than others. But the overall thrust of this volume is exciting. It offers us a work-in-progress picture of a new business paradigm in the making.

What is still missing from this paradigm is a strong link between emergent Third Wave management thinking and Third Wave economics. One reason for this is a disparity in the relevant rates of change. While business theorists and management consultants like those in this book are exploring many aspects of the new business reality and rapidly reporting their findings, economists, with some notable exceptions, remain imprisoned by their own previous successes, seldom venturing into Third Wave territory.

A good example of the current disparity has to do with knowledge—the primary factor of production in the new system for wealth creation. An increasing amount of work is being done by consulting firms on questions of knowledge management—the assessment of knowledge assets, new approaches to organizational and individual learning, attempts to create a metric for dealing with knowledge. By contrast, mainstream economists, for the most part, ignore or underestimate knowledge as a factor of production.

If 'thinking outside the box' has become a buzzword among smart business people and their advisers, economists do so at far greater risk to their reputations in the profession. As a result, Third Wave economics is still in its pre-natal stage, and the intellectual framework that might unify management theory and economics is not yet in place. The task of creating that framework still lies ahead.

What business practitioners—as well as their economists and advisers—will need, however, is an even more comprehensive model of the oncoming Third Wave reality, not just focusing on economics and management issues, but showing how these must respond to social, technological, political, cultural and religious shocks—of which there will be plenty in the years immediately ahead.

Many of these can be anticipated, as can their impact on business, and they need to be taken into account, since a sudden massive swing in any one could wreak as much havoc on a company or industry as could an economic change. Unfortunately, these broader issues still lie outside the frame of reference of most business thinkers and economists alike.

Nevertheless, the distinguished contributors to these pages provide important conceptual components out of which the next business paradigm will be built. The chapters teem with provocative, illuminating ideas, good questions, fresh insights and alternative ways of thinking about the competitive/cooperative combat to come. As the Third Wave system for wealth creation spreads, marked by hypercompetition, successive technological revolutions and social dislocation and conflict, it is creating high unpredictability and non-linear conditions. Business leaders and strategists who wish to flourish in so turbulent and revolutionary an environment will ignore this book at their peril.

Alvin and Heidi Toffler

ACKNOWLEDGMENTS

MANY INDIVIDUALS HAVE contributed to this book and I gratefully acknowledge my large debt to each of them. *Rethinking the Future* would not have been possible without the generous cooperation of Warren Bennis, Stephen Covey, Eli Goldratt, Gary Hamel, Michael Hammer, Charles Handy, Kevin Kelly, Philip Kotler, John Kotter, John Naisbitt, Michael Porter, CK Prahalad, Al Ries, Peter Senge, Lester Thurow and Jack Trout. These special people, who for years have been shaping our thinking on the future of business, were kind enough to give of their time and share their invaluable insights with me for the sake of this project. I am indebted to them all.

My deep thanks also go to Alvin and Heidi Toffler, the grand masters of future thinking, for kindly agreeing to write the foreword.

I owe a great debt to my business partner and friend, Frans Kömhoff, co-founder of International Business Communications plc and Euro-management bv, without whom this book would have remained nothing more than an exciting idea. His generous backing, his unfailing belief in me and his extraordinary access power were the crucial factors in making the impossible possible.

Special thanks go to Nick Brealey of Nicholas Brealey Publishing, who joined the project at an early stage and succeeded in transforming my rough material into a book, providing excellent editorial guidance along the way. Also a big thank-you to Sally Lansdell Yeung for her brilliant editing of the manuscript and for being so very helpful at all times.

My grateful thanks to Melinda Adams, Managing Director of Euromanagement, Irene van der Meulen of European Business Studies, and Jan Bommerez for helping to set up some of the vital early interviews.

I owe another large debt to the personal assistants who represent the direct links to this book's contributors. They include Laureen Austermann, Doris Cunneen, Barbara Devine, Wendy Donnelly, Doris Hagen, Linda McLean Harned, Stacy Horvack, Mary Lane, Jean MacDonald, Karen Moss, Patti Pallat, Linda Paul, Lyn Pohl, Cappy Reed, Grace Reim, Vicki Tweiten and Hannah Beal Will. Thank you all for your patience and assistance over many months.

Peter Barratt-Jones and David Champness of Two's Company-Euro RSCG have been 'soul brothers' since the beginning, and I am thankful to David for his useful input to my introduction. Robert Heller was kind enough to read the chapter and give his comments, and Nick Carding suggested some last-minute refinements.

My thanks also go to Ilonka van Sweevelt, Astrid Jacobs, Sandra Schiavone, Joëlle Sandberg, Suzanne Spock and Carolien Ligtvoet for their help in correcting and printing the manuscript, as well as with organizing some of the correspondence. The team at AVAILABLE Sound Studio duplicated many hours of interview tapes, and Marian van Dorst transcribed them all in record time, for which I am very grateful.

Throughout the project, I have been cheered on by Gérard Dufour, executive vice-president of EURO RSCG Worldwide; Cathal McKee of Communication Online; Peter Frost, CEO of OfficeSMART Ltd; and Hans Huismann of the American Book Center in Amsterdam, who provided me with a constant stream of helpful information.

Lastly, I would like to thank my parents, June and George Gibson, for instilling in me a love of books, as well as my parents-in-law, Waltraud and Dr Felix Netthöfel, along with Heike and Joachim Kammer, for tirelessly taking over the many family responsibilities which my work on this book forced me to neglect.

Most of all my heartfelt thanks go to my wife, Anke, who flew the family 'plane' on one engine for over two years, caring for our first son, Henry, and the recent arrival of his brother James. I will never forget all the sacrifices she made for the sake of my crazy adventure.

Rowan Gibson
August 1996

RETHINKING BUSINESS

Rowan Gibson

BACK IN THE 1960s and early 1970s, there was a general sense of certainty about where we were going and how to get there. Successful corporations, powerful post-war economies and long-established institutions were driving to the future like large luxury sedans on a wide open freeway. They imagined they saw a long, straight road stretching out before them into the distant horizon, one that could be traveled in much the same way as the road they had left behind. The future, it seemed, belonged to them.

Nothing could have been farther from the truth.

The lesson of the last three decades is that **nobody can drive to the future on cruise control**. Business books are replete with examples of apparently invincible corporations who fell asleep at the wheel and paid a heavy price. For many, the punishment came unexpectedly from foreign competitors, who had appeared to be insignificant dots in the rear-view mirror, but who raced past in the mid-1970s and early 1980s to become the new industry leaders. Others were overtaken by smaller, more entrepreneurial players who took advantage of the intersections—or entry points on to the freeway—that rapidly advancing technology began to create. In the space of just a few years, the roads that many once thought they owned became crowded, competitive arenas. And the journey turned into a race.

During that period, hundreds of companies dropped from the *Fortune* 500, falling behind to become laggards or bystanders on the road to the future, as Gary Hamel and CK Prahalad refer to them. Not a few of the former leaders left the race altogether and skidded off into oblivion. The 'excellence' myth, which was born and so widely believed at the beginning of the 1980s, was dead before the end of the decade.

Economically, too, our journey to the future has turned out somewhat differently than we expected. In the immediate post-war period, the supreme economic power was of course the United States. In the 1950s, the US was so far out in front that it seemed ridiculous to consider anyone else as a contender for economic supremacy. Except perhaps the Soviet Union. At the time, the USSR was growing faster economically than the US, and if this trend was extrapolated the Soviet Union would actually overtake the United States in terms of GNP (Gross National Product) by the mid-1980s.

In an effort to balance the power of the USSR and contain the threat of Communism, Washington maintained a policy based on helping the rest of the world catch up economically, without really worrying about what would happen if it eventually did. In the end, contrary to everyone's expectations, the Soviet Union suddenly shifted into reverse gear, falling apart seemingly overnight as the 1980s gave way to the 1990s. By that time, the US had already found itself competing with two formidable new economic superpowers which it had helped to create, namely Japan and the House of Europe, centered principally on Germany. In fact today, as Lester Thurow points out, it is by no means clear which of the three superpowers—the US, Europe or Japan—will win the race for the global economy.

There have also been other major changes over the years which were largely unanticipated. Three decades ago, for example, our lives and our societies were held together by powerful institutions—the government, the law, the education system, the church, the family, the work organization. We respected them. We entrusted them with our future. We allowed them to manage and control us. But not any more. Like ancient rock formations pounded by turbulent seas of change, these old sources of authority have been relentlessly eroded by new technologies and ideologies that have shifted power irreversibly from the institution to the individual.

And what about capitalism itself? That great road to progress and prosperity—or so we thought back then. **Many voices are now asking where capitalism is actually leading us. Or why we are racing to get there.** And what that race is doing to our lives, to our communities and to our environment. These are uncomfortable questions. These are uncomfortable times.

Today, as we look to the future, there is no certainty at all about where we are going or how to get there. We no longer see a long, straight freeway stretching into the horizon. Instead, we find ourselves staring at the end of the road! For the close of the twentieth century might be said to represent the end of a whole order of things. The end of the industrial paradigm. The end of the post-war world. The end of US predominance. The end of the welfare state. The end of Communism and of post-war capitalism. Perhaps even the end of history (according to Francis Fukuyama).

What lies beyond the end of the road? In his book *Powershift*, Alvin Toffler describes it as *terra incognita*—the uncharted landscape of tomorrow. Up ahead we see a world of chaos and uncertainty. A world of accelerating change. A world where economics will be based not on land, money or raw materials but on intellectual capital. Where competition will be fierce and where markets will be merciless. Where small companies will outsmart giant corporations on a global scale. Where customers will have infinite access to products, services and information. Where networks will be more important than nations. And where you'll either be doing business in real time, or you'll be dead.

In place of certainty, there is a sense that our industrial societies are in deep trouble, as we drive collectively towards what scientists call the edge of chaos—a period of violent transition when the old order of things finally gives way to the new. Yet, at the same time, there is also a sense of tremendous adventure and of opportunity for all.

Preparing for tomorrow

As we prepare to drive off the road and on to the unfamiliar terrain that lies ahead, it becomes clear that we are going to require a new kind of vehicle, some very different driving skills and a whole new sense of direction. But, even more fundamentally, we will need to challenge all our personal and organizational assumptions about the world we are heading into—the very different world of the twenty-first century. **In short, we need to rethink the future. But since the future is so all encompassing, how do we actually go about rethinking it?**

In this book, I have gathered together the views of some of the world's leading business thinkers—not by rehashing their many books, articles and speeches, but by engaging them in personal conversations about their visions for the twenty-first century. In these one-to-one dialogues, which took place over a period of several months, they shared unique insights with me about tomorrow's world. And how to prepare for it today.

The thoughts which they express on these pages are stimulating, provocative and sometimes controversial. Inevitably, there are also tensions and differences between them, as well as some overlap between the various chapters and sections. But nowhere else, to my knowledge, will you find all these ideas contained in one book.

My goal was to make this examination of the future as multifaceted as possible, in order to synthesize a more holistic point of view about where things might be going. For this reason, you will find conversations in this book with specialists from widely different fields: trend forecasting, global economics, management practice, marketing strategy, business process reengineering, information technology, organizational learning and the art of leadership.

What you will not find are any easy answers. There is no 'yellow brick road' to the future, no quick short-cut, no 'one best way'. Instead, by giving you a panoramic view of the whole landscape, I have attempted to help you find a pathway through that landscape that is uniquely your own.

To this end, I have refrained from using the introduction to this book as a forum for summarizing our discussions, or for recycling or repeating the ideas of the contributors. My objective is not to present some great universal solution that is the sum total of all the thoughts contained within these pages. Rather, it is to let the specialists speak for themselves, affording you the opportunity to listen to each of them, to reflect on the implications of their words and to draw your own conclusions, thereby clarifying and deepening your personal vision. After all, by definition, rethinking the future is a process which we have to go through individually.

However, in the process of conducting and editing the interviews, three common themes emerged which, to me, represent the most important messages of the book. The first of these themes is **'the road stops here'**— the realization that the future will be different from the past. This may sound obvious, and most of us have always known it to be true. But we behave as if it were not so. Many of today's leaders still cling to the idea that things have somehow gone wrong but that they can be fixed, so that we can return to the way things are supposed to be. This is delusionary. The past is gone. The road that we have been traveling for decades is coming to an end. From here on, the journey to tomorrow will be an off-road experience, and we need to change our mindset accordingly.

The second theme is **'new times call for new organizations'**. We won't get far driving a luxury sedan in a Paris–Dakar rally. What we need is a completely new kind of organizational vehicle that can handle the rough and uncertain business landscape into which we are traveling. One that reflects the information age of the future, rather than the industrial age of the past.

The third theme is **'where do we go next?'**. President Bush won the Gulf War but lost the subsequent election mainly because he failed to articulate a clear vision of where his administration was going. The underlying message of this book is that we are going to need a vision, a destination, a point of view about the future, a direction in which to channel the efforts of the people we work with. We will not develop such a vision by looking at a map. There are no maps of *terra incognita*. Instead, leaders will have to look ahead and explore the horizon for themselves. They will have to create their own ideas about where they should be going, and then point the way forward for their organizations in a compelling way.

The road stops here

For a long time we have known deep down that the future will be different from the past. Every science fiction writer, from Jules Verne to William Gibson, has reminded us of that. But what we have stubbornly refused to believe is that the future will be different than we expect it to be. Most of us still behave as if the future will be a linear extrapolation of the present, like a long straight road that stretches into the horizon.

This erroneous attitude towards the future is rooted in our culturally ingrained notions of predictability and control. In their book *The Great Reckoning*, James Dale Davidson and William Rees-Mogg talk about 'false conclusions programmed into our lives like a computer virus'. They argue that our world view has been shaped for centuries by a Newtonian perception of reality, in which change appears to be linear, continuous and, to some extent, predictable. Where A leads to B leads to C leads to D.

Chaos theory tells us that the opposite is true. As Michael Crichton writes in *Jurassic Park*: 'Chaos theory teaches us that straight linearity, which we have come to take for granted in everything from physics to fiction, simply does not exist. Linearity is an artificial way of viewing the world. Real life isn't a series of interconnected events occurring one after another like beads strung on a necklace. Life is actually a series of encounters in which one event may change those that follow in a wholly unpredictable, even devastating way.'

As our world becomes more complex and interdependent, change becomes increasingly non-linear, discontinuous and unpredictable. Therefore the future becomes less like the past. And less like we expected it to be. We find that A might lead to E, then on to K and suddenly to Z! This realization calls for an entirely new way of looking at the future in our corporations, in our societies and in our personal lives.

Rethinking the Future is about replacing the old mindset—the idea that we could to some extent control, order and predict the future—with a new mindset based on discontinuous change. It is about accepting aberration as the norm.

The fact is that the future will not be a continuation of the past. It will be a series of discontinuities. And only by accepting these discontinuities and doing something about them will we stand any chance of success and survival in the twenty-first century.

The exciting thing about discontinuity is that it breeds opportunity. It means that nobody owns the twenty-first century. But in order to grab hold of the future we have to let go of the past. We have to challenge and, in many cases, unlearn the old models, the old paradigms, the old rules, the old strategies, the old assumptions, the old success recipes.

On this, all of the book's contributors agree. Here, for example, are some of the statements that await you on the pages ahead:

Charles Handy: 'You can't look at the future as a continuation of the past...because the future is going to be different. And we really have to unlearn the way we dealt with the past in order to deal with the future.'

Peter Senge: 'We have to stop trying to figure out what to do by looking at what we have done.'

Michael Hammer: 'If you think you're good, you're dead. Success in the past has no implication for success in the future... The formulas for yesterday's success are almost guaranteed to be formulas for failure tomorrow.'

CK Prahalad: 'If you want to escape the gravitational pull of the past, you have to be willing to challenge your own orthodoxies. To regenerate your core strategies and rethink your most fundamental assumptions about how you are going to compete.'

These messages could not be more explicit. They are telling us that the road stops here. That we have to stop seeing the future like some great imaginary freeway stretching into the horizon. That, despite the title of Bill Gates's bestseller, there is no road ahead.

Roads are linear, and **linear thinking is useless in a non-linear world**. Instead, we have to make an intellectual leap from the linear to the non-linear. From the known to the unknown. From *terra firma* to *terra incognita*.

This book offers insights into some of the major areas of discontinuous change that will affect us all in the twenty-first century. The contributors examine the following issues:

❑ Why is the nature of competition changing so drastically? And what should we be doing about it?

❑ What exactly is the new 'network economy'? How will it work? And why will it be so fundamentally different from the industrial economy?

❑ Will it be better to be big and powerful or small and flexible in the global economy? Should companies be broadening their product lines in order to serve the world? Or should they become more specialized and focused?

❑ Will technology make geographical location increasingly irrelevant? Or will it make particular locations more important for particular industries in the twenty-first century?

❑ Why will the global economic battle of the twenty-first century be so different from previous economic battles? How important will Asia's role be in that battle? Will the modernization of Asia shift the world's center of economic, political and cultural gravity from the West back to the East?

❑ Now that the old fight between communism and capitalism is basically over, will a new fight emerge between the different forms of capitalism? Does the concept of capitalism have a bright future at all? Or has economic progress turned out to be an empty promise?

❑ As technology democratizes not just our workplaces, but our societies and our world, does it mean the end of government as we know it? Are we heading into a world that is essentially ungoverned, out of our control?

New times call for new organizations

Tomorrow's new times will bring new ways of competing. And the companies who are going to be successful are the ones that will grasp them first and overcome all the normal organizational barriers to doing things differently. As Michael Hammer says, 'In an environment of change, you don't want a very rigid organizational structure. You want one that allows you to adapt.'

Driving into *terra incognita* calls for a completely new kind of organizational vehicle that bears little or no resemblance to the big 'luxury sedans' of the past. **The winners of the twenty-first century will be those who can transform their organizations into something that more resembles a jeep—an all-wheel drive, all-terrain vehicle that is lean, mean and highly maneuverable.** One that can move and shift direction quickly in uncertain territory, reacting rapidly to the changing nature of the business environment, the changing nature of competition and the changing needs of the customer.

Despite the mechanical metaphor, this new vehicle will have to have the nature of a biological organism, not a machine. It will be a distributed network of minds, of people working together and learning together, some inside the organization and some outside. It will be intelligent. It will be driven by the engine of human imagination. It will invite customers and partners to climb aboard and come along for the ride. And it will be conscious about the way it affects the natural environment.

This new vehicle—the organization of the twenty-first century—cannot be created through continuous improvement. It can only be created through radical change. Hammer calls it 'reversing the industrial revolution'. He believes that the only way to turn rigid old organizational structures into ones that allow us to adapt is by abandoning the whole organizational model of the past century, along with the assumptions on which it was based. Peter Drucker anticipated this years ago when he wrote that 'every organization has to prepare for the abandonment of everything it does'.

What we are talking about here is a task of immense proportions. Senge compares it to 'going through the eye of a needle'. But, whether we like it or not, if we want to stay in business in the next century, the change has to be made. For, as Prahalad puts it: 'If you don't change, you die!'

Unfortunately, there is no pit stop on the race to the future; nowhere to rest up and reinvent ourselves. In fact, the process of business transformation has become a race in itself. Those that take too long at this process may become laggards or, at worst, may never get back in the race. Instead, we will have to achieve the radical metamorphosis of our organizations while the race is in progress.

Rethinking the Future examines some of the key issues connected with organizational change for the twenty-first century:

- ❑ How do we go about changing our mental models into ones that are more systemic in nature, so that we can learn to look at the whole organization and not just at some part of it that needs to be 'fixed'?
- ❑ What kind of role will technology play in the business transformation process?
- ❑ How do we go about creating a radically decentralized, network organization? And does federalism provide us with a useful model for making it work?
- ❑ What is it that truly binds a network organization together? Is it merely information technology? Or does it require something deeper and far more meaningful?
- ❑ How does a company make the shift from just spreading information around a network to building new knowledge? Is it really possible to set up a 'learning infrastructure'? And if so, will companies begin to look more like universities than business institutions?
- ❑ What sort of principles will guide the successful twenty-first-century corporation? Should top management give their people a meaningful share of voice in the ownership and the running of the enterprise? And what does it take to build a 'high trust' culture?
- ❑ As corporations and their networks become increasingly complex, how will we control them? And should we even try? Or will companies instead develop a bottom-up kind of control like we find in a flock of birds, or a swarm of bees?
- ❑ If the traditional concept of management is reaching the end of the road, will there be any role at all for managers and for hierarchy in the future organization?
- ❑ Will the shift to a new management model be a global phenomenon? Or will there be different rates of progress in different parts of the world?

Where do we go next?

It will not be enough to race into the future with a new kind of organizational vehicle. We also need a clear point of view about where we are going—a vision about where we want to be tomorrow and about which direction to take today in order to get there successfully. Otherwise we may find ourselves driving aimlessly into the future—missing opportunities and stumbling into crises—while others are racing ahead and taking charge of their destinies.

Today, many corporations pursue operational efficiency as if it were a destination in itself. Lacking a sense of strategic direction, most of them sooner or later find themselves spinning their wheels. As one CEO put it; 'On your marks, get set, get slim…then what?' Organizations of this kind are all revved up with nowhere to go.

Reengineering, benchmarking, continuous improvement, total quality management, lean production, time-based competition—these have all proven vital for survival. But getting better at what we do is just about keeping ourselves in the race—it's not about winning the race. To win, we will need to get out in front of the competition, decide where we should be going and make sure we get there first. CK Prahalad's view is that 'Ultimately, the race to the future becomes a mad dash to the finish line.'

In the twenty-first century, the winners will be those who stay ahead of the change curve, constantly redefining their industries, creating new markets, blazing new trails, reinventing the competitive rules, challenging the status quo. To use Charles Handy's words, it will be those who 'invent the world', not those who respond to it.

Of course, it requires far less effort to follow in the tracks of the leader than it does to find your own migration path to the future, and there was a time when this was an option. But not any more. Tomorrow's global markets will show no mercy to the me-too crowd.

So how will the twenty-first century organization develop a sense of foresight about where it needs to be heading? How will it create a meaningful vision and purpose; a goal that is uniquely its own, and that will give it a sustainable competitive advantage; something that it can stand for in a crowded and confusing world?

The answer, in a word, is leadership. Not traditional leadership, but twenty-first-century leadership. Because the new organizational vehicles will have to be steered by new kinds of leaders.

The new leaders will not be content to sit back and let the cruise control do the driving. They will be looking forward, scanning the landscape, watching the competition, spotting emerging trends and new opportunities, avoiding impending crises. They will be explorers, adventurers, trailblazers. Advanced technology will give them an interactive, real-time connection with the marketplace; and they will get feedback from sensors at the peripheries of the organization. But they will be led just as much by their own intuition. Sometimes they will decide to ignore the data and drive by the seat of their pants.

Tomorrow's successful leaders will be what Warren Bennis calls 'leaders of leaders'. **They will decentralize power and democratize strategy by involving a rich mixture of different people from inside and outside the organization in the process of inventing the future.** They will be comfortable with the concept of discontinuity and will understand how to use it to create opportunities. They will love change and encourage a pro-change culture in their organizations. According to Bennis, they will gather people around them 'who have the future in their bones', and they will be adept at fostering creative collaboration among these people—achieving what Gary Hamel calls a 'hierarchy of imagination'.

Above all else, leaders will have a vision, a passion, an exciting aspiration. And this aspiration, once shared by everybody in the organization, will unleash tremendous human energy. It will provide the fuel to push the organization out in front of its competitors. And drive it on to win the race.

In connection with rethinking leadership and strategy for the twenty-first century, this book examines the following issues:

❑ Are organizations spending too much time managing the present and not enough time creating the future? Why is it so challenging to think strategically about the future? And how do you create the incentive within an organization to do so?

❑ Who should a company involve in the process of developing and implementing strategy? What should be the role of senior management in this process?

❑ How strategically focused can a huge corporation be? And should small companies take a more flexible view of strategy than their bigger competitors?

❑ How important will technology be to creating a competitive advantage in the future? Will it have a long-term effect on strategy, or will it be more of a tactical element?

❑ How can companies balance the need for radical change with the need for strategic continuity? When does it actually become necessary to change your competitive strategy?

❑ What can companies do to make the most of emerging opportunities? And how can they de-risk those opportunities?

❑ What will be the essential differences between twentieth-century leadership and twenty-first-century leadership? Will it take a special kind of leader to succeed in the global economy? And what impact will information technology have on the way leaders lead?

❑ Why will it be so important to a be 'leader of leaders'? And how can we encourage leadership at all levels of the organization?

❑ What can leaders do to ensure that their corporate culture will be a strategic asset rather than a change anchor?

❑ Is it the organization's responsibility to give people a purpose in life?

Six steps to rethinking the future

The six sections in this book provide us with a broad agenda for rethinking the future. They set out to create a framework for reexamining business, economics and society in the light of discontinuous change. They help us view the world from a fresh, new perspective—one that supersedes the conventional wisdom of the past. And they identify specific actions which we can take in the present in order to build a winning position for the future.

Rethinking Principles looks anew at the principles which guide our organizations, our societies and our personal lives. It recognizes, optimistically, that we have the power to create the future. But it asks us to question what we are actually creating and why. It focuses on finding sense in the increasingly uncertain world in which we live, and it offers some practical advice on finding pathways through paradox.

Rethinking Competition deals with the fundamental changes taking place in the nature of competition. It provides new ways of looking at competitive advantage as we prepare for the global economy of the twenty-first century, and it helps us to focus on building opportunities for tomorrow. It also identifies some of the key steps which corporations and governments can be taking right now to gear up for future competition.

Rethinking Control & Complexity is concerned with how to structure and manage our organizations for the twenty-first century. It centers on the need to challenge the old assumptions and organizational models, which no longer make sense in a post-industrial world, and to create a new mode of operating based on high-performing processes and empowered individuals. It describes an organizational infrastructure where collective aspiration and systems thinking can be nurtured, where people in the organization can be proactive rather than reactive, and where they can learn how to learn together in a transformational way.

Rethinking Leadership helps us to see leadership in a new light: as a way to release the brainpower of the organization and to generate intellectual capital. This section suggests how to decentralize power successfully in a network organization, and how to lead transformation efforts that actually work. It points out why the true source of power in the future organization will be a meaningful sense of purpose, and why a new generation of leaders will be needed to provide it.

Rethinking Markets examines major changes in the nature of the customer and in the essential marketing relationship between the customer and the corporation. It previews the dominant demographic forces for the early twenty-first century, along with the attitudes and demands of new kinds of consumers in new kinds of markets. And it looks at how technology is revolutionizing the way we market products and services.

Rethinking the World is about the unprecedented changes which are taking place in business and society at the most global level: the shift in the nature of worldwide economic competition; the changing role of governments in a world that is increasingly based on networks; the potential of Asia once again to become the dominant region of the world; the impact of 'network economics' on every sector of business; and the way discoveries in science are changing our view of the world at the dawn of the twenty-first century.

Today, a simple choice faces every individual, every corporation, every government and every society on earth. That choice is: rethink the future or be forced to rethink the future.

Those who choose the first option will have the best chance of surviving and thriving in the turbulent terrain ahead. They will spot the emerging opportunities and impending crises while there is still time to take appropriate action. On the other hand, those who procrastinate, in the belief that the future will be a continuation of the past, will quickly find themselves overtaken by change. They will be forced to rethink where they are going, and how they are getting there, when it is probably too late to avoid the inevitable.

The purpose of this book is to help you make the right choice. To assist you in rethinking and then shaping the future, before it shapes you.

Perhaps the most important lesson I have learned personally while preparing this book is that rethinking the future is a never-ending process. Tomorrow will always be a moving target. Which means that, when we've finished rethinking the future, we have to start all over again.

Rethinking

PRINCIPLES

Finding Sense in Uncertainty

Charles Handy

Putting Principles First

Stephen Covey

“The great excitement of the future is

that we can shape it.”

FINDING SENSE IN UNCERTAINTY

Charles Handy

“ WE ARE LIVING in very confused times, because many of the things that gave structure to our lives are disappearing. Institutions which we relied on, particularly the work organization, are no longer so sure or so certain.

For one thing, work organizations disappear rather rapidly these days. One-third of the *Fortune* 500 companies aren't even there seven years later. Second, even if they do survive as institutions, they don't necessarily give us the kind of lives that we were led to expect by our parents. If we look at other institutions too—the law, the political structures, the monarchy—these are all being questioned. They turn out to have feet of clay. They turn out to be run by ordinary mortals. Understandably, therefore, people are very unsure of where the future is going.

To give ourselves some sense of cohesion, I believe that, to the best of our abilities, we have to try to work out what the future is going to be like. So that's what I'm trying to do. I want to persuade people that there is, after all, some sense in what appears to be all this nonsense around us.

You see, the picture may seem chaotic, but chaos is perhaps the wrong word to describe it. In science, chaos isn't chaotic. Chaos actually says that there are underlying patterns in things, and that there are reasons why particular things happen. But there are also spaces in the reasons, so that you can actually make a difference to the way things turn out. And that is what I find so terribly exciting in the midst of all this uncertainty, even anarchy, that is around us. Because it means that the future is not completely preordained; even in science it is not preordained—which means that one little flutter of a butterfly's wings, or just me doing something, can actually make the world shift a little.

In a sense, therefore, I am pessimistic about the future because I see it being a troubled time. But deep down I am very optimistic, because I see it as a time of great opportunity for a lot of people who never thought that they could actually make a difference to the world.

Paradoxes

If we are going to make any sense out of all this confusion around us, we have to find a way to organize it in our minds, so that we can start to understand what is actually happening in the world and then try to do something about it.

My way of doing this is to accept that there are never any simple or right answers to life, that **life is full of contradictions and surprises, that it is, in fact, full of paradoxes**. But if we can learn to understand and accept these paradoxes, then I believe that we can eventually find pathways through them. We can live with them and manage them.

This is especially necessary as times become more turbulent, because at such times the world becomes ever more complex and difficult to understand. In fact, everywhere we look today, paradox seems to be the companion of economic progress.

What paradox says to me is that two opposite thoughts can both simultaneously be true. For example, you can be in love with a person and also, at times, dislike that person too. You can want both continuity and change, and have them. So what we need to do is to learn how to balance the opposites.

It's like a riding a seesaw. You need to understand that, for the seesaw to work, to move, there has to be a pattern of ups and downs, that both opposites are necessary in order to make the process work. Once you know how and why it works, then you can play the game. Life is like a seesaw, a game where the movement and the excitement come from a balance of opposites, because it will always inevitably be full of paradox. I believe that the key to progress and even to survival in life and work is to be aware that contradictions can coexist, and to learn to live with them.

For instance, I argue that organizations have to be centralized and decentralized at the same time. They need to be both global and local. Differentiated and integrated. Tight and loose. They have to plan for the long term and yet stay flexible. Their workers should on the one hand be more autonomous, and on the other hand be more of a team. But the point is, we mustn't let people get confused by all that. We've got to find a way to live and work with these kinds of contradictions, to reconcile the opposites instead of trying to choose between them.

I don't think most people can manage paradox very easily, so we will have to try and make life a little simpler to understand. The first thing to do is to make people aware that there is paradox, and that there is no simple solution. There is no golden route to glory and happiness in life. But, at the same time, we need to give some structure to things so that managing paradox becomes easier for people to handle.

The doughnut principle

I use what I call the doughnut principle, which basically says that life is like an inverted doughnut, in which the hole is on the outside and the dough is in the middle. In the doughnut view of life, the core is fixed and the bounded space around the core is where we make the difference.

The core gives us the bit of security and certainty which we all need, while the space gives us the flexibility which is necessary to ride the seesaw.

So we can say, for example, that there are some clear core activities in organizations—these are the essential jobs and the necessary people to carry them out—but surrounding this core there needs to be an open space filled with flexible workers and suppliers.

Already we see many new-style organizations that don't own the whole doughnut. They are essentially networks that have a small core of key people who, hopefully, provide them with their lasting core competence, and a collection of partnerships with allied organizations, suppliers, a part-time peripheral workforce, independent professionals and customers which gives them the flexibility to survive in a chaotic world.

The strategic issue for organizations in the twenty-first century will be how to balance their activities: what to put in the core and what to put in the space around it. For example, an organization has to be small enough to be human and flexible, but at the same time in some areas it has to be big, because you need a certain clout in the marketplace, you need research or global reach. That's why, everywhere we look today, we see organizations grappling with the need to decentralize and centralize at the same time.

This idea, in itself, is not new at all. In fact, since Aristotle we have been experimenting with the same principle in politics, and it's called federalism.

In federalism there is always a strong center but considerable space is left for local decisions. It's centralized in some respects and decentralized in others. It's big and yet at the same time it's small. It's regulated in some aspects and deregulated in others. So, if you like, it's the doughnut principle in practice. Except that federalism is made up of a variety of doughnuts of varying sizes and shapes in a multipolar construction.

Organizations achieve this by creating work groups where people are responsible for discharging a particular task, but where they also have a lot of space to decide how they think it should best be done. What you get is a series of cores throughout the organization, so that responsibility is spread across many decision points. But there's always some overarching thing there—a core to the whole set of doughnuts—that coordinates activities and holds the whole thing together.

Rethinking jobs

Of course, the doughnut principle also applies to the individual. If you're going to employ people who are intelligent, and who like to think for themselves, then you've got to give them a lot of responsibility, a lot of power. Otherwise they will leave you, because nobody wants to be a robot or an instrument—they each need their individual doughnut.

In the past, jobs were all core and no space. You had a long, detailed job description that gave you no space for self-expression, no space to make a difference. You weren't empowered at all. There was no opportunity to reshape your individual doughnut or that of your immediate group.

Today, conversely, **we sometimes take empowerment too far**. To say, for instance, that there is no core in your doughnut, that it is all space, can be frightening, because then there is no structure and no certainty. To say, in addition, that there's no boundary to your doughnut is even more frightening, because then there can be no end to the job or task.

One of the challenges for organizations, therefore, is to give people space for their initiative, but also to be able to define success. The reason that some people work so hard, too hard it often seems to me, is that there is no boundary to their doughnuts. Their managers keep saying that they could work harder, they could have made more money, or made more deals, sold more of this or that. They can never look back and say, 'It was a great year', because they always think it could have been greater.

That's unfair. That's throwing the whole burden of paradox back on to the individual, and few of us can cope with that. The result can be burnout or at least a lot of stress. So to get the best out of people we have to put limits to this confusion. We have to design their doughnuts correctly.

Portfolio lives

In the twenty-first century, we will see more and more people adopting a 'portfolio' approach to their lives and to their work. What I mean by this is that life will be a collection of different activities, almost like a share portfolio. A part of the portfolio will be the core activities for providing the essentials for living, whereas the rest will be other things that we think of as personal fulfilment, as responsibilities towards other people or even just as fun.

Instead of having a career in the traditional sense, you will, for part of life, have a 'portfolio career', where part of your time will be spent earning wages or fees, and the rest will be for community work or study or whatever. A lot of it will be work of some form, even if much of it is unpaid, and it will all go to make up a portfolio of activities which will increasingly define you.

Some businesses will recognize the advantages of these portfolios. They will encourage people to take on some voluntary work in the community for the sake of their personal development. And they will arrange portfolios of different kinds of work within the same organization to bring out people's different talents.

We have to remember that **the very definition of work is changing**. Work used to mean having a job with an employer. But today, it increasingly means working for yourself and even by yourself. In the near future, half of the workforce of the developed world will be working 'outside' the organization. Traditional organizations now employ only 55 percent of the workforce on a full-time basis. The rest are temporary, part-time or contractual workers. Our portfolios will increasingly be collections of different work for different clients.

But being outside the organization is going to make life very confusing at times. Those that choose to 'go portfolio', or are forced to by corporate downsizing, will have to learn to cope with their newly found independence. They will have to carve out different chunks in their lives for doing certain things, and not let one chunk take over the other. They will have to learn to sell their services or to find an agent to do it for them, to plan their futures rather than take them as they come, to update and upskill themselves continually and, most crucially of all, to work out what their goal in life should be, now that they and no one else are in charge of that life.

What I am saying is that it helps us to manage the paradoxes in life when we realize that there are some things that are fixed, but there is an awful lot of space around those things which we can move into. **And when we move into that empty space around the core, that's when we become creative.** That's when we become the disturbing bit of chaos which actually sets new things in motion. And that's the exciting bit.

Beyond certainty

These days almost nothing is certain. In the old days, when organizations were younger, there was a feeling that we would in due course arrive at some sort of scientific law about organizations. Companies would succeed because they would be able to predict the future and be able in some sense to even manage the future. So back then we designed and constructed our organizations on the basis of planning, predictability and control. We used words like plan, operate, control, measure. But in my view, all those words are now wrong. They are not terribly useful in a world which is flowing rather than standing still. **All we can really do now is go with the flow, and try to steer things a little.**

Like Heisenberg and his principle of uncertainty, you can make predictions in the aggregate—when you put all things together, for example, you can say that markets will behave in certain sorts of ways—but when you get right down to looking at the little atoms that make up the aggregate, then all you can do is measure their velocity and direction, you can't actually pinpoint them with any accuracy or define where they are exactly. So while it is possible to get a sort of general view of the way the world is going, and the way business is going, you can't actually predict with any kind of certainty where you'll be in that future, more than two or three years ahead.

Nevertheless, you still have to act. You sometimes have to take ten-year decisions, and you have to be prepared to reverse those decisions or abandon them if they're wrong. So it's a different kind of world that we're living in. **We've got to learn to live with chaos and uncertainty, to try to be comfortable with it and not to look for certainty where we won't get it.** As I say in *The Empty Raincoat*, life can best be understood backward but you have to live it forward. You can only do that by stepping into uncertainty, and then by trying, within that uncertainty, to create your own islands of security.

We're not talking here about contractual security within an organization, such as a contract of employment and so on. The new form of security will be very psychological and personal. It will be a belief that if this doesn't work out, you could do something else. You are your own security.

We have to find a personal security in our relationships too. We were not meant to stand alone. We need a sense of connection. We have to feel that it matters to other people that we are there. Because if it makes no difference whether you're there or not, then you really begin to feel like a meaningless person. If you have no connection to anybody, you have no responsibility and therefore no purpose.

Inventing the future

You can't look at the future as a continuation of the past. The things that got you where you are are seldom the things that keep you there. But, on the other hand, if you don't know where you are coming from you will find it hard to go forward.

Actually, we've got to see the future as a series of discontinuities, and we've got to learn to take these things in our stride.

I use the metaphor of the second curve, the second part of what is called the Sigmoid curve. The Sigmoid or S-shaped curve describes the way things go in life. They start out with a dip and then, with luck or good management, they grow and move up the curve, but eventually they wane. Everything wanes. It's true of empires, of corporations, of product lifecycles, of relationships, even of life itself. The way you get continued growth in the future is by building a new curve before the first one begins to descend, which means constantly being inventive and creative.

Recently it has been fashionable for companies to think of themselves as problem-solving organizations. That is actually wrong because, by the time you've discovered the problem and you're solving it, you're already out of date. You have to be ahead of the problem. You have to invent the world. You have to think 'second-curve'.

But in order to recreate themselves for the future, organizations must be prepared to let go of the past. Otherwise they'll just get locked into their present curve and sooner or later they will come to an end. The trick is not to let go of the past all at once. You can't abandon the first curve until you have built the second one. So, for a time, the past and the future have to coexist in the present. And that's the pathway through the paradox.

The way you make sense of the future, in organizations and in societies and in your own life, is by taking charge of the future. Not by responding to it.

I wrote a book called *The Age of Unreason*. The reason I chose that particular title was because George Bernard Shaw once wrote that the reasonable man responds to the world, while the unreasonable man tries to make the world respond to him. Therefore, he said, all progress (and I have to add all the disasters too) comes from the unreasonable person; the person who actually tries to change the world. What that means is that we can't wait for people to offer us secure jobs and long careers. We have to decide what kind of life we want to lead and go out and make it happen.

This will require us to change our whole educational system. We have designed our schools on the implicit assumption that all the problems in the world have already been solved and the teacher knows the answers. So the job of the teacher is to tell the students the problem, then the answer, and, literally, to 'school' them. In my view of the world, the future world of constant discontinuity, the problems are not there yet. We have to invent the world. Traditional education is, therefore, in danger of being deskilling, rather than the reverse. Many of the assumptions of my education were that there were 'knowable' things about the world. And that if I knew those things then I could proceed with some certainty through that world. I think I've had to unlearn a lot of that.

Life seems to be a succession of open-ended problems with no right answers, but problems, nevertheless, which demand an answer. We used to think that life was a closed problem. That everything had a right answer, only we didn't know what it was yet. But somebody did, usually somebody older or more expert than us. And with a little bit more investigation we could find it. A closed question would be: 'What is the quickest road to London?' There is an answer to that. But an open-ended question is: 'Why do you want to go to London?' There is no right answer to that, but nevertheless we have to find an answer. It seems to me that more and more of life is like that. My answer may not be the same as yours, but still I've got to have an answer and I've got to proceed along it. Most of our education has not prepared us for this.

I believe we need a totally new kind of schooling which is not about learning knowledge and facts. Those are still necessary, of course, but those things are easy to get at now. I want to equip every kid with a Macintosh Powerbook and a CD-ROM drive so that, potentially, he or she can know everything, through their fingertips. The job of the teacher, then, is to help them to know what to do with all this knowledge, and *how* to do it.

That's how we make sense of the future. We have to make our own sense, our own future. And organizations have to make their own futures. **The world is up for grabs. That's both very frightening and yet very exciting.** To make the future happen we need to be self-confident and to believe in our own worth. That's what schools should teach us.

➤ *Do you think we will have to rethink our whole perspective about the way the world works?*

Yes. We used to think that the world was, in a sense, a rational place which was governed by rational people. We are rapidly discovering that it's a pretty confused and messy place and that there isn't anybody in charge, really. For instance, we like to think that we can put a figure on the earnings of Britain. But how can we really do that in any credible way? The weekly throughput of the City of London is more than the annual GDP of the UK. This tremendous flow of business is rushing to and fro and we really can't count it because it's literally invisible.

A large amount of what we actually do, these days, no one can see or count. We are living in a virtual economy and we are really guessing at the wealth of our countries. If you can't count it, you really can't control very much of it either. Governments can no longer control what people do, or where they do it, or how they do it, because they can no longer see much of it or count it.

In other words, we live in a world which we used to think was governed, and which I think is largely becoming ungoverned. A world where the old methods of control no longer work. That is, the old sources of authority no longer hold sway.

Since I wrote *The Empty Raincoat* I've been looking at the history of the European Renaissance, and I'm reminded of the early days of the printing press. Before the invention of the printing press in the early 1400s, we really had to believe that institutions like the monarchy and the church knew best. They were, after all, the only sources of knowledge and wisdom that we had. Then the printing press came along and we could actually read the Bible in our own language, in our own homes, and we could make up our own minds about life, morality and the social order. We discovered that a lot of these traditional institutions had feet of clay. The kings and priests were suddenly just people, no better, many of them, than the rest of us.

That was very exciting because it allowed us to be creative and entrepreneurial. We got the Renaissance and all the great things that it brought with it. But, at the same time, we got a lot of insecurity, a lot of uncertainty, factions and fighting as men vied with each other for the vacant authority. I think that the same thing is happening now. Whereas, back then, it was the printing press that made the difference, today we have television, computers, Internet and CD-ROMs. We have this mass of information about everything, so that all of us can now know almost as much as any prime minister or president can, and we probably have more leisure time to digest it than they do.

We can, and do, make up our own minds about things, and that tends to rob institutions of their authority. We can all watch the President of the United States or the Queen of England on television and some of us will think that they're only ordinary people and not necessarily that great.

The same is true within companies. As soon as you put a computer on every desk, the average worker becomes far more powerful. He or she can know as much as the boss does, and often much more. So these 'knowledge workers' take on greater responsibilities and they become, in a sense, liberated from traditional corporate authority.

Society, therefore, is out of control because we are systematically destroying all of the authority and all of the control that our institutions once had. **We are giving society a mind of its own.**

On the one hand that's very exciting because it may lead to a new renaissance in the twenty-first century. We will see a lot of creativity bubbling up everywhere, just as we did back in the fifteenth century. But at the same time it's very frightening, because people aren't used to having no authority around.

That's what I mean when I write about the 'edge of chaos'. This is a term scientists use to describe times of great turbulence when new life is born out of the decaying of the old. When complexity and confusion gel into some kind of new order. And when you are at that place on the 'edge of chaos' there is this great potential for creativity, but it's also by definition a very troubled, very difficult time and place.

I believe that that is where we find ourselves today.

The empty promise of progress

Economic progress has turned out to be an empty promise. We had hoped to have a fairer society. A more ordered society. A society where people basically lived sensible, quiet, decent lives. And it's not turning out like that.

We have societies which are much more divided than we wanted them to be, because in our relentless search for 'efficiency' we are polarizing ourselves into the 'haves' and the 'have-nots'. We're finding that work is increasingly priced either very highly or at zero. So the rich still get richer while the poor get poorer, sometimes in relative and sometimes in absolute terms. We have an emerging underclass and a growing overclass.

For years, we have placed the pursuit of efficiency and economic growth above all else, because we understood that to be the path to 'progress'. But we have done so at the expense of our workers, our communities and, as we have become acutely aware in recent years, our environment.

We have also applied the idea of global competitiveness to things that aren't actually globally competitive. I'm referring to activities such as healthcare, education, local government, welfare organizations and small service industries. They do not have to compete with the world in terms of cost efficiency. But by insisting that they do we are making efficiency more important than output, the methods more important than the result. That's bad thinking and bad economics. In the process we are creating a society that is not at ease with itself.

This is a very difficult thing to cope with because it's confusing to the mind. It's not like a war-time situation where you basically know who the enemy is. **Now the enemy is us and our own societies, because what we're fighting against is our own sense of values, our own principles.** We're discovering that what we thought was fine, which was to be more efficient, harder working and richer, doesn't actually lead to the Nirvana that we hoped for. At least not for everybody. In fact, those who are making the most money are not sure that it's worth it. Who wants to be rich in the graveyard? And those who aren't making any money think that the world doesn't make sense, because money is supposed to be the only thing worth having and they can't get any.

➤ *Do you have worries about the future of capitalism?*

Yes, I do. Capitalism depends on people working terribly hard to make other people rich, in the hope, often misplaced, that they will get rich themselves. Under capitalism, growth depends on making people envious of other people so that they want what the others have. I find this a rather distasteful view of the world. On the other hand, if we don't create wealth then everybody will be as uncomfortable as they were before the Industrial Revolution. It was Adam Smith who said that economic growth did actually remove poverty, make people more comfortable and help them live really healthier lives. Therefore, he said, no right-thinking person can be against it.

But he also said that unrestricted growth can lead to an economy of 'useless things'. So I think we'll find ourselves going down a dead-end road if we pursue economic growth as if it's the only thing that counts. Success sometimes carries a very high price.

We recently went on a visit to South China, and Guandong province next to Hong Kong, where the growth rate has been 12 percent per annum. And in Shentzen City, a New Economic Zone, it's 21 percent per annum.

When something is growing at that rate, people don't walk, they run, with their mobile phones to their ears, and you can see this happening everywhere there. It's called the 'wild east of capitalism' by some people, and rightly so.

But they are causing a tremendous amount of destruction. The red earth is razed, everywhere, to a uniform base for new buildings or highways. The pollution is horrible. People fall off buildings and get killed every day, because there are no laws or rules of industrial safety. There are few effective laws at all, in fact. It is truly like the old gold rush.

Yet you wonder why they are doing this, because they seem to be creating a horrible society. After all, in the long run, who would want to be rich in that social desert, or to grow old in a wasteland like that?

The same applies to capitalist societies everywhere. **Who would want to be successful in the kind of social desert that we're in danger of creating in our own countries?** We might eventually have to surround ourselves with high fences and armed guards, rather like the rich suburbs of northern Johannesburg, in order to survive in this land we have created.

So we have to ask ourselves what we are doing this for. In the process, people are working so hard that they're in danger of losing their humanity. Life is for living, and of course part of living is working, but there is always more to it than that.

This is one lesson I've learned from Italy, where I spend a lot of my time: that the process of living is actually quite a full-time occupation. In Italy, just living—the talking, the shopping, the cooking, the eating, the family and all that goes with it—actually consumes a whole day. It's a miracle that the Italians ever get any other work done. But it does make life rich; there's a texture to it, and more of a point.

Elsewhere, we see people scurrying off every day to an office and coming back with their briefcases full, so that they can sit and read the documents all night and then go back to the office the next day and empty the briefcase again. You have to believe that this must be in the cause of some magnificent religion or crusade, or it's just a colossal waste of time. Why do it all just to make the shareholders rich? **So we still have a lot of fundamental rethinking to do if we don't want to miss the road to the future that we thought capitalism had won.**

Rethinking capitalism

Communism had a cause—which was, ideally, a sense of equality and prosperity for all, that all people were and could be equal—but it didn't have an appropriate mechanism to deliver that cause. Whereas capitalism is a mechanism, but it seems to me that it lacks a cause. Is it all just to make ourselves rich, or is there more to life than that? Because when we get the money, that seldom seems to be enough. The question is, are we in danger of throwing the baby out with the bathwater? The bathwater is the inefficiency and intolerance of communism, while the baby is its idealism. And that is what capitalism is sadly lacking. There is a cancer in the heart of capitalism. It is the lack of a cause that can stir the heart. What's it all for and for whom?

The first stage in rethinking capitalism is to be absolutely clear about what it's all for and *who* it's for. I don't think the answer that it's for the financiers—i.e. the shareholders—is a very adequate answer at all, either practically or morally. We have, for instance, to realize that the new source of wealth is intelligence. It's not land or money or raw materials or technology. It's the brains and the skills of people.

For years, corporate chairmen have been talking about their people as their primary assets. It's time they woke up to the fact that it's actually true, because their only hope for future security lies in the brains of those people.

But, in the age of intellectual capital, who owns the capital? It's not the shareholders. It can't be, in any real sense. The people who own the intellect are the core workers of the company. In other words, it's the assets who own the assets. Because we can't in any real sense own other people. They can always walk out on us. Nor does it seem right to own another person. We used to call that slavery.

So a model that says that the company is owned by the people who finance it—and that the people who are in it are just instruments of those owners—is no longer pertinent in this day and age, and it certainly won't be appropriate in the future. It just isn't the right sort of concept.

If we don't change company law, we are going to see the stock exchange becoming just one huge casino and that is not going to be a sensible basis for any economy. We've got to change the law so that the financiers are actually just financiers and not owners. That is, they are like mortgage holders. They have some ultimate security in what is in the company, but they don't have the right to tell people what to do. They have the right to demand a reasonable return on their money and that's about all. We've also got to rethink the share of voice that the new assets have in the ownership and the running of the enterprise. Presently, the only people with a vote in most organizations are the top management and the shareholders. I believe that this is wrong. We need a fairer balance of power. We need to give more rights to the people who work there because, after all, they are the real assets of the company.

In tomorrow's economy, when intelligence is property, we will also have to make sure that everyone has the right to own some of that property and the wealth that it brings. Everyone has got to get intelligent—in its widest sense. Organizations will have to recognize their role in training and education. Governments will have to invest in the intelligence of all their citizens, otherwise society will become even more divided than ever.

Of course, each of us bears an individual responsibility for this too. We have to realize that our future prosperity depends on our competencies and our education, so we will need continually to develop and update our skills. In fact, we must learn to see education as never ending if we want to be of any use to the organization and to society. And if we want to have any share in the new form of property.

Finding a new purpose

I find that it helps, sometimes, to stand back and realize that we are just a little thing in the eons of time and the oceans of the world, and we are here for a very short space of time, a sparrow flying through a dark hall. We can't change everything or make the world a perfect place. Nevertheless, we should do the best we can, because I think there is a purpose to us being here—even if it is just to keep the show on the road.

I actually have some worries about that because more and more people are finding it a bit of a bore keeping the show on the road, having kids for instance or keeping the organization going, so even that begins to disappear as a purpose. Instead, it becomes, for many, a very temporary, existential, even selfish existence, when all we're actually trying to do is to live in the moment. There are few great causes anymore.

I was very struck by the book *The End of History* by Fukuyama, which was not the triumphalist cry that many people interpreted it as, the ultimate triumph of the liberal democracies over communism. What I understand him to say is that the combination of economics and liberal democracy means that we elect politicians to keep us happy and that is what they have to aspire to do if they want to be reelected. We end up behaving like dogs; we just want to lie in the sun and be fed. Comfortable selfish survival becomes the only point of life.

I sense, however, that more and more people want life to mean more than that. They no longer expect politicians to deliver it, but look instead to other institutions.

Therefore it becomes the organization's responsibility to provide a purpose if they want to retain good people. If you want to retain talent, you've got to create a cause. Otherwise you get a purely instrumental relationship in which I'm working for you purely because I'm earning money, or because it's teaching me some skills which I will go somewhere else and use. Then you get very short-term thinking, very selfish thinking.

The great and most satisfying thing in life, I think, is a sense of purpose beyond oneself. If the purpose is only for yourself, it rapidly dissipates. If you sit and drink a bottle of wine by yourself, it's OK for the first glass, but by the fourth glass it's getting a bit intolerable. There's nobody to talk to. Nobody to share it with. I think that if one doesn't have a purpose beyond oneself, bigger than oneself, then one ends up disappointed in the end.

So I think we will have to change the meaning of business from being an instrument of the owners to make them rich, and which employs other people as instruments of the organization to help make that aim come true, to being something more like a community with a purpose.

➤ *What advice would you give organizations, societies and individuals to help them prepare for the twenty-first century?*

I would say remember the past, and celebrate it if you want to, but put it behind you. Don't let the past stand in the way of your future. Because the future is going to be different. And we have to unlearn the way we dealt with the past in order to deal with the future.

Of course the past is important. We need a sense of history. But you can't walk into the future looking over your shoulder. **You can't stumble backwards into the future.**

If you go into a business and it has a display of its history, you should be worried. On the other hand, if you go into a business and it has a display of what the future might be, you should be excited.

Because the great excitement of the future is that we can shape it. **"**

Charles Handy

Charles Handy is without doubt Britain's foremost business philosopher. Perhaps best known for his ideas on the changing nature of work and organizations, Handy's wide-angle thinking has more recently been concerned with the implications for society of these dramatic changes, and with rethinking the whole concept of capitalism. Educated at Oxford and the Sloan School of Management at the Massachusetts Institute of Technology (MIT), Charles Handy was formerly an oil executive and a business economist with Shell International and a Professor of Management Development at the London Business School. Today he is an independent writer and educator. His books have sold over one million copies all over the world.

Recommended reading

Beyond Certainty: The changing worlds of organisations (1995) US: Harvard Business School Press/UK: Random House.
The Empty Raincoat: Making sense of the future (new edn 1995) US (as *The Age of Paradox*): Harvard Business School Press/UK: Random House.
The Age of Unreason (new edn 1995) US: Harvard Business School Press/UK: Random House.
Gods of Management: The changing work of organisations (3rd edn 1995) US: Oxford University Press/UK: Random House.
Waiting for the Mountain to Move: And other reflections on life (new edn 1995) UK: Random House.
Understanding Organizations (4th edn 1992) UK: Penguin.
Understanding Voluntary Organizations (new edn 1990) UK: Penguin.

"Tomorrow's successful leaders will value principles more than they value their companies."

PUTTING PRINCIPLES FIRST

Stephen Covey

IN MY BOOK *Principle-Centered Leadership* I said that my hope was to bring about an important paradigm shift in management. That paradigm shift would be from the 'human relations' and 'human resource' model—which is based on treating people well and then using them well—to a 'principle-centered leadership' model. This new model includes the first two principles but it goes a lot further, because it deals with helping people find meaning and fulfilment, based on the awareness that, ultimately, natural laws or principles will always govern anyway. So it's about creating an empowered workforce around a common sense of meaning and vision, around a value system that is principle based, and then tapping into the power of that workforce in order to compete in the global economy.

I am personally convinced that what I am talking about here will come about just through the natural force of international competition. In the global economy you cannot compete, you cannot be viable, if you don't have high quality and low cost. And you cannot achieve high quality and low cost without a 'high-trust' culture. It is high trust that gives you the ability to make meaningful partnerships inside and outside the organization, with employees, with customers, with suppliers, with everybody. In turn, you cannot achieve a high-trust culture—based on absolute trustworthiness throughout the organization—without being principle centered. **Trust comes from principles.**

The principles I am referring to are the basic universal principles that pertain to all human relationships and organizations, for instance fairness, justice, honesty, integrity, trust. They are self-evident, self-validating. These principles are like natural laws that operate regardless of whether we decide to obey them or not. I call them 'true north' principles because they don't shift. They are always there, always reliable, like the 'true north' on a compass. And they provide us with rock-solid direction in our lives and in our organizations.

They are also principles that no one argues with. Everyone buys into them. There is a universal common sense about them. And almost all organizations are beginning to talk this way now; about translating these principles into their culture and into their different practices. I go to their meetings all the time and I hear this. Because they are realizing that, in the quality movement of the past, the emphasis was on technologies and on structures, systems and processes, and not on the building of high-trust cultures.

High-trust cultures

If an organization has not yet been competing globally—if it has been in a local economy or a regional economy where it hasn't had this kind of tough competition to benchmark against—it may so far have been able to succeed at the bottom line with the old approach. But the global economy is going to have a huge impact on the entire world. And this has already raised the bar so high, so significantly, that it requires organizations to have high-trust cultures. Otherwise they won't survive.

Some of the companies that are already implementing high-trust cultures include the automobile company Saturn. It has a very different quality of relationships inside its organization, as well as with the union and with other organizations. Or take Ritz Carlton, the hotel chain. The principles on which it operates have produced a culture and a level of empowerment that are totally amazing.

The great value of a high-trust culture is that it brings together idealism and pragmatism. It becomes the basis for both empowerment and quality. **How are you going to get people empowered if you don't have high trust?** When there's low trust you've got to use control. You can't empower people in a culture like that, otherwise you'll have loose cannons all over the place. And everyone will be pointing in different directions and saying, 'This is north, this is north, this is north'. They don't have a common vision and a common set of values based on principles that they all buy into. You also won't get quality, because quality requires that everyone up and down the entire process has quality in their heart and in their mind. They have to really believe that 'quality begins with me', and they need to make their decisions based on the right principles and values. So empowerment and quality are totally integrated in a high-trust culture. Trustworthiness precedes trust which precedes empowerment which precedes quality.

Believing in human potential

If you want to make great gains in human performance—and I'm talking here about 500 percent, not 5 percent—you have to change fundamentally the way you think about people. You have to believe that people are the most valuable organizational assets, and that they are capable of immense achievement. And you have to help them believe it, too. In other words, you have to see the oak tree in the acorn, and you have to understand the process of helping that acorn become the giant oak tree.

This is why I say that it's not enough just to treat people well and then use them well, like the old model taught us. You have to help people find meaning and fulfilment in what they do. They don't want to be 'used' by the organization like victims or pawns. They want to have stewardship over their own resources. They want to feel that they are making a personal contribution to something meaningful. And that's when you get real motivation and real fulfilment. That's when you truly release the human potential and all that tremendous energy and creative power that is hidden inside people, waiting to be unleashed. Goethe said: 'Treat a man as he is, and he will remain as he is; treat a man as he can and should be, and he will become as he can and should be.'

So you have to believe in the unseen human potential. Otherwise you will only get status quo performance—business as usual. And that's not going to cut it in the global economy.

This reminds me of what happened when Chuck Yeager broke the sound barrier and introduced the era of supersonic flight. Before that happened, some predicted that the 'barrier' was impenetrable—that Yeager and his Bell Aviation X-1 plane would disintegrate as soon as they hit Mach 1. But, of course, it wasn't impenetrable at all. The barrier was only a myth. He later wrote in his autobiography that 'the real barrier wasn't in the sky, but in our knowledge and experience of supersonic flight'. Similarly today, some executives pilot their organizations at slow speeds and low altitudes because they believe that there is a 'human barrier' to higher performance, beyond which they cannot go. But a few courageous leaders are breaking the 'human barrier' and their organizations are achieving supersonic performance.

The fact that most organizations have a human barrier is evident by the response I get from large audiences whenever I ask them about this. I just traveled through places in Europe, South Africa, South America, all through Asia and North America. And I said: 'How many in this room would agree that the vast majority of the workforce in your organization possess more talent, more creativity, more initiative and more resourcefulness than their present jobs require or even allow them to use?' Almost all of them raised their hands.

Most people are capable of achieving much more than their present jobs require or even allow. But the problem is that management doesn't believe it. The late Konosuke Matsushita, president of the giant Japanese consumer electronics company, put it this way: 'We are going to win and the industrial West is going to lose out; there's not much you can do about it because the reasons for your failure are within yourselves... For you, the essence of management is to get the ideas out of the heads of the bosses and into the hands of labor.' In other words, what has to change is the management mindset, the old paradigm that most companies are locked into.

It's almost like the old medical paradigm of blood-letting. The thought used to be that the bad stuff was in the blood. Therefore, you had to employ blood letting to cure the problem. But then Semmelweiss, Pasteur and other great scientists discovered the germ, and that changed the essence of medicine. Now the same thing is going to have to happen in management and leadership. **Its fundamental paradigm will need to change.**

What has happened in most companies is that they are trying to bring in new technologies and the new language of 'empowerment', 'team building', 'partnering' etc., but the old benevolent-authoritarian paradigm has stayed the same. The problem is that you can't put new wine in old bottles.

You can't talk yourself out of problems you behave yourself into. If you want to solve chronic problems and achieve long-term results, you need more than an aspirin solution. The new techniques, the new technology, the new language, the new-style planning—they're all cosmetic. And they're like fluffy cotton candy. It tastes good for a short while and then it's gone. Then the cynicism returns and it's deeper than ever. People don't believe it next time around.

Uprooting the old paradigm

Bringing in this new and different way of thinking is a process that takes a great deal of patience, because you have to work at it from the inside out. Every person in the organization must change inside their hearts and minds, so that they themselves become principle centered. You have to get right down to the individual, hopefully starting with the people at the top. But we've also seen the pragmatic fruits when people at the middle and even the lower levels become like a leavening influence throughout the entire organization, and ultimately transform their organizations. It takes longer and is more difficult this way. For a while, they have to buffer the adverse environment around them. But they become like islands of excellence in a sea of mediocrity, and they get noticed. It starts to get other people's attention. They wonder: 'How do you have such a large span of control? How are you able to produce that level of quality at that low cost?' And they pragmatically start to leaven the entire organization. There are all kinds of illustrations of this, and it is something that is going to go on and on.

It is very difficult to go through a fundamental paradigm shift, especially on an organizational level, but it is possible—even when the old paradigm is deeply ingrained. And it's the only way to have any kind of success in the new global economy.

Principles in practice

Colin Hall, who represents the Covey Leadership Center in South Africa, is also the chief executive of the largest retail group in the country, with billions in sales. As you know, South Africa is going through a profound metamorphosis throughout its entire society. It is still on tenterhooks, and it has to go along a very frail, thin pathway in order to bring off the political stability it will need to merit the confidence of the international communities so that it can get foreign investment etc. And it takes a person with such moral authority as Nelson Mandela to do this. Colin Hall was part of the old paradigm of white superiority—the apartheid system. But he came across the material on principle-centered leadership and it started to make a change from the inside out, deep inside his heart. So he started to follow it and to have his managers in various stores throughout South Africa trained along these lines. Now they're gaining tremendous market share because of the level of empowerment that is taking place and the principles on which they are operating. The business results flowing from these principles—which generate high trust and get deep commitment and loyalty on the part of the workers—are gaining the attention of all kinds of businesses in South Africa.

To give you just give one illustration, the company opened up a brand new line of stores called No. 1, and the very day it opened up its maiden store, the old squatters—the local hawkers who sell vegetables and fruits— moved right in front of the store and even in front of the doors so that it was very hard for people to get in. The normal tendency would have been to bring in the law, the superior structure, and drive them off. But is that smart? Is that principled? These people have been there for 20 or 30 years. They have psychological ownership of the place and you have legal ownership. So what do you do? Remember the Seven Habits? If you apply Habits 4, 5 and 6 at the organizational level, you are going to go outside and 'Think Win/Win'. You are going to start to listen to them, you are going to 'Seek First to Understand...Then to be Understood', and then you are going to 'Synergize'. You will come up with the synergistic solution so that both parties can trade better. So that is precisely what they did. They entered into a partnership with these people in which the hawkers promote the store, and in return the store promotes their fruit stands. In addition, the hawkers identify thieves in the culture so that the store has almost no theft taking place. They also sweep up and clean the place out front, and invite people to go in.

The No. 1 stores are really starting to take market share in those markets. And the other stores—with the old benevolent authoritarian approach—say, 'This is our property, this is what we are going to do.' They're not principle centered. They are violating the culture, and their market share is getting smaller. We took a film crew down to South Africa and made 15 films showing this very thing I'm describing and what took place. Colin Hall and I presented this concept at the Young Presidents' Organization's international university in South Africa. I presented the principles, and then he talked about what he was doing with them, so it was not just theory but also practice. He discussed how our whole society must move towards this or we won't be viable in the international economy. He shared his deep conviction that if we can do it in South Africa, we can do it anywhere in the world.

Then people asked him: 'Colin, how could you do this yourself?' Formerly, he was deep into the old Afrikaans way of thinking—the idea of white superiority and of preserving a distinct society. He said that the hardest part was the change that he had to go through inside himself. But he added that for years he had felt in the deepest part of his heart that the old regime, the old thinking, was wrong and flawed, even though he had covered it over with rationalization and justification. He said: 'Now I am totally behind this thing, right from my heart.' And people sense his sincerity. There were hundreds of people sitting there—half of the group were from South Africa. They had heard about the market share that he's taking and they wanted to listen to this guy. They just sat there with their mouths open.

➤ *Many initiatives start well, but tend to fall into entropy after a while. How can you keep the momentum going year after year?*

You need more than words and rhetoric and nice ideas. If you are really doing principle-centered leadership, you build the principles into all your structures and systems. They govern the way you gather information, the way you reward people, the way you promote people, even the way you make people at the top accountable. You establish what we call a 360° review, in which, at least annually, every person, every department, every team and every division in every company is accountable to those principles with all of the stakeholders they interface with on a consistent basis. And no one is exempt. Those people who cannot adapt their styles, their structures and systems to get high grades against these principles cannot stay. They shape up or they ship out. So, little by little, this purifies the culture, and it overcomes this tendency towards entropy. **Because when you apply the principles consistently, they become behavioral habits, and this enables the fundamental transformation of individuals, of relationships and of organizations.**

When you bring new people in, you say to them: 'We want you to join us but you'd better analyze what you're coming into. You'd better be prepared to live by these principles or your future will be jeopardized.' In other words, they have to buy in. And if the culture is a high-trust culture, they get socialized into it. They come to realize that it isn't just words and slogans on the wall. This is the veritable constitution by which every person is evaluated, and by which their future career in the organization is governed.

Habit 7 is 'Sharpen the Saw'. It's the unique endowment of continuous improvement or self-renewal. So how do you sharpen the saw or achieve renewal at the organizational level? You've got to continually go back to your roots. You've got to be constantly improving, innovating and refining. Otherwise you will fall into entropy and things will eventually break down. You must never be too busy sawing to take time to sharpen the saw.

That means you've got regularly to do these 360° accountability reviews, with every person. Some time ago, I was involved in training one of the premier national airforces, and I was talking about this 360° accountability to a gathering of all of the generals. And they were all nodding their heads. So I said, 'You mean you do this already?' And the commanding general, the one who was in charge of them all, said that every one of his generals has a 360° review once a year. I asked, 'How do you do it?' He answered that they get a computerized, anonymous print-out from all of the people that they interface with over time, and it evaluates each of them against the principles and the vision of the airforce. It is for their eyes only. But if they want a promotion, they have to show it, and no one is promoted unless they have high marks from everybody—including from their subordinates.

When times get tough

Everyone can shine when the sun is shining, but it is the storm that tests the character of a person or an organization. **When you have a high-trust culture and times become tough, it's analogous to a smallpox vaccination shot. It triggers off an immunity, so that the culture joins together to cope with that reality in a synergistic way, instead of becoming split and divided.** But if you have a low-trust culture, when times get tough you have accusations and legal fights all over the place.

They say, 'To heck with all this stuff', and throw the principles right out of the window. That's what happens when you have low trust and high pressure—when you have a cosmetic principle-centered culture.

Whereas, if you really have a principle-centered culture, and you have tough times, that's when it becomes most evident.

Principle-centered leaders

You can't get principle-centered leadership without principle-centered leaders. This whole thing has to come from inside people. It isn't some artificial psych-up system, it has to come out of the hearts of people like Colin Hall. They become the catalysts. They become the small rudders that move the big rudder that moves the whole ship.

Tomorrow's successful leaders will value principles more than they value their companies. In other words, they will be more loyal to principles than to any institution. For that is actually the highest way of serving their company.

They will be men and women who have both character and competence. Character without competence is as insufficient as competence without character. So they will be people who are deeply involved on a continuous basis in personal and professional development. They will be constantly expanding their competence, developing new skills, reading, training, listening to others, learning and growing, sharpening the saw.

But the key is that they will work on the basis of natural principles, and they will build their lives and their organizations around those principles. That's what it means to be principle centered. You put principles at the center of your life, at the center of your relationships with others, at the center of your agreements and contracts, at the center of your management processes and at the center of your mission statement.

The marketplace will force leaders to break with the past and begin to live according to the new paradigm. Think of General Electric. It's taken Jack Welch something like eleven years to get a set of values that everyone can buy into. And look at the metamorphosis that GE has gone through. It was deeply bureaucratic and very rule infested before. But today, some of its divisions have levels of empowerment that would knock your socks off. And the major achievement, Jack feels, is the formation of a set of values or principles at the center of the organization that guides everything it does.

The leader as farmer

I think we need to get away from this idea that there is a quick, easy approach to building a high-trust culture. As I said, it took Jack Welch eleven years to do it, and it's still an ongoing thing. You just can't change a corporate culture in a weekend. It's not something you can do with quick-fix, short-term thinking.

That's why I use the farming metaphor. The only thing that endures over time is the law of the harvest. And there is nothing quick and easy about it. We're involved in a process of planting, of watering, of weeding and of cultivating the growth of a beautiful crop, and we may not see anything happening for a period of time. So, too, in an organization, you have to keep on working on the principles over the long term, and eventually you will have a beautiful harvest. All real growth and all progress is made step by step.

The trouble is, many leaders view the organization like a machine. They think if something is broken you can go right ahead and fix it. You just take out the part that's broken, put in a new part, turn it on and it will work again.

But the organization is not mechanical: it's organic. It lives and it grows, and it's made up of living, growing people. You can't 'fix' people. You have to nurture them over time. **You have to create the right conditions, the right climate, for growth and opportunity.** Like the farmer, who has to choose the best seed, then take care that the soil is right, the temperature is right, that there's enough sunshine and water and fertilizer, that the weeds are removed and that the crop is cultivated, so that growth can be maximized. But it takes time. Lots of time. You can't rush it, even if you want to. The law of the farm is a natural law; it's based on universal principles.

We have to learn to view the organization with an agricultural paradigm, not a mechanical one. Just like the way medicine moved from the mechanical to the organic—the awareness that body, mind and spirit are really inseparably connected together, and that we're not just a bunch of mechanics playing around with body parts. The same thing is happening in the new physics. It's moved away from mechanical concepts—such as

Newton's clockwork paradigm—into the uncertainty principle, chaos theory, complexity theory. And it's changed the way we look at the world. Now this paradigm shift is coming into organizations, and I believe that it's going to change the future of management and leadership.

Ultimately, principles will govern. Therefore we'd better align towards principles. That's why I believe that the highest quality of a leader is humility; the strength to acknowledge that you are not really in charge, that principles are in charge in the long run. And the next quality the leader needs to have is the courage to align with those principles, in the face of very powerful social forces and of old paradigms—including the leader's old habits.

➤ *What can organizations and their leaders do right now to become more principle centered, and to improve their chances of success in the future?*

I believe that every organization should get into a reflective state of mind, go deep inside and ask the question: 'What is this company really about? And what are the principles we're going to live and work by?' Then they should write it in the form of a mission statement, philosophy statement or whatever people want to call it, and then start to make sure that their actions conform to it—that they literally live by it, so that true integrity comes from it. I believe that to be the beginning of the process. And it is a process that requires the deep involvement of everybody, like at Ritz Carlton for example, where the janitors, housekeepers and secretaries play an equal part in the process.

You can't announce a mission statement. You can't have it come down from Mount Olympus. It has to come out of the hearts of people. Otherwise the mission statement will be ignored. And it will be a source of cynicism inside the culture.

To the leaders, I would say the same thing. Start with your own personal mission statement. What kind of a legacy do you want to give to your organization? And to your own children? What kind of person do you want to be remembered as? A person of integrity who gave significant contributions and service? Or one that just put the ladder up against a wall of money-making, then climbed it only to realize that it's leaning against the wrong wall? **99**

Stephen Covey

Dr Stephen R. Covey is founder and chairman of the Covey Leadership Center (CLC), an international leadership development company based in the Rocky Mountains of Utah. For over a quarter of a century, he has been teaching leadership principles and management skills to leaders in business, government and education. Covey has a Harvard MBA and a doctorate from Brigham Young University, where he was a professor of organizational behavior and business management at the Marriott School of Management. He has been a consultant to over half the Fortune 500 *companies, as well as thousands of other organizations, and is sought after internationally as a speaker and as an executive mentor to leaders of companies and countries. Covey's book,* The Seven Habits of Highly Effective People, *is one of the bestselling books of all time. To date, it has sold seven million copies and has been translated into 28 languages.*

Recommended reading

Daily Reflections for Highly Effective People: Living the seven habits everyday (1994) US: Simon & Schuster.

First Things First (1994) US/UK: Simon & Schuster.

Principle-Centered Leadership: Strategies for personal and professional effectiveness (1992) US/UK: Simon & Schuster.

The Seven Habits of Highly Effective People: Powerful lessons in personal change (1989) US/UK: Simon & Schuster.

Rethinking

COMPETITION

Creating Tomorrow's Advantages

Michael Porter

Strategies for Growth

CK Prahalad

Reinventing the Basis for Competition

Gary Hamel

"The important thing is to try to shape the nature of competition, to take control over your own destiny."

CREATING TOMORROW'S ADVANTAGES

Michael Porter

" As we enter the twenty-first century, there is a pressing need for clear strategies. Because unless companies have a clear vision about how they are going to be distinctly different and unique, offering something different than their rivals to some different group of customers, they are going to get eaten alive by the intensity of competition.

There was a time when markets were forgiving, when there weren't that many rivals and companies could drift along with 'me-too' strategies. But now 'me-too' strategies are punished quickly and mercilessly. So the stakes of having a clear strategy are higher.

I also sense that most companies have spent the last decade or so doing the reengineering thing, doing the downsizing thing, doing the overhead-reduction thing; and now the question is, what do they do next? **Companies have to find ways of growing and building advantages rather than just eliminating disadvantages.**

Organizations everywhere have been rushing to implement all the latest ideas on management, sometimes to the point of overuse. And they've been struggling to fit all the pieces together: TQM, time-based competition, benchmarking etc. Most of these ideas are about doing things better, about improving operational effectiveness. This improvement is necessary just to stay in the game. But staying in the game is not sufficient.

If everybody is competing on the same set of variables, then the standard gets higher but no company gets ahead. And getting ahead—then staying ahead—is the basis of strategy: creating a competitive advantage. Strategy is about setting yourself apart from the competition. **It's not just a matter of being better at what you do—it's a matter of being different at what you do.**

Many companies have atrophied in their ability to think and act strategically. In the US we have so much short-term, quarter-to-quarter thinking. It's all about immediate results—let's cut staff or outsource to boost earnings next year. Companies seem to have gotten out of the habit of investing, and US capital markets are reinforcing those tendencies. This is true to different degrees in other countries as well.

A fresh look at competitive strategy

The whole field of strategy is, in the scheme of things, relatively new. There was no serious research on strategy until the 1950s or 1960s. And in a sense, the field of strategy and the understanding of competition remain emerging management disciplines. We are still learning and accumulating knowledge about competition very rapidly.

It's also important to recognize that, as we learn about competition and as this knowledge of how to compete diffuses, it creates the need to keep learning. Because, if all companies are doing whatever it is that is supposed to create an advantage, then it's no longer an advantage.

So there is a need to keep learning about strategy. First, because we still don't know all that there is to know. And second, because the process of learning itself creates the need for new learning.

Pitfalls in strategic thinking

There is no strategy that can be stretched beyond the boundaries of a particular business. **One of the great mistakes that has been made over and over again by companies is the attempt to apply a universal strategy.** This thinking leads companies into a trap.

The first trap was that companies thought they had to have the largest market share, because this was the only way to win. The idea is wrong, because there are lots of companies with small market shares that are more profitable. What is worse, if all companies are trying to get the largest market share, a destructive battle ensues which is hard for any company to win.

Another trap was the idea that all companies should reduce their cycle times, and speed up the time to market. Again, as a universal 'truth', this isn't true. In some markets, it's better to take more time to get it right, rather than introduce new products with short development cycles. In other markets it's different. But if all companies reduce their cycle times, then what results is a time race that nobody can win. In fact, everybody loses, because faster time to market eventually starts to drive up costs or reduce revenue, which dissipates profit.

So the idea that there might be a universal strategy for the twenty-first century, that could be applicable across the board, is obviously wrong. And to think otherwise is, in my opinion, a very big mistake.

➤ *What are the underlying principles that define a good strategy?*

A good strategy is concerned with the structural evolution of the industry as well as with the firm's own unique position within that industry. Effects in the industry can overwhelm a good strategy. If a company finds itself in a bad industry at the wrong time, it doesn't matter how well positioned it is, to put it bluntly. So managers have to look at the dynamics of their industry and at its future trajectory. A significant part of any company's success will depend on the industry. And when I refer to industry, I mean the specific business a company is in. It's not banking, but cash management, for example.

Increasingly, the companies that will be the true leaders will be those that don't just optimize within an industry, but that actually reshape and redefine their industry. The question is: 'How can we make this industry a better competitive environment for ourselves?' Instead of just responding or reacting to the industry's present structure, leaders will take action to influence and even restructure it. There are limits to this, of course. But industry structure is not fixed, so companies do have some leverage. The important thing is to try to shape the nature of competition, to take control over your own destiny.

The second principle is that a good strategy makes the company different. It gives the company a unique position. And a unique position involves the delivery of a particular mix of value to some array of customers which represents a subset of the industry.

The fundamental truth in strategy is that a company simply cannot be all things to all people and do a very good job of it. **Strategy requires choices.** You have to decide what particular kind of value you want to deliver to whom.

It might be that a company has a broad customer target, but it should not try to deliver every kind of value that customers might want. Rather, the broad competitor should concentrate on common, cross-cutting needs and concentrate on being unique in meeting them.

Third, **it's not good enough just to be different. You've got to be different in ways that involve trade-offs with other ways of being different.** In other words, if you want to serve a particular target customer group with a particular definition of value, this must be inconsistent with delivering other types of value to other customers. If not, the position is easy to imitate or replicate.

So there must be trade-offs between what your competitors do and what your company does. If there are no trade-offs, then everything can be easily and costlessly imitated. And that leads, of course, to the mutually destructive battle that I talk so much about. Companies end up competing for the same set of customers using the same set of inducements. This is usually a loser's game.

The trouble is that companies hate making choices, because doing so always looks dangerous and limiting. They always want the best of all worlds. It's psychologically risky to narrow your product range, to narrow the range of value you are delivering or to narrow your distribution. And this unwillingness to make choices is one of the biggest obstacles to creating a strategy.

Adapting to change

Change has to do with evolving customer needs. Change has to do with evolving technologies for meeting customer needs. Change has to do with evolving managerial practices. We are constantly learning how to manage large complex institutions such as companies, and the way we do that is a great deal better today than it was 20 years ago. So there is a constant change in the potential for competing.

But what is important in thinking about change is to make the distinction between improving your operational effectiveness—or just the quality of your management—and shifting your competitive position. In other words, rapid change has to be addressed squarely in the area of improving operational effectiveness. You can't afford to be two years behind in your service delivery process. You have to employ the latest methods, techniques and ideas.

But, having said that, if competition is just a race to see who can perform service the best, it ends up being a self-destructive race and nobody wins. Companies must decide what particular kind of service they want to deliver if they are going to have a chance to have an advantage at the end of the day.

Continuity of strategy and rapid change are not inconsistent. In fact the two go right together, if we make the very important distinction between strategic positioning and operational effectiveness in executing that position.

Again, positioning is a strategy in which the goal is to be different, and in which trade-offs are necessary between what a company is doing and what its competitors are doing. In order to create those conditions, however, one needs continuity in the basic positioning—the types of products it offers, the essential core of the value it is delivering. But within that continuity should be a feverish and on-going process of change.

If one examines high-performing companies, and by that I mean those that regularly outperform their industries, one finds that they don't change their strategies. Instead of change, we see stability. We see continuity. But we also see a lot of change in the details—the product details, the service details etc. So there is a consistent strategy, but continuous improvement in how the strategy is manifested.

There is a tendency to fixate on the pace of change. There's an 'action produces a reaction' phenomenon in competition, and I have a feeling that we will see some countertrends. Linearizing some of the trends we have seen in the last 10 or 15 years is dangerous.

➤ *When does it become necessary to change your competitive strategy?*

It becomes necessary when the fundamental needs of the customer group shift. Or when the particular type of product is no longer distinct. A strategy must also change when the trade-offs are eliminated by new technology or customer changes.

Changes of this magnitude don't happen very often. Strategy should rest on dimensions that are not like the difference between a short hemline and a long hemline. You don't want to base the success of your company on a particular definition of value that is transient. Instead, it should be things like intensive after-sales support, the sheer durability of the product, the ruggedness of the product in the face of abuse out in the field. These more enduring sources of value are the basis of really great strategies.

The importance of innovation

As I stress in my book *The Competitive Advantage of Nations*, the ability to sustain an advantage from cheap labor or even from economies of scale— these are the old paradigms. These paradigms are being superseded. Today, the only way to have an advantage is through innovation and upgrading.

But this innovation, this upgrading, has to involve a consistent strategic direction. There has to be a strategic vision within which you are innovating. A company has to have something distinctive at the end of the day that it is reinforcing.

To me, innovation means offering things in different ways, creating new combinations. Innovation doesn't mean small, incremental improvements— these are just part of being a dynamic organization. Innovation is about finding new ways of combining things generally.

The role of technology

Technology is a very underdefined term in discussions of competition. One can define technology narrowly to mean things like semiconductor technology or biotechnology. It can also be defined very broadly to include the technology of management—how you organize, how you control large production processes or logistical systems.

I tend, in my own work, to define technology very broadly, because I find that competitive advantage comes just as often from things like controlling a large distribution system as it does from science in the traditional sense.

I believe that every company has to master—or at least have the capacity to assimilate—the range of technologies that are affecting the way it goes about delivering value to its customers. I would say, from looking at many industries, that a sheer scientific breakthrough—or the ability to have the most scientific technological capability in a particular field—does not seem to be that important. It's more the ability to apply technology that is the source of advantage. And to apply technology you've got to integrate it with a lot of other things. So we find over and over again that the first one to market with a new technology is often not the winner in the marketplace. The winner is the one that figures out how to incorporate that technology into the broader system of the company.

➤ *Whom should a company involve in the process of developing and implementing strategy?*

The essential core of strategy is cross-functional or cross-activity integration. It's not the ability to come up with a better production process or the ability to come up with a great ad. It's the capacity to link and integrate activities across the whole value chain and to achieve complementarities across many activities. It's where the way you do one thing allows you to do something else better.

Consider Wal-Mart's strategy. Its success was based on a whole series of integrated activities. It was location plus warehousing, plus MIS, plus store manager autonomy, plus, plus, plus. So for K-Mart to match Wal-Mart, it would have to match a lot of what Wal-Mart does. It's like a recipe: if you leave out one ingredient, the cake can collapse. To have a sustainable advantage, a company has to integrate across many activities to create a unique positioning involving trade-offs with rivals. **It must be illogical or difficult for rivals to match everything you do, otherwise competition will be mutually destructive.**

So much of the writing on strategy is based on the premise that there is only one ideal way of competing, and that the first company who discovers it wins. This one ideal way of competing is often seen as arising from a few activities. **Instead, the essence of strategy is cross-functional, cross-activity integration.**

As a result of that, strategy shouldn't only be the province of the leader. I believe that strategy should be developed in a multifunctional team, involving the leader and the people who are responsible for the principal activities in the business. And that strategy must be the joint product of those people. It's a great mistake to try to subdivide strategic planning into pieces and then attempt to put the pieces back together. Ultimately, the essential issue is how to integrate across the pieces.

Traditionally, strategy was developed by planners, and that was fine when nobody knew what strategy was. In that era, however, strategies were often not implemented, because nobody paid any attention to the planners. It was an isolated exercise. Strategies have also tended to gravitate towards slogans, like 'you have to have the biggest market share'.

Now what has evolved is a healthier process in which line managers are in charge of developing strategy. Planning departments have a diminished role. But, in too many companies, strategy is viewed as something that one person can set. Or as a process where the task is to staple a marketing strategy and a production strategy and a finance strategy together and call the whole thing a competitive strategy.

Strategy for small companies

The need for strategy is universal. And, indeed, you could argue that it's even more important for small companies who lack the sheer resources and momentum to buffer them from competition.

The small player has to have a position that is hard to imitate—or that competitors choose not to imitate—because if it's easy for the large competitors to do so, they soon will.

My view is that the small competitor ought to focus on that position, that niche, that they will serve uniquely well, and where larger, more broadly targeted competitors won't be as effective.

If you examine the economies of countries like Italy and Germany, what you very quickly realize is that it is the small and midsize companies who are really the backbone of those economies. And they don't jump around from product to product; they become the world's leading provider in a particular segment. Nobody can touch them in this area, because they have so much accumulated expertise and knowledge, and they've optimized everything they do in that segment.

Rethinking globalization

The first impact of globalization was to diminish the impact of location, by allowing international companies to gain an advantage over companies that were still stuck in a domestic orientation. So, in the first phase of globalization it was globalness itself which provided the advantage. That is, the capacity of a company to martial and mobilize inputs and assets across borders.

We are entering a new phase which is more counterintuitive, because now globalness is assumed. Now, a company *must* source inputs from the lowest-cost location. It *must* source capital internationally, not locally. It *must* locate plants in low-labor-cost nations if it has labor-intensive activities.

The presence of so many global markets and companies has essentially nullified the advantage of globalness *per se*. Anything a company can access from a distance is no longer a competitive advantage, because now everybody can access it.

This new phase of globalization is paradoxically putting a greater and greater premium on what I call the 'home base'—the unique critical mass of skill, expertise, suppliers and local institutions that makes certain locations the innovation centers in a particular business.

There are numerous examples of industry clusters that have become the innovation centers in their fields. There's Silicon Valley in microelectronics, Hollywood in the entertainment business, Los Angeles in multimedia.

A company's odds of being successful in any given field are dramatically improved by location. The odds of becoming a world-class software company are much higher if you are located in the United States. The Japanese are still nowhere in software, although their government has poured millions into developing the industry.

So whereas it used to be that the scale of the firm was important, now it is increasingly the scale of the cluster—the network, the infrastructure—that is important. A given firm's scale can be smaller if there are a lot of good suppliers around, if there are a lot of good supporting companies around.

This evolution in the paradigm of globalization is putting a greater and greater premium on specialization, on doing particular things in particular locations—things that you can do best there—rather than doing everything in one particular location. Honda, for example, now makes its all-terrain vehicles exclusively at its US home base, instead of in different factories around the world.

In the future, nations are going to be increasingly competing for these home bases, because they are the sources of wealth and high wages. That's where the development and innovation capabilities in any given business are going to be concentrated.

Technology vs innovation

Fundamental shifts in technology can have an incredible impact on the importance of geographical location. My perspective is that, as changes in technology diminish the importance of certain aspects of location, these aspects become nullified as competitive advantages. So, in some sense, what happens is that **new technology sweeps away potential advantages and therefore the residual advantages get more and more important.**

It used to be that if you had access to capital at home, you had a competitive advantage. But now having a lot of capital at home is no longer an advantage, because technology and market developments have allowed companies outside of the country to get access to that capital.

It's the same thing if we can have employees working at home and not needing to be at the company. It means that the things those people do will no longer be an advantage, because companies anywhere in the United States can tap in to people working at home through the same technology.

There is a constant process by which technology is nullifying traditional advantages of location. And, as it does that, it's creating and elevating new advantages of location. Those new location advantages are more 'innovation advantages'. This is a very subtle, much misunderstood issue.

It's becoming popular for managers to dream about the virtual corporation that has no people, just a CEO who makes decisions. Nobody works at the company; they're at home wired in on the Internet. Parts come together from India and all over the place. But if that's the way the world is going to look then anybody can achieve it and advantages will be quickly replicated.

So in some sense, I find that managers have a curious fascination with ways of thinking that essentially destroy their competitive advantages.

Recalibrating economies

If we apply this thinking to economies rather than companies, governments have to understand first and foremost that there is a new paradigm of competitiveness. It's a paradigm based on innovation and upgrading. It's a paradigm based on specialization—countries prosper in areas where they can achieve unique specialization and critical mass. They cannot try to be in everything.

Governments have to understand that everything they do needs to be recalibrated around the paradigm of innovation. Regulation has to shift from slowing change down to speeding it up. Countries need to have strict regulation that pushes companies to the next generation of technology, rather than retarding them at the last generation.

Governments also need to understand that the only way economies can be innovative is by having a lot of local competition. The idea that the way to win is to have a single large firm has been made obsolete by the fact that scale is no longer as important as it once was, and only rapid progress driven by competitive pressure will allow prosperity.

If governments can grasp the fact that there is a new paradigm, then many of the policies for improving the competitiveness of their economies become relatively obvious.

▶ *What should we be doing right now to plot a successful strategic course into the twenty-first century?*

First, we've got to set the goal of learning. The companies that are going to be able to become successful, or remain successful, will be the ones that can learn fast, can assimilate this learning and can develop new insights. I suspect that companies are going to have to become much more like universities than they have been in the past. Companies tended to think that they knew a lot, and therefore tried to be efficient in doing what they thought they knew. But it's now a matter of learning.

In addition, companies have to create an environment where people don't resist change but really expect it. An environment where companies cannibalize their own products, instead of waiting for some competitor to do it. Where companies render their own production processes obsolete rather than letting somebody else do it to them.

Finally, and most importantly, companies must reconnect with the whole idea of strategy. Success is more and more a function of making choices, and having the discipline to avoid the incredible pressures for compromise and distraction that are present if we're going to compete successfully in the twenty-first century. A lot of people seem to be coming to the same conclusion. **"**

Michael Porter

Michael E Porter is the C Roland Christensen Associate Professor of Business Administration at the Harvard Business School, and a leading expert on competitive strategy and international competitiveness. He has long been regarded as the world's greatest authority in this field; his work has provided a definitive and practical framework for strategic thinking and his ideas have become the foundation for one of Harvard's required courses. Porter was educated at Princeton and Harvard, where his doctoral thesis on business economics was awarded the coveted Wells prize. Today, he sits on the boards of several companies and is a consultant and internationally acclaimed speaker on strategy matters to leading companies and governments throughout the world. Michael Porter's articles appear regularly in business and economics journals, and he is a guest columnist for the Wall Street Journal. *His bestselling books on competitive strategy and competitive advantage are required reading in top business schools.*

Recommended reading

Capital Choices: Changing the way America invests in industry (1994) US/UK: Harvard Business School Press.
The Competitive Advantage of Nations and Their Firms (1990) US: Free Press/UK: Macmillan.
Competitive Advantage: Creating and sustaining superior performance (1985) US: Free Press/UK: Collier Macmillan.
Competitive Strategy: Techniques for analyzing industries and competitors (1980) US: Free Press/UK: Collier Macmillan.

"Competing for the future means maintaining continuity by constantly creating new sources of profit."

STRATEGIES FOR GROWTH

CK Prahalad

" ONE OF THE underlying themes of our book *Competing for the Future* is that the continuity of the corporation, as an institution, is of value in itself. For example, many US- and European-based companies are at least 100 years old—Ford, Philips, GE, Siemens, Mercedes Benz, NCR, AT&T; IBM is close. The same pattern is true in Japan. If you think about the continuity of the institution, not of specific businesses and products, you find that what enables a company to survive over a long period is the ability to change.

You can look at the histories of any of the companies I just mentioned and you will find that their business portfolios, their products and their technologies have changed over the last 20, 30, 40 years. Change is inevitable to maintain continuity. If continuity is of value in society, then change is a prerequisite: if you don't change you die.

Change used to be a generational issue—one generation of managers left and the next generation moved on to create new businesses and new opportunities. But with the tremendous turbulence and the speed with which industries are changing today, you can't just sit around and wait for the next generation of managers to take charge. It's much more desirable for incumbent managers to have an ability to imagine the future and to influence the evolution of industries.

Essentially, competing for the future means maintaining continuity by ensuring that the company is constantly creating new sources of profit.

This requires a commitment to creating new businesses and new products.

Further, if you are committed to continuity and change, then you need to focus on resources. High levels of profits from existing businesses become a prerequisite. But while high levels of profits are a must, the capacity to reinvest in a consistent fashion to build a skill base and to shape the pattern of market evolution are important.

Competing for the future is not merely about having foresight. It's also about having a strong desire to be very profitable in current businesses, one which puts enormous pressure on the organization to raise the level of performance. It's about creating a virtuous cycle in the organization, where you are continuously inventing new businesses, new sources of profit, and you are also continuously increasing the capacity for leverage and profitability within existing businesses—all of which should be part of a clear corporate direction. It should not be idiosyncratic.

Continuous improvement is desirable—but think about its implications. We are telling employees: 'If you do not become more efficient, you will lose your job to your competitor.' The employees can understand that. But we are also saying, 'If you become very efficient, you will lose your job to productivity improvement'—and that they don't understand. How long do you expect employees to continuously improve without them recognizing that the implication of such improvement is loss of jobs?

What is going to happen? Very soon people are going to learn the words. You're going to get a lot of compliance, but not commitment. You're going to get acceptance of the idea of continuous improvement, but no excitement and enthusiasm for doing it. That is the reason why much of the reengineering euphoria has dwindled. Even CSC Index admits that 70–80 percent of the companies don't see the full benefits of reengineering.

If you want to have continuous improvement, the people who are rendered surplus must be rehabilitated in new opportunities. Of course it's easier to do this if you can create new businesses which are consistent with the existing skill base. That's why we talk about core competence-based diversification, where you can redeploy people (and the skill base). However, you cannot redeploy people if you are not growing, because productivity improvements will result in fewer people required to do the same level of business. Continuous improvement is therefore predicated on continuous growth. Continuous improvement efforts will be stalled if you are not simultaneously growing.

Downsizing can be like corporate anorexia; it can make you leaner and thinner, but it won't necessarily make you healthier. Ultimately, you need to grow and you need to change. There is a need to build future muscle, not simply to cut the corporate fat.

Similarly, many companies are not just fat and lazy; they are also blind. They therefore need to work on their vision, on their view of the future. They need to identify the migration path that will take them to that future and then start to follow it.

Restructuring is generating a lot of cash. Companies are reducing their debt; they have strong balance sheets; they're increasing their dividends— which is nice—but they still have significant cash left over. Many of them are buying back their stock. That includes General Electric, IBM, and AT&T...and the list continues. Suddenly companies are finding that the extraordinary new efficiencies which were possible but never dreamed of are going to create an enormous amount of cash. However, if they don't have the ability to redeploy that cash into growth opportunities, they will be left with only two choices—one will be to make an acquisition, with all its toxic side-effects, and the other will be to become a takeover target.

Whether you look at it from the point of view of an investor, an employee or the customer who wants new functionalities, new benefits, new value propositions and new price/performance relationships—the need for growth and change is inevitable.

Think about how many opportunities may have actually been lost through restructuring. **Think what might have happened if companies had used all the 'redundant' brainpower that they got rid of to imagine new markets for tomorrow, or to build new core competencies that would give them an advantage in those markets.**

Senior managers, however, have been spending less time looking outward and forward, and more time looking inward and even backward. The issue has not been what the implications of a new technology might be or how their industries might be different in five or ten years. It has been how they can reduce overheads, how they can respond to their competitor's last move, how they can improve their quality or reduce their cycle time etc.

Whereas these improvement issues are important and legitimate, they have more to do with competing for the present than with competing for the future. Unless you are growing new markets, new businesses, new sources of profit, you will find yourself on a treadmill, always trying to improve the ever-declining margins and profits from yesterday's businesses.

The traditional view

The traditional view of competition was based on three assumptions which I believe are no longer valid. The first assumption is that the industry boundaries are clear; that you know who the suppliers are, who the competitors are, who the customers are, who the collaborators and new entrants are. **But there is absolutely no way, in the evolving marketplace, that you can know exactly who the suppliers, customers, competitors and collaborators are.** Philips and Sony are competitors, but they are also collaborators. Sony competes with Philips, but at the same time supplies to Philips, just as Philips supplies to Sony. Similarly, IBM and Apple are competitors but they are also collaborators. The industry boundaries, which were assumed to be clean, are becoming totally nebulous and overlapping.

The second assumption is that industries have distinct characteristics. But industries are now merging and commingling, i.e. consumer electronics, computers, communications, components, entertainment and so on. It is no longer clear exactly what the product is and what its value to the customer is. The best example is the PC. What is a PC? Is it home entertainment? Work? Leisure? Is it a productivity tool? It all depends on the use of the PC at a given moment.

The third assumption is that you can plan for the future. However, there is so much change taking place in the underlying structure of the competitive arena that you can no longer do this.

Taking all of these things into account in your thinking—the widely varying technologies, the deregulation, the disintermediation in the marketplace, the commingling of competitors and collaborators and the management of the migration path—requires an enormous amount of synthesis and it is hard intellectual work.

Therefore, most managers shy away from the process of synthesis. What you see is that companies have lots of data, and they often have a data dump, but they still don't understand what the two or three fundamental driving forces will be for their future. They don't know how to synthesize the hard and soft information, how to synthesise information on workstyles, lifestyles and demographics with the hard issues of technology and the reasonably unpredictable issues of politics and deregulation. You need a new methodology like the one we have described in *Competing for the Future*—a strategic architecture—in order to come to terms with it.

Strategic architecture

It's not enough to imagine the future—you also have to build it. You need a blueprint for building future businesses. Many companies have had incredible industry foresight, but they lacked the capacity to execute it. Apple is one of them. Xerox has probably had more technology, and yet missed more opportunities, than any other high-tech company. In order to build the future opportunities which you have imagined, you need to develop this capacity for execution. That's why we talk about architecture—because architects need more than a dream. They need to make a blueprint for turning the dream into a reality.

In a corporate sense, a strategic architecture is the link between the present and the future. It tells you what you should be doing now, which new competencies you should be building, what new customer groups you should be trying to understand, which new distribution channels you should be exploring, in order to create a winning position for yourself in a new opportunity arena.

A strategic architecture is not a detailed plan. It's the big picture. It's the broad agenda for deploying new functionalities, acquiring new competencies, leveraging existing competencies and reconfiguring the customer interface.

Competing for the future is about competing for opportunity share rather than market share. How can we talk about market share in markets which don't exist, markets that have yet to be created? Instead, we talk about opportunity arenas, such as financial services, genetically engineered drugs and home information systems.

The questions we have to ask ourselves are: What share of future opportunities can we capture with our current portfolio of core competencies? And which new competencies will we have to build in order to maximize our share of those future opportunities?

The interesting point is that this is not about imitating someone else. Let me give a simple example. If you look at multimedia, you will find that HP approaches multimedia very differently from the way Motorola does, but both can be equally successful. What this tells us is that multimedia is not just one opportunity. It depends on your vantage point; it depends on what customer functionalities you want to influence and drive. You can have different views on what the multimedia opportunities are. Each company must have a point of view on how its industry will evolve and what will be in its best interest. It then needs to know how to manage the migration path and how to de-risk the opportunities it has identified.

De-risking opportunities

Thinking about the future and creating the future are not necessarily risky. The way you de-risk opportunities is, first, by having a point of view; second, by experimenting at low cost and learning from the marketplace; third, by using alliances, suppliers and partners to share the risk; and fourth, by influencing standards battles so that you are not putting everything in the basket before you know you have a winning coalition. There is a wide variety of ways in which you can continuously reduce the risk and yet still be a pioneer.

Of course, many companies don't see it that way. They think that being a pioneer is inherently risky. But you cannot assume that you can be second to the market and still make money. If you have a sloppy competitor who doesn't recognize how to scale up very fast to capture the opportunity, you may still be able to make some money, but that's not very likely today. The other thing is that in many of these businesses there is a tremendous erosion of margins. If, for example, I look at multimedia products, the margins erode in the first six months. If you are second to market, if you are behind the first entrants by even six to eight months, you might capture some share of the market, but the margin structures may be very, very hard to capture. These are some of the reasons why 'being a quick second' does not necessarily always make sense.

▶ *What is it that characterizes the companies who succeed in competing for the future?*

Two things characterize most of these companies. First, the companies which manage to capture the future have aspirations, **shared aspirations which lie outside the resource base of the company**. Successful companies manage to stretch and enlarge their resource base. Look at Japanese companies like Sony, Canon, Honda and Sharp. They achieved incredible competitive victories, often with considerably fewer resources than their competitors. Their ambition outpaced their resources, and that is a vital element in creating the kinds of future competitive advantages we are discussing.

Second, **successful companies have come to a view of the future through a process of synthesis**—either through a systematic process inside the company, or through some intuitive understanding of the industry. It doesn't matter how. However, the larger the company and more complex the technology, the more pressing the need for a systematic process.

If you take a look at Microsoft, for example, it has a distinct point of view. Whether you agree with its point of view is irrelevant, but it is driving towards it in a very systematic fashion. In fact, it has been so efficient that all you hear are complaints. I look at the company and say: 'Isn't this what we are supposed to do as managers—to be quite systematic and clear, and then to put the pieces in place step by step?' The good news is that every time a good strategy is executed well, it becomes quite apparent, and that is exactly what is happening. Everybody can see where Microsoft is going. The same is true of HP.

Many of the companies who complain are only complaining because they did not have a good strategy. They had no point of view. DEC did not see the opportunity for personal computers. Xerox did not see the opportunity for small, personal copiers.

In companies such as these, strategic planning became a financial exercise. It never provoked these deeper debates about where the company wanted to be in ten years' time. Instead, it became an exercise in positioning the company in a given industry space. It was never a question of how to reshape industries, how to create new opportunities, how to create new functionalities or how to change the price/performance relationship in the marketplace. Instead, it became a ritual.

Companies need to have a strategic intent—to have an aspiration that is widely shared, to have a goal which is clear and to have an obsession with winning—that is the fuel that drives the engine.

It is not enough just to have a strategic architecture. A strategic architecture provides the company with a direction, but it needs to have the emotional and the intellectual energy to make the journey. It needs a shared aspiration which allows the company to stretch itself beyond its current resources—one that provides a sense of direction, a sense of common purpose, a sense of destiny, a single-minded and inspiring challenge which commands the respect and the allegiance of every person in the organization. Strategic intent is not an articulation of means, but of goals. Means have to be discovered as we go along.

If a company's goal is to energize the entire organization, it ought to engage as many people as possible in the organization—especially the people closest to customers and technologies—in thinking about strategy. This is why it ought to involve the younger generation rather than just the senior VPs. In fact, it should be an amalgamation of the collective intelligence and imagination of managers and employees throughout the company. This is happening in company after company today—in Marriott, Steelcase, EDS, Philips, Nokia and many others. The quality of work and the quality of commitment being generated deep down inside these organizations is what is interesting. It is even surprising top management.

The role of senior management is to make sure that the organization develops this broad aspiration, and in addition that it is clearly articulated, understood and continuously reinterpreted. Every two or three years, management should again interpret its aspiration and say, 'This is what it means to us in the next two years', so the challenge is always renewed but the goal remains more or less the same. For example, NEC used to talk about 'C & C'. That meant it would be at the forefront of the convergence of computers and communications. Now, twenty years later, as computers and communications have come together, it has a new 'C & C' called 'Connectivity and Compatibility'. It's the same goal, but it's a new challenge.

➤ *How do you build a 'core competencies' perspective into a company that has been traditionally focused on business units—on particular types of products and services?*

The starting point is to benchmark the company as customers see it, as competitors see it and as people deep within the organization see it. We have to look at the organization as a portfolio of competencies, of underlying strengths, and not just as a portfolio of business units. **Business units are focused on products and markets, whereas core competencies are focused on customer benefits,** such as Apple's 'user-friendliness' or Sony's 'pocketability'. We must identify the core competencies which allow us to create new products as well as be successful in existing businesses; and we must ask ourselves what we can leverage as we move into the future, and what we can do that other companies might find difficult.

Then, in order to change its views about strategy, management needs to start thinking differently about the organization. It must become synergistic. We cannot mobilize the energies of a whole company around a strategic intent using the old ways of managing. The first things challenged by the new ways of managing are the role and the added value of top management. Are they becoming stewards of core competencies? Do they see which new competencies have to be built? Are they creating opportunities for the organization to learn new skills?

We must ask ourselves what the role of hierarchy is, how the administrative boundaries between levels, functions and business units are broken, how the boundaries between customers and the company and between the suppliers and the company are broken, and how the boundary between top management and the operating management is broken. Lastly, we must ask ourselves how the boundary between investors and employees is broken.

There are many operational things to do. It is clear that these questions will not be resolved overnight or in a single step. It is a process which requires deep thought. Depending on the organization, the path that it will follow to this Holy Grail will be different. You can't say: 'Give me a couple of one-liners and I'll know how to get there.' You have to discuss these issues, come to terms with them and experiment.

In other words, just as there is a process of evolution of markets and evolution of capabilities, there is also a need for the internal governance process within organizations to evolve.

Unlearning the past

Companies are going to have to unlearn a lot of their past—and also to forget it! **The future will not be an extrapolation of the past. Like a space rocket on the way to the moon, a company has to be willing to jettison the parts of its past which no longer contain fuel for the journey and which are becoming, in effect, excess baggage.** That is particularly difficult for the senior managers—those who actually built the past, and who still have a lot of emotional equity invested in it.

If you want to escape the gravitational pull of the past, you have to be willing to challenge your own orthodoxies, to regenerate your core strategies and rethink your most fundamental assumptions about how you are going to compete. Most often it takes a crisis before a company is willing to do that. It takes a sense of urgency, a sense that the company's future success is not inevitable.

Some companies even manufacture a 'crisis' in order to produce this sense of urgency in the organization. Boeing created a video for its employees that was presented like a future news report about the sad demise of this once-great company. It was designed to help the employees understand the need for change and the need for heroic goals for the future. Motorola conducted a similar exercise. It created an awareness-building program called 'Rise to the Challenge', which confronted employees with the early warning signs of impending doom and described the competitive challenge facing Motorola in the future. It's not easy to unlearn or to forget the past, but it must be done, even if you have to face a real or an imaginary crisis to do so.

Of course, to create the future you do not have to abandon all of your past. There is a need for selectivity. But essentially, the success recipes from your past may no longer be the success recipes for your future. For example, quality was a source of competitive advantage in the past. That is where the efforts of many companies have been focused. But in the twenty-first century, quality will be merely the price of market entry, so there is a need to move on, just as the Japanese are doing. They were the ones who created competition based on quality. However, Japanese managers realize that today's competitive advantages may no longer be differentiators tomorrow. In a recent survey, the source of competitive advantage that Japanese managers rated first for the future was not quality—it was the capacity to create fundamentally new products and businesses.

Global pre-emption

The biggest bonanza that anybody could have hoped for is to have three and a half billion people peacefully join the global market economy. Even if this translates into only 600–800 million new customers, it represents an extraordinary opportunity!

The global economy does three things for me. First, it certainly increases the size of the markets for everyone. Second, it creates new competitors in the marketplace. I expect Chinese, Indian or Indonesian competitors to become global during this decade. These will be not just competitors in terms of cheap labor, but new kinds of competitors because they sit on some of the world's largest and newest markets. By their sheer size they can influence the cost structure of an industry worldwide. For example, the size of the Chinese market will influence the cost structure of companies in the television business, the bulk chemical and pharmaceutical businesses or the education business. The same thing is true of India. There may be a new dynamic in terms of who influences cost structures because of where the critical markets are. Third, innovation will take place across the world, not just in North America or in Europe. I think that's a very important issue, because if innovation is going to take place in different places around the world, we have to have sensing mechanisms and people watching and carefully monitoring those movements.

Ed Artzt, the Chairman of P&G, put it this way: 'If we don't do it early on globally, someone else will.' There is a need for global pre-emption, and it is going to become more important than ever because the appropriate scales of operations that you want to accomplish are going to be dependent on this global pre-emption. With new product development costs escalating, if you want an appropriate return on your investment, you have to develop products for a global market. In other words, you have to get access to critical channels of distribution around the globe and then quickly drive the new product to the market in as many of these countries as possible. The issue becomes, not just time to market, but time to global pre-emption. **Ultimately, the race to the future becomes a mad dash to the finish line.**

There are several examples of companies who are already doing this successfully. P&G is one of them. It put Pampers Phases, which was a new innovation in the disposable diapers business, on the shelf in 90 countries in less than a year. And Gillette put its Sensor razor into 19 countries almost simultaneously.

➤ *What is the best way to convince senior managers, particularly in large corporations, about the need to develop a competitively unique point of view about the future, and to pursue growth by building new business opportunities?*

The best way is to tell them to look at all the large companies that no longer exist. In fact, go back and look at the *Fortune* 500 or the *Fortune* 100 over the last 50 years, and ask how many companies have disappeared from the list and what the survivors do to stay in that league. You will find that they are continually looking forward, not backward. They are continually changing the rules of competition, rather than following the accepted rules. They are regularly defining new ways of doing business, pioneering new product concepts, building new core competencies, creating new markets, setting new standards and challenging their own assumptions. They are taking control of their future.

You can't do that if you are not willing to change and to move from where you are today. The opportunities are out there for everyone, but capturing new business opportunities is like shooting flying ducks—you can't do it with fixed gun positions. **"**

CK Prahalad

CK Prahalad is Harvey C Fruehauf Professor of Business Administration and Professor of Corporate Strategy and International Business at the University of Michigan's Graduate School of Business Administration. Together with Professor Gary Hamel, his work has helped to redefine what it means to be strategic, by looking beyond the current ideas on business transformation to the more visionary concept of industry transformation. As a consultant, Prahalad has worked with many multinational companies, including Eastman Kodak, AT&T, Cargill, Philips, Colgate-Palmolive, Motorola, Marriott, Oracle and Whirlpool. Two of the Harvard Business Review *articles he co-authored with Gary Hamel won coveted McKinsey prizes. He is co-author with Hamel of the bestselling business book* Competing for the Future, *and with Yves Doz of a pioneering book on multinationals,* The Multinational Mission.

Recommended reading

Competing for the Future (1995) Gary Hamel & CK Prahalad, US/UK: Harvard Business School Press.

The Multinational Mission: Balancing local demands and global vision (1987) CK Prahalad & Yves L Doz, US/UK: Free Press.

"You cannot create the future using the old strategy tools."

REINVENTING THE BASIS FOR COMPETITION

Gary Hamel

" MOST OF WHAT companies have been doing for at least the last four or five years has had an internal focus. The restructuring and the reengineering and so on have all been about: How do we get better internally? So what companies have been working on is closing a performance gap along known parameters of competitiveness. That's the foundation of benchmarking: let me go out and see who is best in class and make sure that at least I get to that level.

I would argue there is a substantial difference between benchmarking and path breaking—between improving the capabilities of the organization and creating fundamentally new markets. And it is only the latter that, in the long term, is going to produce any new wealth. **Simply catching up to where others have been is necessary to stay in the game, but I believe that the winners will ultimately be those with the ability to invent fundamentally new games.**

When you look at any economy, whether it is Europe or the United States or Asia, what you see are two kinds of companies. You see the 'laggards' who essentially have fallen behind the change curve, and you also see the 'challengers' who are in front of the change curve, or at least at the edge of the change curve. What most consultants and most companies have been worrying about is: How do you deal with the problems of the laggards? And those problems typically go under the broad banner of organizational transformation. So we have books like *The Transformational Leader* and *Transforming the Organization*. My argument is that this is really a secondary problem. The primary problem is one of *industry* transformation. And the laggards, who are all wrestling with organizational transformation, have those transformational problems typically because they failed to see the future coming. They fell out of the driver's seat of industry transformation. They ceded that role to somebody else. And now they are fighting a rearguard action to catch up.

In fact, something that has become almost accepted wisdom in many large companies is that strategy is the easy part and implementation is the hard part. I think that's dead wrong. I think they are both very, very difficult. But what I say to a lot of companies, those that are perhaps a little bit laggard, is: 'Most of your implementation problems are foresight problems in disguise.' **In other words, they didn't see the changing basis for competition. They didn't see the changing nature of the customer.** And their reaction to that is: 'Well, we have to shorten product development cycles; we have to cut costs.' The point is, what appear today to be operational problems are really there because these companies didn't see the opportunities to change the rules of the game in some way.

A classic example would be what has happened to the US automobile industry. I would go so far as to argue that there has not been one fundamental strategic innovation in the automobile industry in the last 40 to 50 years that has come out of Detroit.

The pressure for fuel economy was exerted by OPEC, and Detroit reacted. Then they thought that, once the prices of gasoline in the US went down—and they are now down again to the levels they were in real terms in 1973—people wouldn't want to buy fuel-efficient cars any more. That's not the case. People still say, 'Why not? If I drive something that is more fuel efficient, I can save money whatever the price of gasoline.'

The pressure for safety came from folks like Ralph Nader. And for a decade or more Detroit fought to prevent having to put in rear seatbelts and airbags and so on.

The pressure for quality came from the Japanese.

So the people in Detroit were laggards again and again and again. I once said to one of the senior people at General Motors, 'I don't even know why GM needs a strategic planner. All you have to do is call Toyota when you've finished doing one thing and say, "We've done that. What do we do next?" .'

In other words, it's not enough to play catch-up, to pay for the sins of the past, to come up to world benchmarks. You've got to learn how to do two other things. First, how to reinvent the existing competitive space you are in, and there are a variety of ways in which you can do that. Essentially it is by changing in some fundamental way the rules of engagement—the basis for competitive advantage within an existing industry—as Wal-Mart did in retailing in the US, or as Ikea did in furniture retailing in Europe.

And second, how to create fundamentally new space, so that you can satisfy a need that individuals or companies didn't even realize that they had.

Restructuring has been about getting smaller. Reengineering has been about getting better. But getting smaller and better is not sufficient. **There is a need at some point to reinvent the basis for competition, and to do that you have to become different as a company.** You have to be willing to challenge many of the fundamental assumptions you have about how you compete in your industry.

Rethinking competition

My view of competition is absolutely complementary to Michael Porter's. They are not in opposition at all—people who believe that they are in opposition simply don't understand. Essentially what Porter did in the early days was to present a view of competition as competition for economic surplus within an existing product market. So it was, for example, competition between Pepsi and Coca-Cola in the carbonated soft drink business. Or between Kimberly-Clark and Procter & Gamble in the disposable diaper business. In those cases, the boundaries of the industry were clear. You knew who was a competitor and who was not a competitor. You could easily describe the value-added structure of the industry—the value chain, if you will—and all of those things were taken as fixed points. They defined the edges of the canvas in which strategy happens.

The dilemma now is that, if you look at many industries today, the clarity in industry structure, in the value chain, in the relative roles of the participants, just doesn't exist anymore. If I look at financial services today, where does that industry begin and end? When General Motors becomes one of the largest issuers of credit cards; when UK banks become some of the biggest underwriters of insurance; when Merrill Lynch can give me a checking account and so on—what has happened to the boundaries in financial services? The same can be said for telecommunications, for healthcare and for many other fields. So we are living in an increasingly boundary-less world.

I therefore see competition increasingly not as competition between players in a well-structured industry to divide economic surplus, but as competition to influence the shape of emerging opportunity arenas. In fact, I don't even use the word 'industry' any more, because I just don't think it's a very helpful word.

Let me give you an example. In the United States and in Europe as well, we talk about the 'supermarket industry'. Sainsbury's is part of it in the UK, as is a company such as Safeway in the US. But the reality is that companies like Safeway or other big supermarkets are increasingly competing against fast-food outlets. They are competing against a very successful company in the US called Boston Market, which prepares ready-to-take-home meals—from chicken with potatoes to the whole thing, and you just take it home and serve it. Certainly in the US, if you tell kids it's time for dinner they're as likely to put on their coats as they are to go to the kitchen or to the dining room. So all of those boundaries have become much less clear, and there is competition for economic surplus in the existing industries, but just as important is competition to shape these emerging opportunity arenas in a way that positions a firm to take the maximum value out of it.

To take a traditional view of competition, imagine that you are holding a can of Coca-Cola. The cost of producing that product is X. The price at which it sells is Y. The question is: Who gets the difference between X and Y? Is it the guys who make the aluminum can? Is it the supermarket that retails the product? Is it the company that transported the cans from one place to another? Is it Coca-Cola that makes the syrup? In the old days it was all quite clear. But in more and more industries today—such as multimedia or financial services—I challenge my students to do a 'five forces' analysis. It cannot be done. At least not at the broadest level of the industry. If you segment it down into narrow pieces you can do it, but then you miss many of the new opportunities.

The most fundamental starting point for strategy has typically been: What is my industry? What is the segmentation here? That is only important if what you are worried about is tactics. Again, let's take Coca-

Cola as an example. I would argue that the people in its management team are probably the world's best tacticians. But I don't think they are strategists. Coca-Cola missed the opportunity for sports drinks. There's a drink in the US called Gatorade and it's now worth well over a billion dollars. Coca-Cola also missed the market for adult drinks. That was grabbed by companies like Snapple in the US, and in the UK perhaps by IDV, with brands such as Aqualibra and Purdey's and so on. So the people at Coca-Cola are wonderful tacticians, but lousy strategists.

Understanding the future

The big challenge in creating the future is not predicting the future. It's not as if there is only one future out there that is going to happen, and that the only challenge is trying to predict which of the potential futures will actually be the right one. **Instead, the goal is to try to imagine a future that is plausible—the future that you can create.** There are some boundary conditions that you have to understand, like what is going to happen to lifestyles, to technology, to regulation and so forth. Those are the edges of the canvas, but it's a very broad canvas. And what you paint on that canvas is a product of your own imagination.

We had the wrong focus for many years when we tried to think about the future. The primary focus was on forecasting and trying to identify some particular future, rather than on developing a deep-down sense of the 'discontinuities'—the things that are driving change, or that potentially could be harnessed to drive change. And then, out of that understanding, trying to imagine or construct a point of view about the unique opportunities we might create.

One of the things that I believe is that **whatever you need to know to create the future you can know**. By definition, whatever Microsoft needed to know, it knew. Whatever CNN needed to know, it knew.

The second premise is that **there is no proprietary data about the future**. But there are very different levels of understanding about the various factors that are going to open up possibilities for industry revolution. Some companies work a lot harder than others to understand these factors at a deep level. The data are there for everybody, but there is an enormous difference in people's abilities to construct imaginative, compelling new opportunities out of that understanding.

Take an example. Why was it CNN rather than the BBC that created the global news network? I don't think it was a prediction issue for CNN. It wasn't that somehow they had some wonderful planners who saw what the BBC could not see. All of the things that you needed to create CNN were totally visible. You had cable television eroding the monopoly of the traditional broadcasters. You had people who didn't come home every night at an hour when they could watch the 6 o'clock news or the 9 o'clock news or whatever. You had satellite technology that made it possible to put a team anywhere in the world and get a signal out. Anybody who was willing to challenge their own assumptions could see those things.

Why should what is intuitive for one person be out of the realm of possibility for another? Certainly some people are more inherently creative or imaginative than others. Some people are, by nature, contrarians. And I believe that the beginning of strategy is a contrarian nature. Somebody who is willing to challenge the existing wisdom, challenge the assumption base, turn it on its head and say, 'Now, what do we have here?'. I also believe that people who have that capability—or companies that have that capability— are just inherently more curious. They are paying attention to a much wider spectrum of input than others.

Another fundamental belief I have is that, **if a company is interested in understanding the future, most of what it needs to learn about the future it is going to learn outside of its own industry**. And that's a very radical thing to say when most managers think about strategy by starting out with their own particular industry to establish the boundary lines.

For example, I was talking recently to a chief executive of one of the US's largest hospital corporations and he said: 'We've spent the last year trying to understand financial services.' I said: 'Isn't that interesting. Why have you done that?' He said: 'Because a lot of the issues that you see there, in terms of consolidation, dealing with overcapacity and deregulation etc., are the same issues that are confronting the American hospital industry. And that's where we're going to have to look if we want to understand what is going on.'

I sat recently with a bunch of utilities executives and I said, 'If you want to understand the future of utilities, go look at the companies in telecommunications. They've had to deal with the separation of production from distribution, with privatization, with deregulation, with new competitors who come in and "cherry pick", and so on. Go look there. Don't look at your own industry.'

Innovation in organizations

When we see companies create new industries and invent the future, we tend to personalize the act of imagination. We say: 'Well, it's Fred Smith or it's Ted Turner or it's Anita Roddick, or it's somebody else.' And we forget that for every one of those people who had a brilliant idea, there's somebody who ended up in failure. And we also forget that in most large companies you don't have that one brilliant, intuitive leader at the top.

If you want to do this kind of thinking in a large company, you cannot depend on having the right, single brilliant person. In fact, I would argue that we've done ourselves a disservice by the emphasis we have put on the leader. So we write about the leader as if these insights were theirs alone. I can guarantee you that, even for people like Ted Turner, the insights did not come to Ted Turner alone. They came from a very rich mix of creative people that he had around him, that he talked to, that he interacted with. And out of that he slowly built—he synthesized—a point of view about what might be possible.

➤ *In* Competing for the Future, *you talk about the need to get to the future first. But a lot of companies believe that's it's better to let others do the risk taking and the trail blazing, and then to come in and exploit the opportunities that the pioneers have created.*

Yes. A lot of companies say, 'Pioneers usually get the arrows in their back. Let somebody else take the initial risk.' There are two assumptions that this point of view is based on, both of which I think are questionable.

The first assumption is that the pioneers will stumble or fail. Now sometimes that has happened. If you look at IBM and Sears when they established Prodigy, their on-line computer services business, they stumbled in some fairly profound ways. They built a network that was inflexible; they made some wrong assumptions about how people would use these services; they thought the first use would be a kind of electronic commerce, which ultimately will come, but the early uses were actually people talking with each other—chatting across the network—and they built a network that was not easily reconfigured for that. This stumble gave an enormous opening to America Online. But it's very dangerous to bet that the leader is going to make a mistake like that.

I remember one time having a conversation with some very senior people at IBM. This was when Akers was still there. And they said, 'We've been the second to market many, many times, and we've always managed in the end to prevail. We did it in PCs, we did it in minicomputers and so on.' My argument was, 'You guys were living off the past. You were living off an age when you actually had been pioneers—that's back to the mainframe and the 360. Out of that you built an extraordinarily powerful global brand and global distribution capability. And because you had that global distribution capability and others did not, you could afford to wait and see others experiment, and then when you decided to enter the market you could prevail because of your sheer distribution might.' Typically other companies—for example, Apple in the computer business—made all kinds of stumbles. They were very slow to innovate. They had capacity constraint problems and so on. But I said: 'You can't bet that every company out there is going to make the same mistakes.' And the case in point is Toshiba. IBM was number two to Apple in the PC business, and it ultimately passed Apple. But it has never caught up with Toshiba in the laptop business. Because Toshiba also has global distribution capabilities. And Toshiba did not stumble. It did not introduce lousy products. It churned over its product mix very, very quickly. It never gave IBM a window to get in there in any significant way. IBM is there, but it has never taken the leadership away from Toshiba. So I wouldn't want to bet the future of my company on an assumption that the competition will stumble in some profound way.

The second assumption is that to get there first you have to take bigger risks. We say today that we want more risk takers in our organizations. I think that is absolute nonsense. **What I want is for people to have greater ambitions, but also to understand how to 'de-risk' those ambitions.**

When you're competing for the future, you're trying to walk down a fairly narrow road without falling off on either side. On one side of that road is what I would call **undercommitment**. An assumption that you actually can't know anything about where the new opportunities may be. That you are merely going to be responsive or agile. When a company says to me, 'We're going to be very responsive, and very quick on our feet', my reaction to that is, 'What you're telling me is that you're going to be a follower and that you don't have a point of view.' To me that is dangerous. Because, in so many cases, if you want to create these new opportunities, there are five or ten years of experimentation, investment and work that go into them.

When the BBC wakes up ten years later and says, 'There is an opportunity for global news', how long is it going to take the BBC to catch up with CNN? It's not going to happen. Not unless there's some catastrophic failure at CNN. So if you undercommit, if you're not building the new competencies, if you're not repositioning your brand, if you're not experimenting in the marketplace or understanding where customer needs and demands are going to be, some years ahead of the actual opportunity, you're not going to get there.

It's like running a marathon. You don't enter at mile 24. You've got to be there from the beginning—it's 26 miles long. So undercommitting and saying, 'We'll just wait', is not a viable option. You end up in a position where you don't have the competencies, you don't have the capabilities and you don't get into that opportunity set.

The next thing you're trying to avoid—on the other side of the narrow road—is **overcommitment**, which is where you are committing resources far in advance of having enough detailed information about this particular opportunity to know exactly where to put your chips.

I'll give you an example. People have looked at the Apple Newton as a failure. Now I don't agree with that. I mean, at one level it is a failure; if you judge it by Apple's hype: 'Here's the best thing since sliced bread. It's going to totally change your life. It's the coolest thing ever.' If you look at it this way, it is a total failure.

But if, on the other hand, you see Newton as the first shot in what will actually be a ten-year battle to redefine computing away from the desktop and into the pocket, you realize that it's just one of the necessary first battles in what is going to be a very protracted war. Now the problem for Apple is that it overcommitted. Should it have been on the market experimenting with something like Newton? Absolutely. But what could Apple have done differently? Well, number one: you give Newton to 500 of your employees, and you let them fool around with it for a few months, and you see the problems. You don't go and tell the whole world that this is the greatest thing ever, and then have your problems publicly displayed on a global stage.

So the way I describe it is that you are trying to find the lowest-risk way of accumulating, as rapidly as possible, insights into where the ultimate center of demand is going to be located. What the right product or service configuration is going to be and so on. It is what I call 'maximizing the ratio of learning over investment'. In other words, **I want to learn one day earlier than my competitors about the technology and the demand etc., while betting one dollar less to get that insight**. So I don't believe that you can wait and let others make the mistakes—because, increasingly, we have very sophisticated competitors out there on whom you cannot rely to make those kinds of mistakes. Neither do I believe that getting to the future first is about betting the farm.

➤ *Why is it that so many companies fail to anticipate the big opportunities and seem instead to drive backwards into the future?*

There are some fundamental reasons why so many companies have not been able to do this kind of thinking. And why so many companies are laggards. Strategy and strategy making in most companies are extraordinarily élitist processes. And while we are saying to employees, 'Bring your brains to work', we are only really allowing them to participate in operational improvement. In other words, we are saying, 'You can bring your brains to work to sit in the quality circles; you can bring your brains to work to get involved in reengineering our processes; but creating strategy and direction?—No, no; that's a job for top management.' So we limit the creativity available to the organization by turning strategy making into a very élitist process.

For example, if you draw an organizational pyramid with senior management at the top, you need to ask the question: Where in that pyramid do you find the least genetic diversity when it comes to thinking in radically different ways about the future of an industry? And where in that pyramid do you find managers who have most of their emotional equity invested in the past? It's at the top. Then you ask: Whom do we give primary responsibility for strategy setting and direction? The same guys. No wonder we don't get anything very creative out. So this is one of the huge dilemmas that we have in large organizations, and we have to destroy this élitist view about how you create strategy.

The great irony to me is that the individuals in the organization who have the greatest stake in the future are the young people, because their whole careers are at stake. You know, when John Akers has to take early retirement at 58 or 59, or whatever it was, he sacrifices three or four years of his career. But when you lay off 200,000 people, and a lot of them are young, it's a different story. Most of them will find other employment, but they have much more at stake. And those individuals, who have the greatest emotional stake in the future, are typically those who are least involved in defining the future of the enterprise. After all, it is those people, the young people, who live closest to the future.

Creating the incentive

There are several steps in creating the incentive within an organization to think seriously about future strategy. First of all, you have to create a **deep sense of restlessness with the status quo**. You have to get people to understand that current success is very impermanent. That whatever economic engine—whatever profit engine—the firm is relying on is, by definition, running out of fuel. You can look at it like a rocket: it blasts off and its energy carries it up and up, but ultimately, at some point, gravity reasserts itself. Most rockets follow a parabolic curve and come down the other side. But very few organizations understand the inherent limitations of their current economic engine.

Take EDS (Electronic Data Systems). It used to write ten-year computer service contracts and it would go to an insurance company and say: 'We'll process your insurance claims for however many cents a claim, and we'll guarantee a fixed price for the next ten years.' The insurance company thought this was a wonderful thing: how can these guys guarantee a price for the next ten years in an inflationary world? Of course, EDS knew that the price of computing is constantly going down, so the out years in that contract become an annuity. But customers are not so stupid any more. Slowly, customers have woken up to the declining cost of technology. Nowadays, no one is going to agree to a ten-year contract with fixed prices. They want you to take out 20–30 percent of the price every year. So at EDS, that economic engine was running out of steam. And the first thing to be done at EDS was to create this deep sense of restlessness with the status quo.

All too often, top management is not willing to be brutally honest and to share that information. I think it was a huge problem at Philips. I remember listening to Van der Klugt—the ex-CEO—make speeches, with lots of his people in attendance, and I remember him saying that the problem was that the Japanese cheat. So if we could get the Japanese to stop cheating, then it would all be OK. He was not being open about the problems that Philips had, and the mistakes top management had been making and what the inherent limitations were. So finally, those issues only got resolved in a crisis. And, typically, companies do not create an internal incentive to reinvent themselves and their industries until they are in a crisis mode.

At EDS we designed a two- or three-day experience for 300 of its key people that really brought them face to face with the declining efficiency of their profit engine.

Second, we had to create in those people a whole new way of thinking about strategy. To think about opportunity arenas instead of industries. To think about core competencies instead of strategic business units. To think about functionality instead of existing products or services. To think about competition as a process of shaping the evolution of new space, rather than competing within existing space. **All of those new tools had to take root, because you cannot create the future using the old strategy tools.**

So when I work in companies, the three things I do initially are: first, create that sense of restlessness. Second, equip people with new tools. And third, identify the natural pro-change constituency in the organization: the people who are already itching for change.

One of the most mistaken assumptions we make is that people don't like to change. I think that is garbage. There are some people who don't like to change, but think how many people you know who go back to the same holiday spot 20 years in a row. There are some that do—I don't want to meet those people because they're going to be very boring. But there are many people who one year go hiking in Kathmandu and Nepal, and the next year go to Vietnam, and the next year do something else interesting. Those are the people I want to find in any organization, because those are the people who do not look at change as a problem; they look at it as an enormous opportunity. And if you can give them that sense of restlessness, and give them the right set of tools, then you just stand back and let them work.

Of course, you have to focus their work—there is a set of what I would call 'domains of discovery' that every organization has to go through. You have to understand those discontinuities that you could harness: the technologies, the lifestyles, the regulations and so on. You have to scrape away the superficial view of the company as units of products and services, and get down to the underlying view of core competencies. You have to work systematically to understand where the opportunities are for industry revolution. But first of all you have to create that constituency with the right level of energy and the right tools, otherwise nothing else will happen.

What I am trying to do in my own work is to move towards something I describe as the **'democratization of strategy'**. It's not a democracy in the sense that 'one person gets one vote', but it's a democracy in the way that the ancient Greeks would have understood it, which is on the basis of what you can contribute intellectually. It is a process of creating strategy that has nothing to do with hierarchy. A process where the strategy-mak ͜ responsibility is distributed, but where, ultimately, you come to a singular point of view that can encompass the entire enterprise. That's how you create strategy in a deeply and broadly involving way, and how you end up with something that is common and shared.

Global competition

We have tended to describe global competition as Europe versus the US versus Japan versus the newly industrializing countries. This is misleading because, wherever you go in the world, you find companies who are wrestling with the problem of transforming their industries. Japan has probably the biggest structural transformation challenge of all. Europe has an enormous challenge ahead to catch up with the information revolution. The newly industrializing countries have their own challenges. So I don't think that there is any one part of the world that, somehow, has this all figured out, and that represents the model for the rest of the world. Japan is absolutely not the model. Neither is Europe. Neither is the US. You find examples of good and bad practice all over.

I don't see competition as competition between nation states. I see it as competition between firms. There are laggards in Japan: Sanyo, Aiwa, Suzuki, Isuzu. There are laggards in Europe: Air France, Crédit Lyonnais, Volkswagen and so on. And there are laggards in the United States.

I see two big races going on today. There is the race to the future, which is essentially the race to intercept and profit from the information economy. And there is also the race to Asia, which is the race to capture the wealth that is going to be created there. What most people will tell you is that, over the next 10–20 years, 40 percent of the new purchasing power in the world is going to be created in Asia. Now who is going to get a hold of it?

The reality is that, if you look at who is investing in Asia today—where the direct foreign investment in the South-east Asian nations is coming from—primarily that money is coming from Japan, secondarily from the United States and Europe lags way, way behind. The chairman of one of the biggest Japanese companies recently said to me, 'We're very happy about the broadening of European integration. We're very happy that the Czech Republic and Hungary and Poland have emerged out of Communism and are becoming part of Europe.' I asked, 'Why? They are not huge markets, and you don't have much of a presence there.' And he replied, 'Yes, that is true. But all of our German and French competitors are concerned with eastern Europe. And while they are busy with that, we're going to take China.' And he added, 'Eastern Europe is a side show', which I believe it is.

I would go further than that. I would say that, today, Europe is affected by a continental myopia. European companies are maintaining their market share in Europe, and they are losing it outside of Europe. That is just fact. So the race to Asia is a big issue. And who will win that race will largely be governed by who is investing there already, who is building the deep relationships in those countries.

There are two very distinct points of view on the Asian opportunity. There is the view that I hear a lot in Europe and the US, which basically looks at it as a threat: here are these potential one billion new wage earners; here are these PhDs sitting in India who are willing to work for $10,000 a year instead of $100,000 a year; this is going to put an enormous damper on income growth in the West and so on. While this is true, I don't think that it is the right way to look at it.

Even today in the developed world, in the OECD countries, only about 4 percent of imports are coming from countries whose wages are less than half of the OECD average. We are not hugely at risk from all these new industrializing countries. Certainly, Europe was not impoverished by the growth of the United States as an economy. It provided a big market for Europe and we've managed to coexist.

We also saw in the United States and in Britain that agriculture's share of the economy went from 60 or 70 percent down to 4 or 5 percent of the economy. We were not impoverished. I don't think we're going to be impoverished in any way by the growth of the new economies in Asia.

Japan is already running a huge balance of surplus with these countries because it is arming them with the capital, the equipment and the components they need to compete globally. And we are not going to be impoverished if it is Taiwan, Korea and Singapore that end up making our gadgets and widgets and whatever else, as we move ahead to create the new information economy.

But if we try to compete in the old economy with those countries then we are going to have a problem. We moan about the threat to wages and our balance of payment deficits with these countries. And why? Because we haven't got in there early enough. We're not working hard enough. We're not investing enough. And I think Asia represents the greatest opportunity going. It is not primarily a threat.

> *What should organizations be doing right now if they want to win the race to the future?*

Most importantly, they should recognize that the existing hierarchy in most organizations is a hierarchy of experience and not a hierarchy of imagination. And there is a big difference between experience and imagination.

If you want to create a point of view about the future, if you want to craft a meaningful strategy, you have to create in your company a hierarchy of imagination. And that means giving a disproportionate share of voice to the people who up until now have been disenfranchised from the strategy-making process. It means giving a disproportionate share of voice to the young people. It means giving a disproportionate share of voice to the geographic periphery of your organization—because, typically, the farther away you are from headquarters, the more creative people are: they don't have the dead hand of bureaucracy and orthodoxy on them. And it means giving a disproportionate share of voice to newcomers.

That, to me, is leadership. Leadership is when the senior group of executives has the combination of confidence in their ability to contribute and the humility to recognize what they can learn from others. Those are the attributes that make them willing to create a hierarchy of imagination. And to involve many new and different voices in the process of charting the future. **99**

Gary Hamel

Gary Hamel is Visiting Professor of Strategic and International Management at the London Business School. The Economist *calls him 'the world's reigning strategy guru'. Along with Professor CK Prahalad, with whom he has worked closely for many years, Hamel has been credited with creating a new language of strategy, using an approach that is centered on the concepts of 'core competence', 'strategic architecture' and 'strategic intent'. Founder and chairman of Strategos, a company dedicated to helping its clients get to the future first, Gary Hamel has consulted with senior managers in companies all over the world, including Rockwell, Motorola, Alcoa, Nokia, EDS, Ford and Dow Chemical. He is a member of the editorial board of the* Strategic Management Journal *and, together with CK Prahalad, he has co-authored several ground-breaking and award-winning articles on competitive strategy published in the* Harvard Business Review. *The two professors are also co-authors of the bestselling business book* Competing for the Future.

Recommended reading

Competing for the Future (1995) Gary Hamel & CK Prahalad, US/UK: Harvard Business School Press.

Competence-based Competition (1994) Gary Hamel & Aime Heene, US/UK: John Wiley.

Rethinking

CONTROL & COMPLEXITY

Beyond the End of Management

Michael Hammer

Focusing on Constraints, Not Costs

Eli Goldratt

Through the Eye of the Needle

Peter Senge

“The traditional concept of management

is reaching the end of the road.”

BEYOND THE END OF MANAGEMENT

Michael Hammer

" THE TRADITIONAL MODEL that organizations have used for the last two hundred years is a 'command and control' model, which is similar to what was started in the Roman legions.

The basic idea is that the individual should carry out orders, and orders start at the top. All intelligence, all wisdom, resides at the top of an organization. A handful of people make the fundamental strategic decisions. And everybody else in the organization is either a 'spear-carrier' who does the actual work, or a middle manager who conveys directions from the top down to the bottom and information from the bottom up to the top.

Think of it like the human body, where the brain is at the top and the work gets done in the fingers and the toes, and the nervous system is what carries the information from one to the other.

Except that, in organizations, the speed of information transmission is not that of electrical impulses through the nervous system; it's more similar to the speed of an advancing glacier!

That is, from the time that something is decided at the top to the time that it's conveyed down to the bottom, or from the time that a situation arises at the bottom and it's conveyed up to the top, days, weeks, months, even years can pass. And if you've got a relatively stable, slow-moving environment, then this is satisfactory. But in the twenty-first century and, indeed, in the latter part of the twentieth century, this is a ludicrous model.

We live in an environment that's bombarded by change—this has become a cliché by now but it is nonetheless true—and we've not even begun to come to terms with what it means.

There has been so much accumulated knowledge that change is now happening exponentially. It's not that every bit of additional knowledge adds a little more change to the world. But rather, because it interacts with all the other knowledge and experience that we already have in so many domains, it has a cumulative effect. That's why the rate of change has become so astounding.

I heard someone back in 1994 talking about telecommunications who said: 'In the next six years, we will have more technological change than we had in the last ninety-four.' And he was right of course. The rate of change in all technological areas will continue to increase.

There's another important factor that is radically changing the way organizations have to do business—and that's the customer.

Customers have come to expect that we do things their way, rather than that they do things our way.

The traditional organization really came of age in a supply-constrained economy, where people were standing in line for whatever they could get. There was more demand than there was supply. So all we had to do was organize ourselves to maximise the utilization of our capacity. To maximize our output. Which, of course, gave us mass-market standardization. And if customers didn't get exactly what they wanted, something was certainly better than nothing.

Today, in the global economy and with improving technology, most industries are in an oversupply, overcapacity situation. So it's no longer 'we'll make whatever we like and the customers will take it because it's the only option they've got'. The customer now has many options. Many choices. There are many people competing for the same order and for the same customer dollar.

So success will lie with those who can do things the way that the customer wants, whether that is in tailoring a particular order, or tailoring a particular product, or doing business in the way that suits the customer best.

The idea of a standard operating procedure, which is decided at the top and then relentlessly executed and carried out by those on the bottom, doesn't make sense in an environment where you need a lot of flexibility and responsiveness to individual customer needs.

This new customer primacy, along with today's intense competition and the constant technological and contextual change going on all around us, makes a mockery of the centrally planned, 'command and control' model of the traditional organization. And it simply won't do.

What we need is a very different mode of operating. We need ways of operating in which decisions are made by those much closer to the work.

We need a model in which people at the front lines, armed with a basic strategy decided by the senior management of the company, are given a lot of autonomy and responsibility for deciding things on their own. A model where management exists, not to direct and control or to supervise, but rather to facilitate and enable.

Reversing the industrial revolution

If we persist in the fiction that all wisdom resides at the top, then we're bound to have poorly performing organizations.

We've traditionally started with the assumption that people are limited and simple. This means we have had to design very, very simple tasks and jobs for them to do. Which, in turn, has led to complex organizational processes and systems, because when all the work that is being done is fragmented, atomistic and small scale, then we need a lot of overhead to tie it all together.

Complex processes, however, are by their very definition rigid, inflexible, low quality and high cost. All that overhead makes it hard for them to deliver what's needed competitively and quickly.

We have to start with the other end of the stick. **We have to start with the premise that what we need is high-performing processes.** High-performing processes have to be simple (complexity never performs well). And simple processes require complex jobs.

This means that individuals must do larger components of the work that needs to be done, rather than just isolated fragments. And larger jobs require more sophisticated individuals. So, in effect, this represents a reversal of the industrial revolution.

Prior to the industrial revolution you had artisans who were skilled craftsmen, who did whole lots of work, entire processes—to use our reengineering terminology—to create value for a customer. They were, to use a contemporary term, 'professionals'. They had responsibility for doing the work, responsibility for ensuring that the outcome was achieved.

The industrial revolution really introduced the idea of the mindless worker, of the worker who had no responsibility or decision-making power, but merely had a mind-numbing task to perform, and did so under the watchful eye of a supervisor.

For a period of time, where we had economic expansion and a supply-constrained economy, where standardization and uniformity and just 'getting it out the door' were the requirements, the industrial revolution was splendid. Except that it's reached the end of its useful life. We don't need what it can give us any more.

We need to go back to an idea where people are focused, not on their task, not on their isolated activity, but on the end result. And what is it that produces the end result? A process. Not an individual task, but a collection of tasks.

Since processes can't always be performed by single individuals, we revert to the idea of a team. No longer is it an assembly line, it's a collection of individuals. A group of people with collective responsibility for creating the end result. For performing the whole process, not bits of it. And for getting their outcome to the customer.

So it is a customer-driven, a customer-focused environment, in which teams of professionals, with autonomy and responsibility, create a result. And they do so, not under the basilisk eye of a stern-faced supervisor, but under the benign tutelage of an advisory manager.

In effect, this 'manager' becomes a coach. Somebody whose role it is to advise, to support, to facilitate. To enable the team members to get their work done. But not based on the premise that the managers are really better equipped to do it. Because, to be blunt, if they were better equipped to do it, then they'd sure as hell be doing it. But rather their capability is in leveraging and enhancing the work of the team.

Personal development

One of the phenomena that interests me is how quickly we tend to associate transient conditions with permanent conditions. We tend to think that, just because something happens to be the way it is, then 'thus it has always been and thus it shall always be'. In fact, nothing of the sort is even vaguely true.

We have come to terms in the last 50, 60, 90 years perhaps, with a hierarchical organization in which the model of personal development was hierarchical promotion. And we've come to behave as though that's the way it shall always be.

The idea is that, if I do good work, I will get promoted to a position in which I can supervise others doing the work. And after this to a supervisor of supervisors and so on and so on. This is delusionary. This only makes sense if you believe that the most important work to be done is that of supervision.

In the kind of environment that we're discussing, **the real work, the craft, the added value, is in the work being performed by the teams of professionals**. And advancement is not hierarchical; advancement is lateral, through growth.

The model that I revert to is that of professionals and professional service organizations.

If you think of a medical group, for example, a physician's objective is not to be promoted from physician to supervisor of physicians, then to supervisor of supervisor of physicians. But rather to go from being a young doctor able to perform simple procedures, to a more sophisticated physician able to perform more sophisticated procedures, and finally to a leader in his or her field who can handle the most complex cases.

The nature of the work doesn't change. The nature of the position doesn't change. It's rather the individual's ability and the degree of sophistication that he or she is able to bring to the job that changes. And the complexity of the situations that he or she is able to handle.

That's the model of personal development that the twenty-first-century corporation will offer—if people are good at doing their work, then they're too valuable to be put into management.

Management then becomes a very separate profession. It's like in sport: the correlation between being a great player and being a great coach is really very minimal. Just because you were great in the field, it doesn't mean that you're great on the sidelines. And vice versa.

We have to recognize that management is its own real profession, with its own identity, and that it's not simply a matter of 'once I've done a bit of work, I become a manager'.

If I have the talent and the capacity to leverage others, then I become a manager. Other than that, I should stick to my knitting and do what I do best. And learn more. And do more. With the objective that over time I will do better; whether it's in handling orders or answering customer inquiries or developing new products.

I will do more of the work myself, add more value to my team, be able to handle more complex situations and create more value for the company and for the customer. And, thereby, I will have a better future assured for myself, both in terms of status and recognition within the organization, and in terms of financial compensation.

➤ *So what will happen to the traditional concept of management, as we know it today?*

The traditional concept of management is reaching the end of the road. The notion of management as a significant idea in itself, and as a major part of the organization, is obsolete.

I think we will have three kinds of people in the future organization. We will have the overwhelming majority who are the value-added performers, the people who do the real work—whether it's routine or highly creative work. We will have a small cadre of coaches to facilitate and enable them. And we will have a handful of leaders, who are the people who direct the organization.

These leaders will have the wisdom, talent and insight to determine the direction of the organization, and to create the environment in which everyone else can operate. They will not be bureaucratic managers who have risen through the ranks. They will really be entrepreneurs, even in a large organizational setting.

Today, entrepreneurs can just as easily be 30 years old or 60 years old. So I think the idea that the oldest people reside at the top of the organization will not necessarily be the case.

You may have front-line performers who are senior in age, and who have grown through their career, but whose influence is felt not through commanding others but through the wisdom that they have gained, by their ability to share with others and the exemplary performance they are able to bring to their work.

So it is talent, rather than superiority, that will bring people to leadership roles in the future organization.

In the intermediate term, I anticipate that the number of managers per capita in organizations will quite quickly decline to about 50 percent of what it is today. And over the long term, I suspect that it will go down significantly further than that.

In the twenty-first-century corporation, we may have only 20–25 percent of the number of 'managers' that we have today. And they will not be the only high-status people in the organization. Individuals' careers will also have trajectories other then merely advancement into management.

If we look for paradigms for this, we could look to sales organizations, where there is quite a difference between being an effective sales representative and being an effective sales manager. In fact, being a sales manager does not mean that one is more highly compensated than a sales representative. There are different models for both positions, different career tracks, and the real goal is not to be promoted but to maximize the performance of the organization as a whole.

Cultural differences

Certain national cultures are more congenial for this kind of model than others. Just as the growth of the industrial revolution saw shifts in the balance of economic power (certain countries adapted to it much more quickly and readily than others), I think similarly the post-industrial, twenty-first-century organization will work better in some cultures than in others.

The characteristics that it requires are, on the one hand, an orientation towards innovation, change and personal responsibility, and at the same time group cooperation, a certain degree of selflessness in order to focus on the customer, and real capability and educational attainment in order to be able to handle the more complex jobs.

There are certain environments which would seem to be well adapted to this and some less so.

For example, the US, which is obviously the place I know by far the best, fits this description in many ways, but of course not in all. The individual is certainly a strong figure in US culture. The ideas of innovation and change are ones that Americans are comfortable with. But US educational standards are not what they need to be; and this is recognized as a problem that both the public sector and the private sector are concerned with and trying to do something about.

On the other hand, if you think about a managerial culture like Germany, the idea of devolution of responsibility and authority from the top of the hierarchy down to the bottom is anathema. The Germans are the masters of the 'general staff' concept, where thorough plans are worked out centrally by the best minds, and then it is the responsibility of operational individuals in the field to carry out those plans.

I think that attitude is deeply imbedded in German society, not only in the central planners and top managers, but even in first-line workers, who don't particularly want the autonomy and responsibility that this new mode of operation will give them.

In Japan, they are quite comfortable with collective work and with customer focus but, on the other hand, less comfortable with the idea of doing things differently and making fundamental, radical changes to the way they manage their organizations. So they, too, may find themselves having more difficulty making the adaptation to this new model.

Each culture has its advantages and disadvantages, so it remains to be seen who will come out on top. I'm not about to be able to pick the ultimate winner. But if I had to guess, I think that the cultures which are likely to adapt well to this would be the US, the UK, some of the Scandinavian countries, Latin America and some of the emerging economies of the Pacific Rim. Several of the more classical and successful 'industrial era' economies are going to find this transition a great deal more difficult.

➤ *Some of the emerging economies never had much to do with the industrial era in the first place. Do you think it's likely that they will go straight to the new model you are describing?*

Yes, I do. They are actually starting with the proverbial 'clean sheet of paper', so they require less adaptation.

It's a well-known phenomenon, for example, that countries that introduce technology at a later stage than others have the advantage of introducing the latest form of technology.

There are those who say that Japan's economic success in the 1970s and 1980s was a result of having their entire industrial plant reduced to rubble in the Second World War, which forced them to start over.

On the other hand, the United States still had a completely intact industrial plant, and so marched bravely into the 1970s and 1980s with plants equipped from the 1930s.

If you start later, you have less baggage from the past to overcome. So I think there is a real opportunity here for relatively younger economies to vault themselves into a very advantageous position.

Organizations as football teams

The model I use to describe the twenty-first-century corporation is that of an American football team. And I don't mean World Cup football, I mean US football.

The details of the sport aren't important. What's important is that the team is organized first around its processes: there's an offensive process and a defensive process, and a team of people who perform each one.

Every individual on the team is focused on the objective, which involves cooperating with others while carrying out your own particular set of duties.

The team as a whole has a coach whose job it is to guide the team in the performance of its processes; but there's also an offensive coach and a defensive coach. At the same time, every individual has what we call a personal coach, whose job it is to see to it that the individual maximizes his or her own potential and is able to contribute to the performance of the team as a whole.

It is this simultaneous focus on both the process and the team collectively, as well as on the individual and his or her capabilities, that I think is a model for where we're heading in terms of organizational structure.

It's a bit loose. It's a bit ambiguous—which is both a shortcoming and its greatest advantage. In an environment of change, you don't want a very rigid organizational structure. You want one that allows you to adapt.

This means that, on an operational basis, there's a great deal of ambiguity and uncertainty. And it requires new attitudes on the part of the people who work in the organization. They will have to learn not to look for definitive control from a single supervisor, but to be able to operate in an environment of competing demands and basically try to resolve alternative objectives that are all simultaneously valid.

The important thing to remember is that this trajectory we've described is not a personal vision of mine. It's not something that I would personally like to see. My preferences really have little to do with it.

The issue is that there's a certain inevitability to this. If you start with the premise that we have to focus on customers, then almost everything follows inevitably. If you make the assumption that we are moving from a supply-constrained to a demand-constrained economy, then again, what I've said is quite inevitable, in terms of being the most effective and desirable way to operate.

➤ *What advice would you give to the leader of the twenty-first-century corporation?*

I have a very simple observation which is based on something I have seen in many companies: **If you think you're good, you're dead.**

The essence of successfully going forward is humility—a recognition that success in the past has no implication for success in the future. And that the world has changed so much that the formulas for yesterday's success are almost guaranteed to be formulas for failure tomorrow.

I think it will be an open-minded humility, and a recognition that we have to reinvent ourselves for the customer, that will be the difference between those who survive and thrive in the twenty-first century and those who become footnotes in the history books. **99**

Michael Hammer

Dr Michael Hammer is recognized globally as the originator of the concepts of reengineering and process centering, ideas that have literally transformed the modern business world. Formerly a professor of computer science at the Massachusetts Institute of Technology, he is the founder of a successful consulting firm as well as several high-technology firms, and works today as a communicator and adviser to some of the world's largest companies. Hammer was named by Business Week as one of the pre-eminent management thinkers of the 1990s, by the New York Times as one of America's most sought-after speakers and by Time magazine as one of America's 25 most influential individuals. His public seminars are attended by thousands of people annually. He is the author of the seminal Harvard Business Review article 'Reengineering Work: Don't Automate, Obliterate', and co-author with James Champy of the international bestseller, Reengineering the Corporation.

Recommended reading

Beyond Reengineering: How the reengineering revolution is shaping our world and lives (1996) US/UK: HarperCollins.
The Reengineering Revolution: A handbook (1995) Michael Hammer & Steven A Stanton, US/UK: HarperCollins.
Reengineering the Corporation: A manifesto for business revolution (1993) Michael Hammer & James Champy, US: Harper Business/UK: Nicholas Brealey.

"The goal is not to save money but to make money."

FOCUSING ON CONSTRAINTS, NOT COSTS

Eli Goldratt

"
ONGOING IMPROVEMENT WILL become an increasingly critical issue as we enter the twenty-first century, because everywhere we look today we see competition becoming fiercer than ever. And what is fueling this competition is advancing technology. Why? Because it continually gives us better and better raw materials, to the extent that in many cases a mediocre engineer using today's components can produce products which are by far superior to what an exceptional engineer could produce with the components that were available ten years ago.

The movement of new products—fueled by this tremendous improvement in the abilities of the materials—is changing and confusing the economy. Because while product capabilities and quality are rapidly improving, the price of these products is falling, or at least remaining stable.

As a result, companies are under pressure to sell more, which means they need a constant stream of new products. In turn, the constant introduction of these new products, which offer better capabilities and better quality at better prices, makes the market more confused and more competitive. And that means that companies need more and more innovative ideas for products to sell. It's a vicious circle. A vicious race, in fact.

This increasing competition has made companies realize that it is not so important where you stand now. What is vital is to embark on the process of ongoing improvement, otherwise in just a few years you will lose your dominant position. And a few years later, you will simply vanish.

In the traditional sense, ongoing improvement—throughout the twentieth century—was based on the concept of what I call the 'cost world'. Think of an organization as a chain, composed of many links. Somebody has to purchase materials, somebody has to design the product, somebody has to produce the parts and so on and so forth. If you want to improve the chain in an ongoing way, on what should you concentrate your efforts? There are only two main choices: either you take actions that will reduce costs or you take actions that will increase throughput (sales). You can try to do both, but it's not so simple. The management philosophy that guides cost reduction is vastly different from the one that guides increasing throughput.

So suppose that you concentrate on reduction of cost. The first thing to ask is: where is cost drained? And the answer is in each and every department, in each link of the chain. It's like asking the question: what determines the weight of the chain? Of course, the weight of the chain is determined by the weight of each and every link. It's the sum total of all these individual weights. So if you reduce the weight of one link by, let's say, 100 grams, the total weight of the chain will now be 100 grams less than before. Thus we get the impression that each improvement in each link is an improvement of the whole chain. The underlying philosophy becomes: global optimum is the sum of local optima. That has been the governing philosophy in business over the last century. Under that philosophy, a process of ongoing improvement—where the focus is on reducing cost— means following the Pareto principle, trying to concentrate on the 20 percent of the problems that are responsible for 80 percent of the waste. But the resulting improvement in performance is much too slow, and this 'cost' thinking can lead to devastating mistakes. In fact, it is at the root of many corporate failures.

Take International Harvester. Back in 1980 they got into some trouble. They lost money for the first time in 30 years. And because of it, they retired the CEO and got a new person. Now, this new CEO came in and said: 'OK, starting now we are going to do it right.' The first thing he did was to ask for a calculation to be done on all the parts they produced—there were tens of thousands of them. For each part he wanted to know: how much money does it cost us to produce this? And what does it cost us to buy it from the outside, if at all possible? Then he decided that every part which cost them more to produce themselves than to buy they should start to outsource, while trimming their excess capacity. And they did this on a major scale.

You can imagine what happened. You can trim some people, but can you trim machines or buildings? The result was that, following the 'cost' calculations, the expenses actually went up, not down. Because on the one hand, he mainly reduced the variable costs but not the fixed costs, and on the other hand he now had to pay suppliers for the parts that they were buying in from the outside.

Three months later he asked that everything be rechecked. And of course the results were misleading. The parts that they were still producing had to carry on their shoulders all the overhead costs that were previously shared with the other parts that he was now outsourcing. Therefore the cost calculations showed that there was no end to the components that would cost less if they were bought in from the outside. And so they stopped producing them and bought them in. On a mammoth scale.

Then the fourth quarter arrived and naturally the bottom-line results were not good at all. The CEO decided to concentrate on his biggest investments—on his assembly plants. They were reported to be quite efficient but he said, 'Wait a minute. We are calculating efficiencies based on two shifts, five days a week. But these investments are there for three shifts a day, seven days a week. On that basis the assembly plants are running at less than 50 percent efficiency.' So he activated all the assembly plants for three shifts, seven days a week. And in the process, of course, he built up finished goods inventory all over the place. Soon the company's financial statements suggested that it was making more net profit. How come? Because he absorbed more overhead into the inventory, and inventory according to our traditional cost accounting is not a liability but an asset. At the end of the year, it looked like the company was profitable again. He got a bonus. And immediately resigned. Subsequently tens of thousands of people were laid off and his successor had a hard job just to save one-third of the company.

Those are typical results of following the assumptions that stem from the 'cost world': assuming that the way we calculate the cost of parts reflects the costs we can save if we stop producing them and buy them in; assuming that activating a resource—making it work more—is synonymous with utilizing a resource—making a profit; assuming that inventory is an asset; assuming that product cost is a base for determining selling price.

> ➤ *So if traditional cost accounting methods are the wrong way to measure improvement in performance, what do you suggest is the right way?*

If you are convinced that to stay in business your company must embark on a process of ongoing improvement, isn't it obvious that the key is not cost reduction? This avenue of improvement is limited. It's limited by zero. **Instead, what really determines the success of the company is throughput.** And by throughput I mean the rate at which the company generates money through sales.

Let's go back to the chain analogy. Throughput is gained only at the end of the chain through the efforts of all the links. If one link drops the ball, then throughput is jeopardized. The shift from looking at cost to looking at throughput is like shifting from concentrating on the weight of the chain to concentrating on its strength. What determines the strength of the chain? The answer, of course, is the weakest link. So if, for example, you improve any other link—even if you triple its strength—are you going to affect the overall strength of the chain? No.

The minute you switch to making throughput the determining factor, you realize that most of the improvements to most of the links do not really help the performance of the chain. **The global optimum is not the sum of local optima.** This way of thinking is a drastic departure from the way we have conducted our business throughout most of the twentieth century.

In the 1980s the Japanese started to teach us that, in fierce competition, throughput is the dominant factor—that the client is king; that you have to do everything to create throughput; and that inventory is not an asset but a liability. So now, more and more, we are seeing these ideas being adopted. The problem is that most managers do not realize the resulting paradigm shift in management philosophy. They have not yet learned how to operate when the global optimum is not achieved through many local optima: when most local improvements don't really contribute to the global performance.

Improving throughput

Once we agree with the dominance of throughput—the strength of the chain—immediately the question that comes to mind is: how do we identify the weakest link of the organization? Because if we don't do it and we just feel satisfied with improving whatever we can, then the chance that we will improve the organization and its throughput is very small.

In my book *The Goal* I outline the ongoing improvement process that is needed when the weakest link is physical—a bottleneck in production, for example. Unfortunately, though, in most organizations the weakest link is not physical. It's a policy that has been cast into a behavior pattern.

How do you identify it? It is not enough to look for wrong behavior patterns or wrong policies or wrong measurements—there are simply too many of them in every company. So the question is: what is the most fundamental weakness that we should concentrate on improving? What is the core problem, the weakest link? And once you have identified the weakest link, you face another question: what to replace it with? Finding the wrong policy—the weak link—is not so trivial for a start. But finding a replacement for the wrong policy—in other words, creating the *right* policy—is even more difficult.

So we are faced with these two questions. The first is: what to change? In other words, what is the erroneous behavior pattern that is the core problem in our company? And the second question is: what to change to?

But then immediately there is a third question. Because, if we are talking about changing an erroneous behavior pattern, then we're changing something deep in the organization. It's a culture change. Which means that if we don't want to crash into the next bottleneck—resistance to change—we had better find the answer to the third question: how to cause the change?

I don't know of any other way to deal with these questions except by using thinking processes that will enable us systematically to find the answers.

Theory of constraints

The theory of constraints (TOC) says that there is at least one constraint on every system—otherwise companies would all be making infinite profits.

The key is to focus on the constraints—on strengthening the weak links in the chain—thereby improving throughput and improving profits.

Now, how do we identify the constraint? How do we answer the questions: what to change? What to change to? And how to cause the change? Well, this is where we need the thinking processes, which is the technique I developed for analysing problems, finding solutions and communicating in the Socratic way. It's a method of mapping out logical chains of 'cause-and-effect' relationships on paper—I call these diagrams 'trees'.

The first tree is called the **current reality tree**. It's designed to answer the question: what's the core problem? And it does this by visually depicting the existing undesirable effects—or symptoms of the problem—and then using known cause-and-effect relationships to find the very few, usually one, underlying root cause—the core problem.

At the top of almost every current reality tree you find loops. You look at one undesirable effect and your intuition guides you to see that another undesirable effect participates in its cause. And then another undesirable effect participates in the cause of the second one, and the first one is contributing to the third one. When the full current reality tree is developed, you realize that towards the bottom there are no loops. You find that there are one or two root causes that create all the symptoms—all the existing undesirable effects. These core problems are not usually realized by the company or, when they are realized intuitively, their importance is not recognized. So the minute that you finish constructing a current reality tree, the clarity about where you have to concentrate and where you don't is amazing.

➤ *What happens when the constraint is the market itself? Would a market survey tell you this?*

No. Market surveys only tell you what the market is complaining about. These are the symptoms. If you try to aim at the symptoms—at the things the market is complaining about—your chances of being effective are low. It's like trying to aim at the symptoms that exist in your own organization. Instead, it's better to aim at the core problem, the cause of all the undesirable effects. If you want significantly to increase your competitive edge in the market, you'll have to aim at the core problem. You'll have to construct the current reality tree of your market.

Most of the problems in the market are things you already know about before you start the survey—unless, of course, you are a total novice in that particular market. In my experience, market surveys are usually a very elaborate way to procrastinate. In most cases, you have all the data you need before you start them.

To identify the market's core problem you have to build its current reality tree. This is the process you need to go through. Then you go and check with two or three people in the market. If you show them your analysis, in terms of your logical 'cause-and-effect' tree, they will immediately find any mistakes or lack of clarity in your tree. In this way, by checking with two or three people, you find that you have something which is extremely reliable.

The length of time it takes to identify the core problem depends on your experience. When we teach this process we demand that managers do it themselves, on a major subject they need to improve. It takes them almost two days. But the learning curves are very steep. The fifth time a person does a current reality tree it usually takes an hour or two.

For my people to do a diagnosis for a client usually requires about an hour of interrogation. But we are trying to do much more. You see, most people come to us with a preconceived idea about what they want to improve. We've learned that most times what the person wants to improve and what the company needs to improve are not synonymous. Many times the things that they want to improve are just some of the symptoms. So, first of all, we have to identify the constraint—the core problem. We do it through questions and answers, while constructing the current reality tree. Then it becomes apparent what the core problem is.

But that's not enough. **We have to continue to ask questions in order to find out what will happen when they succeed in breaking that constraint. Is the organization going to crash into the next constraint?**

Suppose we determine that the constraint is in production and you break that constraint. Will there be enough demand in the market? Because if not, the improvements will result in excess manpower and the pressure to lay off people in production will start. And if lay-offs happen, the whole improvement process will stop.

Or say the first constraint is the market. We must determine whether finding a way to persuade the market to buy will cause the next constraint to be in distribution. If the distribution cannot deliver what was promised it will ruin the company's reliability. This is what I call 'crashing into the next constraint'.

Therefore we have to verify to ourselves what the first constraint is and what the second constraint is, and whether we have to deal with both of them at the same time or if we can just focus on the first one. After that, we have to find out what obstacles are standing in the way of the people we are talking to—obstacles that might block them from bringing a solution to the company. There is no point in turning people into martyrs.

Only then can we formulate our specific recommendation on how to go about improving the core problem. We explain why the company should adopt throughput management, how TOC will bring them the maximum results for the minimum effort and investment, and why it is so important to do it this way. People's intuition is good, and so is their logic. Therefore, in most cases, we reach a consensus. If we don't succeed, then we say goodbye.

➤ *Let's go back. A manager has identified the core problem. Now what?*

The next step is to find a breakthrough idea that will solve the core problem—remove the constraint—and start to produce desirable effects. This is where you need some creative thinking, to work out what to change to. For that, we use the thinking process called the 'evaporating cloud'. It's a simple process that forces people to think out of their box. Next we create a '**future reality tree**', which uses the same 'cause-and-effect' logic to test the validity of the solution. And then you need a '**transition tree**', which is, in essence, an implementation plan. A logical analysis of how you should go from the present to the future.

When managers finish the current reality tree on the subject they have chosen, they usually have some mixed emotions. On the one hand, there is some embarrassment, especially in the cases where they realize that the finger is pointing directly at them. On the other hand, it's like a weight lifted from their shoulders when they realize that they don't have to deal with an ocean of problems, but instead with just one or two.

Naturally, as they construct their solution, and than hammer out the details of how they are going to introduce and manage the change, they become more and more enthused.

Generally, the more skeptical the people are to start with, the more convinced they are when they finish.

➤ *When management teams get together to use the thinking processes, I've heard them refer to the occasions as 'rethinking parties', or 'intellectual white water rafting trips'. Are the conclusions they reach really such a revelation for them?*

Yes. There are actually three revelations. The first is to what extent you can get a true consensus on the current reality tree.

The second is to what extent the basic beliefs of running a business are based on flawed assumptions. Assumptions that were maybe correct in the environment that existed in the past, but that are definitely not correct now.

Some of the assumptions at the base of cost accounting were correct at the beginning of the twentieth century when we had piece payment—one more piece produced, more money paid, one piece less produced, less money paid. At that time, the vast majority of the cost was truly variable. This became incorrect when we started to pay not by piece but by the hour, which means that traditional cost accounting became invalid by the 1930s and 1940s. But it is still dominating even today. So, again, one of the revelations, or surprises, is to what extent the basic assumptions underlying our businesses are wrong.

The third major surprise to people is to what extent there is no resistance to change if you know how to introduce your ideas; if you carefully design their introduction using the Socratic approach.

The way to use this approach to your advantage is to recognize that behind any 'but' there is usually something valid. So, rather than fighting the 'but', managers learn how to lay the reservation out in logical detail. The person that raises the reservation is then normally able to suggest the additional action that is required to treat it. It becomes his or her solution as well. So resistance to change is a function of how you present your ideas. And if you present them right, which takes a lot of logical work, what you get is not resistance to change, but enthusiasm.

Managers are not so naive as to ask for the ultimate solution. They realize that it is a process of ongoing improvement. There is obviously a continual need to solve the next problem. And you never really finish.

If I look at companies that have already embarked on the theory of constraints, a year later you see that the core problem does not exist any more—they have solved it. Instead, there are other problems that prevent further improvements, sometimes new problems. But the people in those companies actually like this because the challenge keeps moving on. And they become more and more confident in themselves—they know how to approach problems now—and the survival pressure is already off after the first time they turn the wheel. They are already profitable. They are already doing very well.

Applying the theory

The Electronics Division of Ford Motor Company has about 16,000 people and it produces the electronic parts that go into all of Ford's cars—from the stereo to the computer that is controlling the fuel injection. A few years ago it decided that it had to reduce its production lead time, which it measures from the release of the first component until shipping of the final product.

Before it started, its average lead time was 10.6 days. Not too bad, considering the complexity and variety of its products. But Toyota was at 5 days. So Ford implemented the Toyota production system, 'just in time'. And after two years of implementing 'just in time' it reduced its lead time to 8.5 days. It knew that was not enough, because, as we said, Toyota was on 5 days. But when managers went and talked to the Japanese, the Japanese told them, 'What do you expect? It took us more than ten years to achieve it. So keep going.'

They couldn't wait ten years, so they embarked on the theory of constraints. In just one year the company has reduced the lead time, on all the products in all its plants, to an average of 2.2 days. Currently their lead time is, on average, less than 2 shifts.

The core problem was that the company was managing inventory. Now it manages time. As a result, it also reports that customer satisfaction has improved by 75 percent in spite of the fact that the customers have become much more demanding. It is also now able to have real-time statistical process control (SPC) on the floor, which is a huge advantage (previously, it was just lip service).

Responsiveness and learning are 300 percent faster. Floor space used is 20 percent lower, allowing for the introduction of new products. Material handling and tracking have been reduced by 50 percent. Facilities investment is reduced by 25 percent.

The two reported results that impress me the most are that the suggestion process—the time between suggesting an improvement and having it implemented—went from 150 days to just 10 days, and the scheduling process went from 16 days to 5 days to 1 day. Which means that, previously, the reaction time to the market was 16 days until it was scheduled, and then more than 10 days until it was delivered. Now, the order is received today and shipped tomorrow.

To take another example, Avery Dennison is a three and a half billion dollar company that produces adhesive labels from paper and plastics. You'll find its products in virtually every office in the United States. It implemented the theory of constraints in about one-third of its operations, and 12 to 18 months into the change process it reported the following: Market share up 17 to 25 percent. Net sales up 23 percent. Customer complaints down 47 percent. Customer order lead time down 80 percent. Total stock lead time down between 50 and 90 percent. Manufacturing capacity improved by 50 to 300 percent, without investments. Capital deferment improved by millions through existing capacity increases. And the company says that all these improvements have enabled it to open up markets that it traditionally could not enter. For me, the most impressive thing was the work it did in organizing its financial reporting the throughput way—detailing the financial reporting of the entire company, through the financial reports of division and plants, right down to how it measures an individual work center. Here I see a real contribution to the body of knowledge.

A fresh view of marketing

The thinking processes can also be applied to marketing. Many managers don't understand what marketing really is. I often use the analogy of ducks. To me, marketing is about spreading corn to get the ducks to come. Sales is about taking the gun and shooting a sitting duck. And if the duck is not sitting, it means that marketing has not done its job. Marketing is about making the market want your product. Sales is about closing a deal with a specific customer.

Look at the way prices are normally set. We come back to cost accounting again. You calculate what it costs you to make the product by allocating all your business expenses, and then you add a profit margin. As a result, you get what you would like to see as the product selling price. And you get something even more devastating: you get the impression that there is one fair price for the product.

But this is only the producer's perception of value. **If you want to be competitive, you'd better concentrate on the market's perception of value.** In the market's eyes, the value of the product doesn't come from the effort and expense you put into producing it. Its value comes from the benefits the customers think it will bring them.

The customer perceives value in terms of what he or she needs, and since different customers need different things there shouldn't be just one price for the product.

We should segment the market—just like the travel industry does, where different customers pay different prices for the same airline tickets or the same hotel rooms, according to their needs or the time they spend in their traveled destination before returning etc.

As another example, one company I work with supplies microchips to computer companies such as IBM and Hewlett-Packard. And it charges very different prices for the same products, according to how fast it has to deliver. There is one price for standard orders and another price for super-rush orders, orders that it is asked to fulfil in one-fifth of the standard lead time. This price is three times the standard price, and super-rush orders account for 15 percent of the company's business. So again, it's not about product cost, it's about product value. It's about giving customers what they need, which is to help them reach their goals. A lot of people seem to forget that the only way to make money is not through the products but through the benefits that those products bring to the customer.

➤ *Your approach always seems to fly in the face of conventional business rules. Why do you think this is?*

It does violate the rules, but it doesn't violate common sense. In fact, because of its logic you will find that it's totally in line with the intuition of most of the people who ever worked in organizations. The thinking processes are essentially a way to map out intuition and experience on paper and to face the unavoidable conclusions.

So if pure common-sense logic violates the rules that exist, then you have to conclude that the rules that exist are not common sense, but common nonsense.

The point is, these solutions don't fly in the face of conventional wisdom. They fly in the face of conventional assumptions. Companies have been almost universally doing things wrong because of the assumptions that were guiding them the whole time—assumptions that were based on the outdated philosophy that an improvement in the link is an improvement of the whole chain. And the erroneous system of measuring efficiency that grew out of this philosophy has kept people from acting in accord with their common sense for decades.

A whole herd of sacred cows has already been slaughtered by these ideas. And there are more to come. Take project management. In project management, everyone believes in the critical path. At least they believe that it's a constraint. But even the smallest example will show you that this is a mistake. Now, you can imagine what happens when you think that something is a constraint and it's not. It means that you end up ignoring the real constraint, and the result is that projects seldom finish on time or within budget or according to spec.

Look at Intel. It was expanding an expensive facility in Ireland, and midway through the project the person that was in charge, Patrick Hickey, realized that the company had already exhausted its spare time and budget. He started to use the theory of constraints and ended up finishing the project ahead of time, under budget and without compromising at all on the initial scope.

Or Ford Electronics again. It was opening up a new production plant in Hungary, and it was doing it with local people, just after they had abandoned Communism. Now, what do you think the chances were that they would meet the initial targets? The director in charge of putting up the plant, who used the theory of constraints, testified in public that it was the smoothest start-up in the history of the division.

▶ *Can we apply the theory of constraints, as a scientific principle, to all kinds of situations and to any kind of organization?*

Yes. I believe that one of the most startling examples is the Transportation Command of the United States armed forces, which is where they coordinate all their transportation logistics. So here we are talking about a not-for-profit organization. And it's a huge organization. Extremely bureaucratic. Nevertheless they testified in public that, using TOC, they succeeded in drastically changing the whole Command in just one year.

We have also tried it already in elementary schools, middle schools and high schools. And, according to the teachers and administrators, it's working. Instead of teaching kids all the 'facts'—all the answers—they use the Socratic method to show them how to derive the answers themselves.

In my book *It's Not Luck*, there are also some chapters that talk about how to solve problems in the family. This has now grown into a whole course that we teach to people in all kinds of organizations. As a matter of fact, most of these courses we don't teach. We teach their own people to teach them. And the impact? They claim that it has changed their entire working environment and unleashed the intuition that exists there. The impact on productivity improvement is completely in accord with these changes.

If managers learn to explain the change process correctly to their people, if they involve them in the logic of what they are doing, if they give them effective tools to think on their own, then they get the full support and enthusiasm from these people. Because we all intuitively feel it when something makes sense. Of course, you have to do the whole thing in a systematic way. You can't have the change process going on in only the top two or three levels. It has to be throughout the organization. And now there is a way to do it. It's amazing how quick and simple it is.

➤ *How would you express to managers the need to change the way they think if they want to perform successfully in the twenty-first century?*

I would say we've got to kill the assumption that the way to increase profits is through downsizing and cost cutting. Instead, we've got to learn how to focus on increasing throughput. How do we do that? By learning how to construct and implement 'unrefusable' offers, giving customers what they need—something that gives them a real advantage.

To top management, my questions would be: Do you know what to change? What to change to? And how to cause the change? With your hand on your heart? If the answer is no, then it's time to learn how to do it. We have proven that success is not luck, it's logic. You don't have to shoot from the hip any more. We now have very simple tools for constructing and communicating logical solutions.

Most managers know that the way to run a business in the future will probably be quite different than the way it was done in the past. They also know that the goal of their company is not to save money but to make money. In order to make money they realize that they must manage in a way that will satisfy their customers and satisfy their employees. But what managers still have to realize is that, no matter what the circumstances are, there is now a way to achieve these goals. **99**

Eli Goldratt

Dr Eliyahu Goldratt is the founder of the Avraham Y Goldratt Institute, and an internationally recognized leader in the development of new business management philosophies and systems. His revolutionary Theory of Constraints (TOC) is currently being used by hundreds of companies to determine core problems, construct detailed solutions and devise effective implementation plans. Dr Goldratt obtained his BSc from Tel Aviv University and his MSc and PhD from Bar-Ilan University. Today, Goldratt is an educator who is sought after by many of the world's largest corporations. He is a frequent contributor to scientific journals and business publications and is the author of the international bestsellers The Goal *and* It's Not Luck.

Recommended reading

It's Not Luck (1994) US: North River Press/UK: Gower.

The Goal: A process of ongoing improvement (2nd edn 1992) Eliyahu M Goldratt & Jeff Cox, US: North River Press/UK: Gower.

The Theory of Constraints and How It Should Be Implemented (1990) US/UK: North River Press.

The Haystack Syndrome: Sifting information out of the data ocean (1990) US/UK: North River Press.

The Race (1986) Eliyahu M Goldratt & Robert E Fox, US/UK: North River Press.

"We're talking about changes in basic assumptions ... few traditional organizations ever go through the eye of this needle."

THROUGH THE EYE OF THE NEEDLE

Peter Senge

" As we approach the twenty-first century, I see three distinct driving forces, any one of which would probably be sufficient to bring about significant change in management and organizations. But the operation of these forces together is what will bring about profound change.

First, there's technology. Then there's the globalization of business, which is related to technology. But the third is the hardest to name and yet probably the most challenging. It concerns the unprecedented growth of total material throughput due to all industrial activity on a global scale, the consequent stress on natural systems, and increasing complexity and interdependence. This third set of forces is one of those things we feel in our gut but it's very difficult to describe succinctly in words. The most obvious symptoms are breakdowns—societal and ecological crises and massive institutional breakdown on an unprecedented scale. It is hard to find any institution in modern society—business, government, public education, the family—that is not suffering breakdown.

Doing what we've always done, faster

Many people seem to believe that technology is the major driver of change—that is a conventional cultural story in industrial societies. Personally, I think that **only the most superficial changes are being brought about by technology**. The sole exception I would make to that is in so far as technology moves information. You can argue that Radio Free Europe did more to break down the Soviet Union than political pressure, so clearly the movement of information is not trivial. But did it change fundamentally how anybody thought? Did it pave the way for the emergence of effective twenty-first-century institutions in Russia and in Eastern Europe? Surely, the events of the past few years would lead us to question that.

Let me tell you something that was told to me years ago by the man who was my mentor in the systems field, Jay Forrester. Jay is an eminent technologist, having led the team that built Whirlwind, the first general-purpose digital computer in the early 1950s. There had been previous computers but they had been scientific tools for very particular laboratory purposes. This was the first digital computer built for a significant practical purpose, which was to coordinate North America's first integrated air-defense system. Along the way, Forrester invented random access core memory, a critical technical breakthrough in the history of digital computation, an invention which put him in the Inventor's Hall of Fame along with people like Marconi and Edison. IBM was MIT's prime contractor in building the machines for the government, which is how IBM entered the computer field. Digital Equipment was started by a few of Jay's graduate assistants on the project. So, when Jay speaks about technological progress he does so with some credibility.

In 1970, when I was entering graduate school at MIT, I asked Jay why he had left the computer hardware field entirely when he was only about 35 years old. 'How could you leave such an exciting field, when you were literally in on the ground floor and in such a central position?' I asked. After all, IBM's Tom Watson Jr later called Jay Forrester one of the five most influential people in his life, and he was on the Digital Equipment board for 10 years. Do you know what Jay said? He said, 'Well, it was quite obvious that for at least three or four generations, people would pretty much use computers to do what human beings had always done, only faster. It would take at least that long before people began to use computers for doing what human beings had never done before.'

Now, most of what is going on in technology, I believe, falls into this category: doing what people have always done, but faster. We westerners seem especially attracted to 'more' and 'faster' as the essence of innovation. We never think we do anything fast enough, so we always want to do things a little faster. This is insane at some level, since no one has ever figured out how to enhance the quality of life faster. Usually, things that enhance the quality of life involve slowing down, not speeding up. But, of course, we are focused more on quantity than quality of life, so speed is very alluring to us.

The second driving force I mentioned is the globalization of business, and the market pressures that come when we operate in a global business environment where we can produce and sell anything anywhere. But I think that a lot of people have already said plenty about that.

However, the third reason for all this change going on is, to me, the most interesting and unquestionably the most important.

A hierarchical nervous breakdown

Jay Forrester said something else that also stuck with me. 'Today,' he said, 'technological progress is more or less a production process—if you put more money and good people into a particular area where there is a solid foundation, technological progress is more or less guaranteed. The really big issues facing mankind concern our inability to understand and manage our complex human systems.'

In fact, you might even add that blind technological progress exacerbates these problems, because it contributes more complexity when we cannot understand the complexity that already exists. **We are out of control, driving down a dark road with little or no light, and most technological progress amounts to speeding up.** On the other hand, Jay felt that technologies like the computer could also play a critical, positive role in understanding the complexity we are creating, but that those benefits were not in the technology alone—but in the interplay of simulation technologies and new conceptual understandings of complex systems.

This interplay seems now to be happening, but it has not yet begun to penetrate into the world of practical affairs, to affect how we think about, lead and manage our social institutions. Hence, we have massive institutional breakdown and massive failure of the centralized nervous systems of hierarchical authoritarian institutions in the face of growing interdependence and accelerating change.

We are everywhere preoccupied with coping with these breakdowns. So it is very difficult to recognize, let alone correct, the collision course we are set upon. By merely speeding up the machine of traditional hierarchically controlled organizations, we are reinforcing the collision course of our 'outlaw' industrial system.

What I mean by 'outlaw' is that we are living outside the laws of nature. No engineer would expect to build an airplane that violated that laws of aerodynamics, that had negative lift, or build a chemical refinery that violated the law of conservation of matter and energy. **Yet we are together running an economic system that violates the basic laws of natural systems, and just hoping that we can keep it going long enough that the problems will have to be solved by someone else.** There is no 'waste' in nature—all outputs or by-products of one natural system are inputs or nutrients to another. But we run an economic system that truly produces waste, visible and invisible by-products of our industrial processes that can go nowhere—they just 'pile up'. Never before in the history of life on this planet has there been a species that systematically destroyed other species— until us. Does any species have a right to do that?

An analogous set of unprecedented changes is occurring in social systems, likewise brought about by accelerating global industrial growth. Just as we are destroying biodiversity, we are destroying cultural diversity, the 'gene pool' for cultural evolution. Probably nowhere today is this happening more rapidly than in China. One of the world's oldest continual cultural systems is being uprooted and destroyed in a mere generation or two. The Chinese language is being reengineered by government. Religious institutions are under attack. Ancient philosophical systems, like the *chi* energy system that explains a great deal about health which escapes our western medical system, are being uprooted. We have no idea of the accumulated knowledge, for advancing understanding of the human condition, for health, for 'beingness', that may be lost. The homogenization of cultural diversity and the destruction of cultural history are central forces underlying societal breakdowns worldwide.

Now, for most businesses such issues as these are 'off the screen', not even remotely ponderable, let alone discussable. Yet these very same businesses are made up of human beings, and these human beings are getting increasingly uncomfortable. They are increasingly uneasy about the environment. They are increasingly uneasy about the breakdowns in family and social structure. They are increasingly uneasy about the continued concentration of wealth and power, and the accompanying growth of the disenfranchised. They would like to pretend that these 'big problems' will just solve themselves, that still more technology will come along to provide the remedies. But then they look out at the world, at the net consequences of the technological progress to date, and they are less certain. They cope with this by not thinking about the future, by busying themselves with reacting to the breakdowns. But they are uneasy. They are fearful. They really do not know what to think. They do not know what to tell their children.

To me, all of this speaks of a new reality. It says that we as a species are confronting a whole new class of problems for which we are completely unprepared. These are 'systemic crises'. They have no simple, local causes. No one is to blame. There are no villains to bring to justice. These problems are the unintended by-products of the way the entire system of industrial progress works, especially as it continues to increase in global scale. Any rational assessment would say 'slow down'. So much is changing that we do not understand, therefore we should at least slow down and try to regain some balance and perspective, to understand these momentous systemic changes. But of course we can't slow down. **Why can't we slow down? Because we literally have no ability to control our behavior at this macro level.** And, of course, this is precisely part of the problem.

So, if you wanted to ask me personally what is the deepest and most profound force driving change, I'd say that it is the awareness, however dim and ill formulated, that we are in deep trouble. As this awareness grows, I think we will increasingly see that the role of business organizations in the twenty-first century must change, because the world we are going to be living in will be radically different. And to play a new role, business organizations will have to develop fundamentally new capabilities for understanding and dealing with complexity.

Learning organizations

When we formulated the 'learning organization' idea, I was personally interested in learning how to control large-scale human systems which are technological, economic, cultural and political, and which can never be understood by focusing on only one of these dimensions. And I was struck by the fact that no one knows how to direct, manage or influence human systems at this scale. **We are, by any technical definition, operating out of control.** It seemed to me that if we were to make any sort of fundamental headway on this, we needed to have a practice domain. We had to have a domain in which we could roll up our sleeves and go to work, to start to see what it would really mean to be able to consciously influence large-scale human systems. It seemed to many of us that the business organization was a logical starting point.

First, business organizations are big enough that nobody can control them. If you talk to any CEO of a large corporation, unless they are a pure egotist, they will tell you, 'I know that I'm not in control'. Nobody, rationally, could say that they are in control of the thousands of variables, the hundreds of thousands of people, the dynamics of the incredibly complex processes. Does anybody really understand how the product development process works? Of course not. I remember talking to a senior product development director in a large firm who was relating how products really get developed. He said, 'You get further behind and further behind, and there are more crises, and people work longer hours, and they throw more money at it, and there are more crises. And then,' he said, 'a miracle occurs. That's how new products really get developed.'

But you could say, 'Why not start with a university?' or 'Why not start with a school system? Why not start with a municipal government? They are all big. And they are all complex. And they are all political, economic, cultural, technological, human systems.' But I think that if you wanted to start any place, and you looked at all these different possibilities, you'd say they are all impossible. But a corporation is probably less impossible, relatively speaking.

One thing in its favor is that the business organization has a greater capacity for innovation than does government—certainly more than do educational institutions. And a greater incentive. It has something called a bottom line which gives a little bit of coherence. You know, there is at least one performance measure that everybody will more or less agree on. Believe me, there is no performance measure that everybody will agree on in education. It's very difficult to know if you are making headway if there are no measurable results people can agree on.

Businesses are also fairly well-defined entities. You can see, more or less, where the inside and the outside are. They are less 'embedded' in other social instutions than is, say, education. Business people might like to complain about how Wall Street or their stockholders limit their ability to innovate, but they should try innovating when there are school boards, state departments of education and parents glaring over their shoulders.

Plus, of course, business is becoming increasingly global. So its scale is commensurate with the scale of the really significant issues I mentioned before. It seems to me that there are really unique responsibilities and capabilities that business organizations will have to develop in order to maintain viability, given the extraordinary interdependency that exists in the world today and that will increasingly exist in the future. I think this will be true whether they are networks or more traditional, hierarchical types of business organizations.

For all these reasons, I think that there is no institution in the world that has a better chance of developing and maintaining a global and systemic view than the corporation.

➤ *How do you suggest that organizations come to terms with the increasing interdependency in our world?*

The first step is to realize that everything is interrelated. That the world is becoming more interconnected and interdependent, and that business is becoming more complex and dynamic. All of which means that we have to change the way we think about learning and interacting with each other at all levels.

We have to develop a sense of connectedness, a sense of working together as part of a system, where each part of the system is affecting and being affected by the others, and where the whole is greater than the sum of its parts.

The way we usually deal with complexity is that we break things down into smaller, more manageable pieces. But that way of thinking assumes that the sum of the parts equals the whole. That is the way we've tried to solve problems traditionally in business, and it won't work anymore in the kind of world we're moving into.

So the way organizations can deal with the issue of interdependency is, first, by seeing the need for a change of mindset, which is by the way very difficult because we have accomplished a great deal with our traditional reductionistic mindset. Second, they need to encourage the innovators. I don't know of any example in history where significant changes were led by majorities, and I see no reason to believe that this will be any different.

Royal Dutch Shell's famous study of 'long-lived' corporations, companies that had survived for 200 years or longer, found that a common characteristic of the survivors was that they had a 'high tolerance for experiments in the margin'. We're talking about changes which are fundamentally cultural, changes in basic assumptions and 'taken-for-granted' ways of operating. Such changes cannot be mandated from the top. You cannot command people to change how they think. Instead, small pockets of people or organizations will start operating differently. They will develop new skills in understanding complexity, in building shared aspirations, in learning how to reflect on their own assumptions and in challenging assumptions without invoking defensiveness. Some of these 'small pockets' might be at the top of organizations, but even that will not alter the basic organic nature of the change process. **Changes in mindset usually don't start on a large scale.**

As far as I know, whenever a new mindset—a new way of looking at the world—does take hold, it happens only over a long period of time. This is not like a light switch that somebody throws and says: 'Now we have a new management paradigm.' There is an old line from studying paradigm change in the sciences, which is that 'most paradigm changes occur at funerals'. The people who are really committed to a particular paradigm in a scientific domain don't change. They never change. It's much too significant a shift for them. Basic changes in how we think involve tremendous uncertainty and tremendous risk.

There are two levels to this change. One is at the personal level of new skills and capabilities, both individual and collective. Today, everyone in business is into 'teams', but learning how to 'think together' involves very high-level skills that few managers have. The second has to do with the extent to which we organize ourselves to support learning. This ranges from the overall design of organizations to more specific features—what we call the learning infrastructure.

The term 'learning organization' is very broad and can mean many things to many people. To most people it means flexible, responsive, adaptive organizations that aren't so bureaucratic and so forth. But in our work, it has really meant **developing specific learning capabilities not present in traditional organizations**.

The 'Five Disciplines' represent one articulation of these new learning capabilities. They include the capacity of people to have a sense of purpose and to build genuinely shared visions (based on people, individually, knowing what they care deeply about); the ability of people to see larger patterns and understand interdependency—by developing what we call 'systems thinking'; and people having increased reflective capabilities, so that they can be more and more aware of their own assumptions— particularly the assumptions that they would not normally question. These have been the cornerstones of our work for a long time.

In the last few years, we have become more and more interested in some of the organizational conditions or organizational features that would enable this to occur. This involves the philosophical 'guiding ideas' that might be more conducive to deep change, the overall design features and the specific infrastructures that would support continual learning.

> *Can you give some examples of new organizational design ideas that might be consistent with learning organizations?*

Sure. But we need to keep in mind that these are just pieces of the puzzle, not the whole puzzle. It is easier to talk about new organizational structures than challenging personal changes.

One thing that I have been intrigued by recently is what we have been learning about as a successful approach to radical decentralization.

There is a man who is advising us now as we rethink the Learning Center consortium, the group of companies working together to develop these new learning capabilities. His name is Dee Hock, and he was the founder of Visa International. Visa International is a pretty interesting example of a twenty-first-century organization. By some measures it is perhaps the largest corporation in the world. If you took all the Visa card businesses together, they would have a total market capitalization of around 400 billion dollars. Yet the organization that coordinates it all has only a few thousand employees. It is a completely non-traditional corporate form. It is a for-profit membership corporation, and it operates based on a few simple principles. It is completely open. If you meet the membership criteria, you can be a member of the club.

There is no formal hierarchical authority that governs Visa at all. It is completely a network organization. But it *is* an organization. It was founded 30 years ago with an original philosophy and design. It is governed by a set of ideas, a very clear purpose statement and a set of carefully worked-out operating principles. In that sense, it is more like a democratic society than a traditional corporation. Its success speaks for itself. It is still growing worldwide at about 20 percent per year.

Now Visa obviously represents just one particular business, but the organizational design is what is really interesting. Dee Hock has an interesting story about the whole thing. After struggling to get people to understand the Visa organizational concepts for almost 15 years—it seemed to succeed despite the belief that it couldn't succeed—Dee left the business around 1980 and dropped out. He didn't do anything in the business world for 10 or 12 years. When he came back, he says, he felt like Rip van Winkle. Everybody was now talking about what he had been talking about—radical decentralization, network organizations, virtual organizations. For the last three or four years, he has been looking around the world and finding many different examples of this new organizational form. He has given it the label 'chaordic organizations', a contraction of chaos and order. **These are organizations that seem to generate order out of chaos, as opposed to traditional organizations that try to impose order (and often end up producing a lot of chaos).**

One especially interesting example of this kind of organization is The Natural Step in Sweden. In my view, it's one of the most important developments worldwide in the environmental movement. It is a non-profit organization that's the center of an environmental movement throughout Sweden. In many ways it is producing more significant change in industrial practices, governmental practices, public awareness and behavior towards a sustainable industrial society than any other place in the world. Today, four million copies of a booklet explaining The Natural Step have been distributed, reaching virtually every household in Sweden, and many of the largest Swedish corporations are working together to see who can develop the most environmentally sound practices. I don't think there's anything else even remotely like it that I am aware of. It's gradually spreading now to several other countries.

Dee believes that what makes The Natural Step work are exactly the same principles that make Visa work. It's based on two cornerstones, the same as Visa: a very clear purpose that everyone understands and supports, and a set of clear operating principles. In the case of The Natural Step, the purpose is becoming a sustainable industrial society, and the 'operating principles' are called 'the four system conditions', a set of 'non-negotiable facts' about the nature of all natural systems, which must ultimately hold for human systems as well. Because such organizations are self-organizing, specific structures will come and go. Visa, for example, is sold through banks and other kinds of financial institutions around the world, and they have all kinds of different structures—but the basic structure of Visa is almost transparent. It's so simple in one sense, yet anything but easy to achieve. Visa International has a very carefully worked-out statement of purpose and a few operating principles, which Dee said took them over a year to work out originally. Karl-Henrik Robert, who founded The Natural Step spent over a year writing letters to 20 leading scientists until they could all agree on the four system conditions. The two organizations, despite worlds of difference, are strikingly similar in their foundations.

We shouldn't generalize too much from these two examples, but they are at least worth taking seriously. Both are very radical, and they succeed in their respective domains in ways that traditional organizations have not.

Creating a learning infrastructure

One key issue is how you design organizations so that you don't leave learning to chance. Over the last couple of years, there has been much thought as well as some interesting experiments on this in the Organizational Learning Center (OLC) companies. Recently, Vic Leo from Ford Motor Company, our liasion officer to Ford for several years, suggested that there are three basic areas in which a learning infrastructure must operate: **practical experimentation and testing, capacity building and diffusion and standardization.**

Most of our projects have been focused on the first area, in particular on developing 'learning laboratories'. The basic idea behind these projects is redesigning particular operational environments so that learning and working are integrated. In Ford, for example, initial experiments with a Car Development Learning Laboratory resulted in the 1995 Lincoln Continental being one of the most effective car development processes ever, breaking many internal company records for timing and quality. In its first nine months of sales, the car achieved some of the highest quality ratings in the Ford fleet, on a par with the Lexus. More importantly, the learning laboratory represents a generalizable set of tools and methods, a 'practice field' or space where people who work together can test out new ideas and learn how to inquire together into complex issues. Without such a learning space, daily pressures, combined with suspicion and lack of common understanding in a very large team, invariably lead people to quick fixes that make things better in the short run but only leave deeper problems unaddressed. These deeper problems invariably are the cause of overruns and suboptimal solutions as a large car development effort nears conclusion. Today, other car development programs at Ford are trying to build on and incorporate the learning laboratory into their efforts.

Capacity building may be addressed by conventional training programs but also requires longer-term development efforts. For example, EDS has implemented an intensive nine-month 'Leading learning communities' (LLC) program that helps middle- and upper-middle managers develop 'transformational learning skills'. The LLC program combines about 30 days of classroom sessions with an equal or greater time on personal coaching and work-related projects outside the classroom, focused directly on the deep personal changes required to inquire continually into our own mental models and to create safe environments for others to do likewise. This program is one of several major capacity-building efforts at EDS, including ongoing developmental programs for the top management.

Diffusion and standardization start with serious efforts to study and capture the learning from innovations like the learning lab and the LLC program. For example, we have begun to train 'learning historians', who are part of all projects we do through the OLC consortium today. Amazingly, I hear top managers complain all the time that 'we can't learn from ourselves', meaning that innovative practices do not spread within their own organization—yet very little serious effort is devoted to studying and documenting new innovations. Managers seem to think that innovative practices ought somehow to spread spontaneously. They give no thought to the infrastructure required for this to happen. An interesting counter example among large organizations is the US army. The army has had historians for 150 years, and army leaders have a sense of history totally unlike their corporate counterparts. What is really interesting is how this understanding of history provides a unique perspective to inform them in a time of radical change, which is what the army is going through today.

➤ *Why do you think that the majority of organizations will not want to make the kind of changes we are discussing?*

First, these changes are personally challenging. In most cases, they represent radical departures from traditional ways of running businesses. But it is especially hard to get people to think about radical changes at the personal level. In some sense, it's often the most difficult thing of all, because it is very hard for people to conceive of themselves as being different.

Think about the personal changes that an individual manager has to be willing to go through to move away from a 'command and control' environment. The façade of control provided by this environment is a little like a drug. It is very soothing. It's really like solving your problems by having six drinks at the end of the day. You know your problems haven't actually gone away but you feel OK about them. That's in some ways what hierarchical control is like. You know deep down that you're not in control. But things look good. The people say, 'Yes boss, we're on top of it.'

Letting go of that, and moving to an environment where people are really candid and honest, feels a lot more chaotic. You feel out of control. You feel uncomfortable. You feel like, are we going to make it? **So reality becomes a much more challenging place to live.** You've given up the drug.

Second, these changes take time. We've been doing work in systems thinking, mental models and building shared vision for almost 20 years, and I have never seen a situation where people didn't say: 'I never understood this until I worked with it for at least a year.' Usually after two or three years people say, 'Now I'm starting to grasp it. I had no idea how significantly it would change the way I look at the world and how I operate, how I actually behave.'

Third, we are talking about redistributing power. You can argue that this is inevitable, that everywhere you look over the last ten years you see the failure of large, centrally controlled institutions—from the breakdown of the Soviet Union to the decline of IBM and General Motors. But it is one thing to have that happen to you and another to bring it about yourself. Dee Hock says that business people get really excited when they start to understand how 'chaordic' organizations can work, when they see their potential productivity and effectiveness. But the love affair is short lived when they suddenly grasp that no such organization could ever justify paying a CEO a million dollars a year. Such organizations naturally deconcentrate and distribute power and wealth.

So, few traditional organizations may ever go through the eye of this needle. People will talk about empowerment, they will talk about learning organizations, but it will be mostly talk. Only a few will have the courage of their conviction and patience to move ahead. **Those that succeed will, I believe, have unique advantages in the twenty-first century, because they will harness the imagination, spirit and intelligence of people in ways that no traditional authoritarian organization ever can.**

Sharing knowledge

Traditionally we're used to hoarding things because scarcity creates value. The unwillingness to share information, for example, is highly cultural. You'll find it most strongly in the West where we treat information and knowledge as if they were something that could be possessed. We think that people own ideas. After all, for us, what could be more personal, more 'our own', than our own thoughts?

In a more collectivist culture like the oriental cultures, even the concept of knowledge is different. When you or I went to school we 'got' knowledge. That's our metaphorical way of looking at it, but it's really quite inaccurate to think of knowledge in that way. What you or I get in school is something we inherit. Nobody learns history as facts, we learn history as selected facts *and* as stories that we tell about the facts. It's all completely social. It's collective. However, there is a mental model that westerners have that knowledge is something that individuals acquire and possess.

Just look at the language we use in connection with knowledge work. We talk about 'knowledge acquisition'—something we acquire, then possess. In our consumer mindset, 'acquire' is tantamount to 'purchase'. And our first instinct with something we possess is to hoard or protect it.

So I think, first, we have to help people to sort out definitions. In the West we have a very weak definition of knowledge. We use the words knowledge and information virtually synonymously, and for us there is no sharp distinction between the two.

As far as information is concerned, individuals do acquire it in a very real sense. It comes from some place and it passes from hand to hand. But knowledge, I believe, is something that is quite different. The definition we use for knowledge is 'the capacity for effective action'. And that's not something you 'get' in the sense of purchasing, it's something you learn.

You may never persuade people to change the accepted colloquial definition of knowledge, but at the very least you can force them to think about the difference between 'knowing about things', which is really information, versus 'knowing how'. That's a pretty standard distinction in most of our western languages; the distinction between knowing about it and knowing how.

In this light, knowledge sharing and information sharing are fundamentally different. Sharing knowledge is not about giving people something, or getting something from them. That is only valid for information sharing. **Sharing knowledge occurs when people are genuinely interested in helping one another develop new capacities for action; it is about creating learning processes.**

Moreover, most capacities for action that are important to organizations are collective. No one could hoard them even if they tried. A football team's knowledge, its capacity for action, is not the sum of a bunch of individuals' knowledge. It is literally a collective phenomenon. We might say that certain individuals are 'team players', but that is meaningless until the team, collectively, develops the ability to play as a team. Different individuals might have relatively more experience of being parts of great teams, but the 'chemistry' of any great team is always a collective phenomenon. In that sense, much of the knowledge that we're really interested in inside organizations is just like the chemistry of a fine sports team. It's a group of people who have learned what it means to function together. That takes a certain mindset and a lot of patience and practice. The resulting knowledge literally cannot be in one person—so there is nothing for any one person to possess.

Interrelationships and interdependencies

If you take a good look at your relationships with customers, you might say, 'We're committed to the customer, we're committed to the customer, we're committed to the customer'—but how do you actually view the customer? One senior executive at a major corporation said that he always felt he was committed to the customer, but he eventually realized that he actually saw the customer as his boss. It wasn't until an environment of real trust started to develop within his organization that he could honestly start to feel truly committed to the customer. It was the first time in his professional life that he felt like it wasn't just about pleasing the boss.

So there might be real connections between the quality of relationships within the organization and the quality of the relationships that extend beyond the organization. Laying a foundation of trust is what will allow people to build really meaningful relationships with partners, suppliers, distributors and customers. **Real commitment is a function of the quality of relationships.** We often forget that. And when times are tough, those relationships will hang in there.

It's like anything in life. Marriages go through a lot of crises. Most don't make it. Those that do have some foundation that comes into play. There is a deep level of trust and mutual regard that can allow you to go through a very difficult time. Companies are no different. And customers are no different. They are just people and it's all about how people relate to one another.

The trouble is that most business relationships work like dysfunctional families. Everybody is basically concentrating on just pleasing the boss and avoiding getting their ass kicked, rather than on building real relationships.

➤ *Do you think that the changing business environment will make it easier for companies to adopt these new management paradigms?*

No. I think most of the forces on organizations tomorrow will make it harder. Increasing competitiveness, for example, will create much more stress. And any psychologist will tell you that under stress most people revert to their most primitive behaviors. Therefore, **the more stress we put on our organizations the more their tendency will be to revert to their most primitive behaviors**. And in a business organization, at least in the West, what are our most primitive behaviors? Management control, time pressure, do it faster, do it cheaper.

You see these problems manifested in the way most companies are trying to speed up basic processes. Of course, fundamental processes in our organizations do need to be more responsive and resilient. They need to be both faster and more adaptable. But the way you get there is virtually the antithesis of what most western business managers do. We know, for example, that it's necessary to develop new products at least one or two years faster. So that is an external stress in a way. But how do we speed things up? Under stress we revert to our most primitive behavior. We put more pressure on the program managers. We put in more stringent financial controls.

The irony is that to do things faster you often have to go slower. You have to be more reflective. You have to develop real trust. You have to develop the abilities of people to truly think together. Why? Because it requires you to go through fundamental changes: redesigns of the most basic sorts. You need to build a shared understanding of how the present system works and why it takes so long. And, you need to have people who can trust one another through difficult systemic changes.

This, of course, is the aspiration of most reengineering efforts—to build shared understanding of how things work today and to redesign the processes. But, the consultant's 'as is' map of the current systems is usually grossly deficient, because people do not trust anyone enough to tell the truth of how things really work. Likewise, there is little deep commitment to change.

Many years of research on how people learn has told us what we all know as parents—learning requires safety. Without some modicum of safety, it is difficult or impossible for people to learn. Stress compromises safety. And consequently most of the organizations that are trying desperately to do things faster are going to fail dismally. They will get a little faster. But as Deming used to say, 'Sure, you'll accomplish the results, but you'll destroy the organization to do it. And you'll destroy the people in it.' So the present environment will, if anything, create more and more pressure to revert.

The leader's role

Very few leaders understand the depth of commitment required to build a learning organization. As Bill O'Brien, a retired CEO, once put it: 'This involves the willingness to change our mental models.' This is much easier said than done. In practice, it is disorienting and deeply humbling, because our old mental models were the keys to our confidence and our competence. **To be a real learner is to be ignorant and incompetent. Not many top executives may be up for that.**

Another way to look at this is to recognize that a learning organization represents a fundamental shift in organizational culture. According to Edgar Schein, most top executives have little understanding of the task of developing culture. It requires patience, reflectiveness and a willingness to find a new balance between focusing on results and focusing on how we are operating while we are trying to achieve those results. So they shy away from it.

At the same time, there is also a question about what the role of the operative leaders will actually be in the new organization. My guess is that we are going through a profound change in the nature of managerial work. In the old model, the job of the people at the top was to figure out what was going on, make all the key decisions and create the control mechanisms that would translate top management's decisions into coordinated actions throughout the organization. Planning, organizing, controlling—the holy trinity of traditional authoritarian management. Today, this is changing. It is no longer possible to figure it all out from the top. Even if we did, top management's insights and decisions would probably be obsolete by the time they reached the front ranks. And even if that wasn't the case, it is pretty unlikely that people would pay any attention anyway.

Consequently, what exists today in most of our big organizations is extraordinary anxiety at the top. And it's not just because of external stresses. That's what most top managers talk about, of course, but only because most of them are afraid to talk about the level of personal stress they feel. Many are starting to get the message that their jobs are changing, and they don't know what they're becoming and they don't know if they're qualified to do them any more. They hear that they've got to empower people, and they've got to push decisions out into the organization. But they are starting to say to themselves: 'If everyone else is making all those decisions, what decisions am I going to get to make?' So naturally they're schizophrenic. They push decisions out for a while, but as soon as things get tough they pull them right back. Because they are terrified that pretty soon they might not have any work. Or even any job at all. So the concern with workplace stress today is justifiable, but most of it is focused on middle management. I think the focus should be on top management stress because, until this is resolved to some degree, stress at lower levels will never improve.

And it's not just that senior managers feel that they are losing control. **Giving up control is very difficult, but it's virtually impossible if you have no idea of what you might be getting in its place.** In this case, the safety required for learning might revolve around having some positive image of the future. We can work and work and work on how to help senior managers not feel anxious about losing control. But it would be better to start helping people formulate a compelling image of what we might be moving towards, something that might be exciting enough and positive enough for people to say, 'I'd be willing to give some of this up in order to try to move towards that.' See, the big question leaders are asking themselves is, 'What ring am I reaching out to grab as I let go of this other one? Because in between I'm hanging in space.'

Now that doesn't mean that we're ever going to find a ring that's going to satisfy everybody. Once again, I don't think we're dealing with the majority. If 90 percent of the human energy is out there trying to resuscitate, revive and revitalize the old system of management, that wouldn't surprise me. But if we have 10 percent available to work on creating something really new, then that might be more than adequate.

Rethinking hierarchies

To find something that will satisfy the 10 percent, we are going to have to rethink what hierarchy is all about. At some level, we need to address the question, 'Why do we need hierarchies at all?' There are some people who say that the future organization is going to have no hierarchy. I don't agree.

Even in extreme examples of network organizations like Visa International and The Natural Step there is still hierarchy. But it is first and foremost a hierarchy of guiding ideas. The hierarchical distribution of power is very different than in traditional organizations.

Perhaps Visa and The Natural Step suggest the first role of hierarchical leadership—the articulation of guiding ideas. In both cases, individuals and small groups of leaders had an extraordinary impact on how the organizations were conceived and how they continue to run. But they exerted this influence through the ideas they developed, which became embedded in the organizations, not through ongoing decision making.

The Canadian organizational theorist Elliot Jaques offers a very interesting way to think about hierarchy in general. He argues that different people at different levels of a hierarchy should be able to see further into the future. On the front lines, if I'm dealing with customers day to day, then naturally my primary time perspective ranges from hours up through days and weeks, because what is most important for my work is making the customer happy now. If I'm a manager, my primary job might be the *processes* that are helping to make customers happy. Improving these processes might involve several months up to a year or so. Extending that argument, Jaques argues for seven fundamental layers of hierarchy, even in the largest organization, based on different time horizons. As you might imagine, when you get to the top, Jaques's last two levels, you're considering a time horizon of 10–20 years or longer. This seems to me to be a very elegant way to get at what hierarchy is all about.

I would also argue that the justification for hierarchy is breadth. Recently an executive from Ford told an interesting story that illustrates this. He was the head of a program to build a prototype car, which involved 500 or so people, and his team wanted to make a fairly radical short-term decision about stopping an assembly process. They had good reasoning and they'd thought it through. They were convinced themselves and they were together, but they didn't make the decision by themselves, they called this executive who was the head of the program. And you might ask, 'Why did they call him? There was this bunch of people in a team, who saw what needed to be done. So if they were really empowered, why didn't they just do it themselves instead of checking with him first?' The executive told me that there were two reasons. One was that, given the existing hierarchy, he still had some authority. But more than that, the second reason was that they called to check it out with him. Because there might have been some consequences of that decision that they couldn't appreciate. **So there is a legitimate role for hierarchy which concerns seeing possible impacts of decisions that people closer to the actual process might not see.** This is the idea of breadth of perspective. It is a natural complement to Jaques's ideas about time horizon.

So, what is the chief executive's job? It is thinking 10 or 20 years ahead or longer, and continually helping the organization to see its impacts on a larger society. This might entail responsibility for guiding ideas that are important over such a time horizon and breadth of scope. It might entail comparable decision making. Neither of these needs to be their sole responsibility, but they would define what the person is accountable for. I believe that if you could paint a picture like this in a compelling enough way, you would find some chief executives who would reach for that ring. They would say, 'You know what? I know damn well that I can't control this organization. I shouldn't even be trying. But I might be able to help this company to think about itself in the future, in ways that nobody else within the organization could.'

If you take that one level down, to where the time perspective is, say, 3 to 10 years, that's your vice president level. What's their job? To work out how the organization is functioning in the most deep ways. How does the organization function effectively or ineffectively as an integrated system, in concert with suppliers, customers, other business partners? What is its infrastructure for learning? How does it learn?

Arie de Geus, the retired coordinator of planning for Royal Dutch Shell, played an important role in reconceiving the company's planning process. He and his colleagues in group planning proposed that people should see 'planning as learning', as fundamentally a learning process that might continually work to improve the mental models of decision makers throughout the Shell group. Planning is a process that is broader than assembly in a way, because it potentially influences everything in the organization. So to think about how you redesign that process, so that it becomes more and more a source for building knowledge in the organization and a source of future competitive advantage, is a tremendously influential job for that next level down below the CEO.

If you start this kind of reasoning going, we'll create some rings which the people up in the hierarchy can start to grasp. It will only be 10 percent, but that's all we need.

▶ *Let's focus on this 10 percent for a moment. If they succeed in making the changes you are suggesting, what do you think will be the most obvious manifestations of improvement in their organizations?*

I would say that there are two obvious distinctions right away. One is that their organizations would be a lot more productive in whatever they were trying to do. They would actually work better, by definitions we would agree on, in terms of business results.

The second thing that would be fundamentally different is that people would be working together differently. I have never met a single person in any organization who if asked, in a way that made them feel safe enough to respond honestly, 'Does this place work anywhere near as good as it could?', wouldn't say, 'Absolutely not.' I have never been around anybody who didn't say that their organization isn't rife with internal politics, game playing and people covering their ass. They say, 'If I brought in my six-year-old kid, who is in kindergarten, to watch how we work, I would be embarrassed. Because all the stuff he is learning in kindergarten, about self-respect and listening to one another and sharing your toys, nobody does here.'

There is such a huge gap between the things we value and the way life actually operates in almost all large organizations. Therefore, the second major dimension that I think would differentiate the new kind of organization is that people would actually say, 'This is more like the way I would really like my worklife to be.' I think the single most dramatic piece of data that you can generate here is that there's a remarkable consistency in the values people have for how they would like their worklife to be. They virtually all value spirit, trust, excitement, meaningfulness and working with people they like. But compare that list to what people actually have in their organization currently, and it's damn hard to find many people who will say, 'Yeah, I've got 80 percent of what I want.'

The learning organization will be fundamentally characterized by dramatic enhancements in productivity and by people who feel like the work environment they are operating in is closer to what they truly value. And I think we are getting enough evidence that both are possible: that these statements are not hyperbole.

We're at the stage right now where we're seeing an abundance of examples. Existence is a good proof of possibility—it's hard to argue that it isn't possible any more. But that doesn't mean that it's easy, or reliable, or easily recreated.

It's like when the first plane flew. From that point on, it shifted the context of the development of aviation. Because until then, every single plane that crashed was one more piece of evidence for the cynics that it couldn't be done. But once the first plane flew, that all changed. Because all that same data from the failures were now interpreted in a different mental model. It became evidence of how not to do it. This is the essence of truly deep learning processes.

In the transformative learning process, demonstrating possibility is a critical step, because then it shifts the interpretive context. All the evidence is, 'Well, that didn't work. We need to try something else.' But now you believe that it's possible.

This sort of belief, based on experience, is really important. I don't think that belief systems, as we normally talk about them, matter a lot—like 'I believe this' or 'I believe that'. But in a creative process, to believe that something is possible is so important because you interpret all the data of failure in a different way.

If you and I grew up and we never saw anybody walking, it would actually be darned hard to learn to walk. The fact that we see people walking is why we know that it's possible. And this is really all it takes. We don't actually have to know how to do it, but we do need to know that it's possible.

 What would be your key message to senior managers today to help them start rethinking the future of their organizations?

I would say that we have to stop trying to figure out what to do by looking at what we have done. And we have to start really looking into our hearts and seeing what we truly believe to be possible. That's literally what it means to have a vision-led change process. The source of the energy comes from your deep belief that something is possible. And it might be something that has never, ever been produced on a large scale, so all your historical evidence says 'no, no, no'—but your heart says 'yes'. **99**

Peter Senge

Dr Peter M Senge is a faculty member of the Massachusetts Institute of Technology, director of the Center for Organizational Learning at MIT's Sloan School of Management and founding partner of the management consulting and training firm Innovation Associates, Inc. His insights into how organizations learn and share knowledge have helped many leading companies around the world tap into a new and very real source of competitive advantage. Senge received a BS in engineering from Stanford University, an MS in social systems modeling and a PhD in management from MIT. He has lectured extensively around the world and has worked with leaders in business, education, healthcare and government. His first book, The Fifth Discipline, *is a widely acclaimed bestseller which has sold more than half a million copies.*

Recommended reading

The Fifth Discipline Fieldbook: Strategies for building a learning organization (1994) US: Doubleday/UK: Nicholas Brealey.
The Fifth Discipline: The art and practice of the learning organization (1993) US: Doubleday/UK: Century Business.

Rethinking

LEADERSHIP

Becoming a Leader of Leaders

Warren Bennis

Cultures and Coalitions

John Kotter

"The major challenge for leaders in the twenty-first century will be how to release the brainpower of their organizations."

BECOMING A LEADER OF LEADERS

Warren Bennis

" THE PROBLEM FACING almost all leaders in the future will be how to develop their organization's social architecture so that it actually generates intellectual capital.

Most firms, with only one exception I know of, have no ways of even measuring this thing called intellectual capital. But when you ask people in organizations how much of their brainpower they think they are using on the job, the standard response is about 20 percent. So if we only added another 10 percent to that, just think what our organizations would be like.

What leaders must learn to do is develop a social architecture that encourages incredibly bright people, most of whom have big egos, to work together successfully and to deploy their own creativity.

That's why my latest book is entitled *Organizing Genius: The secrets of creative collaboration*. During my term as a university president, I found that most of the people in the university were not just well educated but also highly individualistic. And it's that individualism that makes the whole environment so exciting and so very challenging for a leader. I think the best way to describe it is with the oxymoron 'organized anarchy', because, in a way, I always felt like I was 'herding cats'.

Therefore, once again, the major challenge for leaders in the twenty-first century will be how to release the brainpower of their organizations. I think it's the essential challenge, and it's quite different from the challenge that faced twentieth-century leaders.

For the latter, it was much more of a linear world, in which organizations were hierarchical and bureaucratic. It was somewhat similar to the early notion of computing, in which you simply feed information into the system and it disgorges a solution. The old mindset can be summarized in three words: control, order and predict. And that was fine in a stable environment where to a large extent you could control, order and predict.

But that's not how it's going to be in the twenty-first century. We are going to experience increasingly rapid change. And in order to deal with change, organizations are going to have to become unhinged. They are going to be confusing, chaotic places to work in. And they'll be full of surprises.

The whole role of human resources people will have to be changed too, as they develop ways of trying to understand and to generate intellectual capital. They're going to have to work very closely with the top managers, the CEOs and so forth, to foster this creative collaboration within the organization and to translate the intention into reality.

Recreating the company

The truth is that we are undergoing a period of the most rapid acceleration of 'creative destruction' in history. So change really will be one of the key challenges facing leaders in the twenty-first century. And what it means for leaders is that they are going to have to keep recomposing and reinventing their leadership.

One issue that is popularly recognized is that, because of the rapid changes going on, not only the CEOs but all of the leaders within the institution, at every level, are going to have to be continually reinventing themselves and redesigning their leadership roles.

Another issue which is almost always overlooked is this: **twenty-first-century leaders will also have to make sure that they are constantly reinventing the organization too**.

I don't mean this in the sense that most people do. I mean that, rather than just downsizing, leaders are going to have to deploy the creativity of the workforce to recreate the company.

What the world is facing right now is a situation in which we have excess capacity and an oversupply worldwide. And the fact of the matter is that we are going to have excess capacity for at least 15 more years, until the third-world countries develop enough of a middle class to start buying the goods which will help to equalize supply and demand.

India, for example, is just coming out of a long period of economic stagnation, and has a comfortable, growing middle class of almost 200 million people who are now buying such goods as GE appliances. And Bangalore is becoming the software capital, not only of India, but also of that part of the world. But until the point when countries like Brazil, Mexico and Argentina develop enough of a middle class, we are going to have increasing turbulence and increasing problems with what to do with organizations where half of our people can produce three times as much as they could before. Economists refer to this, rather callously I think, as the 'exit' problem, which is an inherent part of industrial democratic capitalism.

But the point is, how do you deploy your workforce so that it is continually moving around and changing jobs, so that, rather than downsizing the organization, we can start reinventing it and creating new opportunities?

Let me give you an example. One of my favorite leaders is a man named Sidney Harman, who runs Harman International Industries. The company manufactures 'up-scale' sound systems.

He's been able to increase productivity by about 30 percent and he hasn't laid people off. Rather, he's begun to do a number of other things. One is that he's encouraging his workforce to think about new possibilities, to create new inventions of their own core competencies. So he's using all of his workforce to invent new jobs that are going to be productive and profitable.

For example, for a long time the company has been cutting perfect circles out of its sound speakers, which are made out of wood, and then it pays a lot of money to have a trucking firm pick up these thousands of perfect wooden circles, ship them off and burn them.

The employees suggested that they make clock faces out of them, because the wooden circles would be perfect clock faces. Or use them as trivets for tables, selling them in retail stores.

Another thing is that the company has begun insourcing what it used to outsource. When productivity went up, Sidney Harman found he had

30,000 extra square feet of space. So what the company used to have produced by another firm in Chicago, it decided to make itself in those 30,000 square feet, rather than continue to outsource it.

Now that is an example of what I think leaders are going to have to do more of: really recreating the company in different forms so that the exit problem will, in part, be alleviated. This is related to the intellectual capital idea, but it's a much more concrete version of it.

Tomorrow's leaders will have to learn how to create an environment that actually embraces change, not as a threat but as an opportunity. I think that's the only way to run an organization in a turbulent world.

▶ *What is it that will make some leaders tremendously successful at this, while others will fail?*

First, the capacity to have enough self-awareness and self-esteem to be able to sense when a different repertoire of competencies will be needed, without being threatened by the need to change. In other words, the diagnostic ability to understand what new things are required, or what things should be *unlearned*, plus the behavioral flexibility to be able to change.

Here, we're talking about leaders like Jack Welch, who have enough diagnostic ability to say, 'Gee, the way I was doing things is not going to work'. So that was the diagnostic part. But then he was also able to change behaviorally. That's number one.

Number two is to have the boundaries of the organization sufficiently porous and permeable, so that you can spot things. So you have the foresight to see things before the curve, before others do.

And the only way you get that is by being in touch with your customers, being in touch with society, being in touch with the outside world, by having the boundaries of the organization permeable and porous enough to get your information. That's why people at the periphery of organizations are usually the most creative and often the least consulted.

Role models for the twenty-first century

Perhaps the best-known example of a leader who could serve as a role model, and someone I know of very well because I've spent a lot of time with him, is Jack Welch. What I most admire about Jack Welch is not just his incredible performance at GE, but this fact that he is continually reinventing himself.

Not too long ago, I asked him what had happened to the Jack Welch who used to be known as 'Neutron Jack'. Nowadays, of course, he's being called 'Transformational Jack'. So we talked at length about how, given changing times, he has continued to learn, to reinvent himself, to redesign and recompose his leadership style.

I can't emphasize this point enough. It's like snakes. What do snakes do? They molt, they shed their outside skins. But it's not just that. It's a matter of continuing to grow and transform, and it means that executives have to have extraordinary adaptability.

Another example that springs to my mind is James Houghton of the Corning Company. He has a human resources person who, before he retired, became Houghton's personal coach. He wanted to use the wisdom of this retiree who had worked for his father too, and who had some institutional history. He just wanted to continue to learn.

So I would say that James Houghton would be an example of a terrifically exciting leader. A leader who keeps reinventing or redesigning or recomposing himself.

Women in organizations

I can't speak for Europe, or any other parts of the world, but I think **the US's industrial competitive advantage will be the leadership of women**. Partly because we have made a lot of progress in this particular area, not to the point where I'm satisfied yet, but far better comparatively than any other country I know.

I suspect that, by the year 2005, about 50 percent of the vice presidents for finance will be women. And I say that because of the number of women now majoring in accounting.

So even though we are still below where we should be, I think in the United States women will be appearing much more often in top management positions, and one of our competitive advantages will be the full deployment of the talent of women in our workforce.

One of the myths that has to be dispelled is that the only way for a woman to succeed is to act like a man. Women don't have to impersonate John Wayne to become successful leaders.

One of the ironies is that male leaders have been trying to shed the same macho character traits that women have been encouraged to imitate—some of the traditional tough-talking, no-nonsense male stereotypes.

Dr Helen Tartakoff, who is a Harvard psychoanalyst, said that, in general, women have exactly the opposite character traits, and that these feminine traits 'contain the potential for improving the human condition'.

Look at the superb performance of women in all the top graduate schools of management. Women already account for over 40 percent of the enrollment in MIT, Harvard and Stanford, and their numbers have been increasing every year.

What has got to change is not women's character traits but corporate cultures, because most of them have just been playing male-chauvinist games for too long. We've got to look more closely at the nature of complex organizations, where the power structures and avenues of opportunity have excluded women for years. And we've got to stop 'blaming the victim', like the title of the song from *My Fair Lady*: 'Why Can't a Woman Be More Like a Man?'

Happily, though, I think it's true to say that corporate cultures in general are moving away from rigid hierarchies and towards more collegial environments, and that organizational values and behavior are changing for the better.

Leadership attributes

What we're learning is that successful leadership doesn't depend on masculinity or feminity. It's not about being tough or soft, or whether you are assertive or sensitive. It's about the particular organizational culture within which you are embedded, and about having a particular set of attributes which all leaders, both male and female, seem to share.

First, leaders need to have **a strongly defined sense of purpose**. A sense of vision. I have said for many years that this is the essential difference between leading and managing—that leading means doing the right things while managing just means doing things right.

Too many of today's organizations are overmanaged and underled because the people at the top are better at making policies, practices and procedures than they are at creating a compelling, overarching vision. They are managers, not leaders. They are looking at how to achieve greater efficiency and how to control their systems and structures more effectively. They are looking at how to do things right.

But that won't work in the twenty-first century. We are going to need leaders who know what is really important to the organization in the long term. Who have a dream, a mission, a strategic intent—call it what you like.

I use the terms vision and purpose, because to me they are the best ways to describe what I am talking about here. And I think the leader's role is not only to have this sense of vision but also to be able to impart it to the whole organization. To remind people continually of what's important and to create an environment where people know why they are there.

So that's the second attribute: **the capacity clearly to articulate a vision**. To communicate it simply, but also compellingly. John F Kennedy rallied a whole nation behind his simple mission to put a man on the moon before the end of the decade. Former president Ronald Reagan was called 'the great communicator'. Why? Because he used metaphors that people could identify with. He once described a trillion dollars by comparing it to piling up dollar bills beside the Empire State Building. And I remember one of his speech writers saying that Reagan could even read the phone book and make it sound interesting.

But to communicate a vision you need more than words. It's not a question of giving speeches, sending out memos and hanging laminated plaques in offices. **It's about *living* the vision, day in day out**—embodying it—and empowering every other person in the organization to implement and execute that vision in everything they do. In other words, you have to anchor it in organizational realities, so that it becomes a template for decision making. If ever there was a truism, it's that actions speak louder than words.

Generating trust is another vital aspect. Leaders will have to be candid in their communications and show that they care. They've got to be seen to be trustworthy human beings. That's why I believe that most communication has to be done eyeball to eyeball, rather than in newsletters, on videos or via satellite broadcasts. The leader will have to be able to generate and sustain trust, and that also means demonstrating competence and constancy.

I would give tomorrow's leaders this piece of advice, told to me by a famous hockey player. He said: 'You miss 100 percent of the shots you don't take.' If there was anything I would recommend, it would be to try as many things as you can. To strike hard and try everything, which is a quote from Henry James. I love that quote, because it really means that **you're never really going to get anywhere unless you risk and try, and then learn from each experience.**

To use the sports metaphor, leaders have to be at bat. They have to play even when it means making mistakes. And they have to learn from those mistakes.

In other words, it's important to be protean—to be able to adapt and be knowledgeable about as many situations as you can be.

This means that, first, you need to have a sort of general bias towards action. Not just reflection, but action. A combination of both of them, of course, is what we all want. And then you need to get feedback on how you are doing, so that you can learn.

You have to develop and cultivate sources of 'reflective backtalk'. That is, to get enough people around you whose counsel you treasure. People who are capable of telling the truth.

These are people a leader can depend on to see the need for change. People who have the future in their bones. And you need these people. You can't do it alone. You need people who can take the vision and run with it.

What effective leaders are going to have to do is to create not just a vision, but a vision with meaning. One with significance, and one which puts the players at the center of things rather than at the periphery of things.

If companies really have a vision that is meaningful to people and which they share, nothing will stop them from being successful. I really believe that. A shared vision is going to be a winning thing.

But I want to emphasize the words *meaning* and *significance*, because not just any old vision will do. Every company says it has a vision, and that just isn't enough.

The vision has to be shared. And the only way that it can be shared is for it to have meaning for the people who are involved in it. Leaders have to specify the steps that behaviorally fit into that vision, and then reward people for following those steps. Then they need some feedback loops, to make sure that the vision is still relevant, still salient and that it has some resonance. Again, without meaning and resonance, vision statements are only stale truths.

➤ *What impact do you think IT will have on the way leaders lead?*

We're living now more than ever in a high-tech society. Information and communication technology will change not just the degree but also the kind of leadership that we're going to need. Because, as we democratize the workplace to PCs, and as we develop the kinds of technologies and digital interactivity that we are now seeing, our communication is going to become more, should I say, rampant.

We are going to be able to talk simultaneously to a lot more people than we ever thought possible. And we are going to have a lot more information at our fingertips.

So, clearly, one of the things this is going to do is to democratize the workplace even more, and it means that leaders are going to have to be very comfortable with advanced technology and the changes that it's going to bring.

Many of them aren't. I have a board in my leadership institute, made up of very terrific leaders, and they all have e-mail. But when I asked how many of them use it, only half of the hands went up, and some of those went up rather lamely. Rather haltingly.

So I think that IT will have profound consequences for how we organize in the future, and also for the sophistication that will be required by those of us who are leaders.

What's interesting is what happened on my 70th birthday. My children were all there; they're in their late 20s and early 30s. And one of their birthday gifts to me was two hours' instruction on using the Internet and the World Wide Web. Two of them gave me gifts of software.

So it's clear that the younger generation has been brought up in a high-tech world. I was born at a time when television was unheard of, when FM radio was virtually unheard of. But now, it's exactly as Naisbitt said many years ago, we're creating a 'high-tech, high-touch' world, and we're going to see a totally new breed of people for whom advanced technology is just a natural part of life.

What will this mean for tomorrow's leaders? Let me draw an analogy. It's sort of like psychiatry and psychopharmacology. My wife is a psychopharmacologist. She was trained as a psychiatrist but she realized that talk therapy wasn't enough. And that a lot of problems, mental health problems, can be dealt with effectively through medication and pharmaceuticals. But she realizes that both are necessary. She still does talk therapy, but she also uses medication.

In a similar way, leaders are going to have to be both comfortable with advanced technology but at the same time probably even more hands-on than ever before. They will need more interpersonal competence and more of some of the other things that I've mentioned.

Big vs small

What we are going to see in the global economy is that both small companies and big companies can be successful. It's just a matter of finding the right scale for a particular organization in a particular industry, and then providing the right structure and the right leadership.

As Rosabeth Moss Kanter pointed out, companies all around the world are becoming PALs: they are 'pooling, allying and linking'. This is particularly true of small companies, who are creating networks, joint ventures, R&D consortia and strategic partnerships that cut right across corporate and national boundaries. In effect, they are 'buying the power of bigness', to quote Jay Galbraith, which gives them the kind of scale in marketing, purchasing and manufacturing that was previously only possible for large corporations.

Small firms also have a lot of new technologies on their side. Like computer-based manufacturing and distribution, sophisticated marketing databases, the latest telecommunications systems—all of which are formidable competitive weapons that today allow tiny organizations to build global markets.

But this in no way signals the end of the large corporation, as some people would have you believe. In the 1980s people were proclaiming that big companies would all suffer the fate of the brontosaurus. This reminds me of Mark Twain's famous line: 'News of my death has been greatly exaggerated.' Because I think it's very misguided to try to assign big business to the ash heap of history.

Giant companies around the world have some very formidable advantages—the economies of scale, the resources, the skilled people, the know-how, the social clout, the long-term planning, the stability and so forth. That's why they are not collectively going to go out of business next week—or next century.

They just wish they could get all the benefits of size without all the problems of bureaucracy and the other diseconomies of scale that size brings with it. They've realized that to compete with small, fast-moving companies in the global economy, these giants have got to behave like small, fast-moving companies.

In other words, they have got to recreate themselves as collections of small, independent, manageable units. Hence the worldwide focus on reengineering, downsizing, subcontracting, decentralization, spin-offs, intrapreneuring etc.

However, I think the real answer to the dilemma is that most successful organizations in the future will in some way combine the best characteristics of both big and small companies. This is why I believe that the most practical solution, particularly for the large corporation, is federalism.

Federations work better than monolithic organizations because, along with strength, they offer the degree of flexibility we need to deal with these turbulent times. They are more nimble and more adaptive to changing conditions. They have all the inherent advantages of being big but at the same time all the benefits of being small.

Everywhere we look in the world today, from ABB to Benetton and from General Electric to Coca-Cola, what we see are new kinds of corporate confederations made up of numerous semi-autonomous units, all collaborating together and joined by a common vision.

Essentially, what makes a federation work are the principles described by Madison in the late eighteenth century. They are just as valid for corporations as they are for nations.

First, you have to diffuse power to all the semi-autonomous units. You have to be non-centralized rather than decentralized.

Second, decision making must be shared between the units and the central authority. Nobody dictates terms and conditions to anybody else. Everything is negotiated.

Third, there has to be an overarching vision and purpose, and some form of written constitution that lays out the company's operating principles. The units may even have their own constitutions, but these must be in harmony with the vision and principles of the federation.

Fourth, the units need to understand where their boundaries are, whether these are business or product line boundaries or, as is the case with Coca-Cola's bottlers and Benetton's retailers, geographic boundaries.

Fifth, you need to balance power not only between the units and the central authority, but between the units themselves, so that none of the units dominates the others.

Sixth, and last, the units have to have autonomy. They have to be free to be self-governing, as long as they don't violate the federation's universal operating principles. And this is the most difficult characteristic of federalism. It's the source of the continuing tension: the power of the central authority versus the power of the constituent units.

In many cases, this tension can be fatal. Because the tendency is to go to one of the extremes. Either the federation overcentralizes, as it did in the old USSR. Or it lacks a unifying vision and constitution to hold it all together, and it finally disintegrates.

So this is where you need true leadership. Leadership that continues to provide the necessary balance. And I think this calls for a new kind of leader.

Leaders of federations don't think of their associates as 'troops'. And the associates don't think of their leaders as generals. The leader of the new federal corporation has to be a leader of leaders.

You can't be the only one making decisions. You can't be the only leader. Rather, you have to create an environment in which other leaders, who subscribe to your vision, can make effective decisions themselves. An environment in which people at all levels are empowered to be leaders.

One of my favorite metaphors for this is Schumacher's balloon man— now perhaps a woman—who holds a fistful of strings attached to balloons, each representing an entrepreneurial unit. She doesn't control the balloons—they all have their own individual buoyancy—but instead, she simply holds them together in her hand.

The leader of today's federal organization has to have faith in the power of people to solve their problems locally. He or she is responsible for establishing the 'why' and the 'what'—in other words, the overarching vision and purpose—but the rest of the leaders are responsible for the 'how'.

Look at Coca-Cola. It's a global federation of fiercely independent franchised bottlers and distributors. Recently, the CEO Roberto Goizueta had a meeting with these folks and he had to ask them three times in one speech to 'please paint your trucks red'. He didn't command them to do it. He pleaded with them.

Percy Barnevik, CEO of Asea Brown Boveri, describes his organization as 'a federation of national companies with a global communications center'. ABB has only 100 employees in its Zurich headquarters, but I've heard Barnevik say he has 5000 leaders. So it's not the central staff that holds ABB together, it's the common vision of globalism and excellence that those 5000 leaders subscribe to. And, again, this is what I mean by a leader of leaders. Percy Barnevik doesn't command and control the 'troops'. He simply enunciates clearly the company's performance standards and then he gives his associates the freedom to find the best ways of achieving those standards. He doesn't try to manage their jobs for them.

A central task for the leader of leaders is therefore the development of other leaders. Which means, primarily, creating conditions that enhance the ability of all employees to make decisions and create change. But, further to this, it means that the leader must actively help his or her followers to reach their full leadership potential.

As Max De Pree, the chairman and CEO of Herman Miller, once put it: 'The signs of outstanding leadership appear primarily among the followers. Are they reaching their potential? Are they learning?'

So tomorrow's leaders are going to have to spend a lot of their time nurturing and developing other leaders within the organization, in order to make the federal corporation work.

▶ *What thought would you leave with today's leaders to prepare them for the challenges of tomorrow?*

Perhaps I can conclude by elaborating on a thought I mentioned earlier. For my new book, *Organizing Genius: The secrets of creative collaboration*, I studied many terrific groups. And of all the groups I studied, in every case where they really reached epiphanies, there was a leader who was able to enrol people in an exciting, insanely significant vision. Someone who was capable of reeling in advocates and supporters to work with him or her. They all believed that they would make a dent in the universe.

What leaders have to realize is that people would much rather live a life dedicated to an idea or a cause that they believe in, than lead a life of aimless diversion.

I think that's what effective leaders are all about and that's what creative collaboration is all about. It's about creating a shared sense of purpose.

Because people really need purpose. Meaningful purpose. That's why we live. And I think that the power of an organization will be that shared sense of purpose. With a purpose like that you can achieve anything. **,,**

Warren Bennis

Dr Warren Bennis is Distinguished Professor of Business Administration at the University of Southern California. His name, more than any other, has become synonymous with the study of contemporary leadership. An adviser to four US presidents (Kennedy, Johnson, Carter and Reagan) and author of more than 20 books, Bennis has been studying the art and practice of leadership since the 1950s. As early as the mid-1960s he was writing about 'the coming death of bureaucracy' and pointing to the need for 'adaptive, rapidly changing temporary systems'. Educated at MIT's Sloan School of Management, he has been president of the University of Cincinnati as well as provost and executive vice president of the State University of New York at Buffalo. Today, Bennis is a consultant to companies and governments throughout the world. His latest book is entitled Organizing Genius: The secrets of creative collaboration.

Recommended reading

Organizing Genius: The secrets of creative collaboration (1996) US: Addison-Wesley.

An Invented Life: Reflections on leadership and change (1994) US: Addison-Wesley.

Learning to Lead: A workbook on becoming a leader (1994) Warren G Bennis & Jean Goldsmith, US: Addison-Wesley/UK: Simon & Schuster.

Leaders: The strategies for taking charge (1986) Warren G Bennis & Burt Nanus, US: HarperCollins/UK: Harper & Row.

"Do we have corporate cultures that are

anchors on change? Or cultures that enable

us to adapt to the changing environment?"

CULTURES AND COALITIONS

John Kotter

" WE HAVE BEEN in a new economic era for a decade or two, in which the central driving force is the globalization of markets and competition, and there is no evidence that this era is going to end any time soon. In other words, this is just the beginning of something that could go on for another two, three, four, five or even six decades.

Globalization is nowhere near finished. There may be a billion people who are currently integrated in the global economic system, but that still leaves another 4.7 billion that aren't. And more are coming in literally every day. So this isn't going to play itself out any time in the near future.

The main impact of globalization is that it's creating both more hazards and more opportunities for everybody. Hazards in terms of a more volatile environment and more competition. And opportunities in terms of more markets and bigger markets. What all of that is doing is speeding up everything and producing more change.

So if we are in a new economic era that's going to continue at least into the first quarter of the twenty-first century, if not throughout the century, and if the major trend in this era—driven by the globalization of markets and competition—is more change and a faster-moving environment, then that suggests that we need to rethink corporate culture.

Because then the key issue becomes: do we have corporate cultures that act as anchors on change? Or cultures that will enable us to adapt to the rapidly changing business environment? And, of course, how can we change the former into the latter?

This, in turn, brings the focus to leadership; because in my view **it's only through leadership that you can truly develop and nurture a culture that is adaptive to change.**

Defining corporate culture

At one level, corporate culture has to do with group norms or traditional ways of behaving that a set of people have developed over time. These group norms are not just the recurring behavior patterns that one sees in a group, but are those actions that are unconsciously reinforced by everybody. Something is 'cultural' when, if a member doesn't behave in the normal manner, the others automatically nudge him or her back towards the accepted ways of doing things.

At a deeper level, corporate culture is about the implicit shared values among a group of people—about what is important, what is good and what is right. Usually, these values are consistent with the group norms. That is to say, the norms of behavior tend to reflect the values, and the values tend to reflect the norms of behavior.

The thing that makes all of this so tricky, of course, is that values and norms are invisible, and actions to reinforce them occur subconsciously. So people are often not very aware of culture, or of the role that they play in helping to maintain a particular culture.

In the latter part of the twentieth century, corporate culture has mostly been an anchor on change. That is to say, if you go into most firms and talk to them about culture, what they will talk about is how it gets in the way of them reengineering, adapting to market developments, trying to implement a new strategy or folding in some new acquisition.

But, as long as you are successful, you are going to have a corporate culture whether you want it or not. The only places that won't have cultures are companies that have just been continuously and phenomenally unsuccessful over long periods—organizations that have gone through huge turmoil and turnover. A place like that won't have a culture. But as long as you have a relatively stable group of people and they are relatively successful, you'll end up with a culture. It just happens.

So, first, you can't just ignore corporate culture; it's going to happen anyway. But more importantly, it is possible to create a culture that will facilitate change, rather than act as an anchor. We have done a number of studies that show that it is possible. Indeed, **we know that it is possible to have a culture that helps you to adapt, that doesn't just hold you back**. In fact, the firms that seem to have those cultures today—or something close to those cultures—and that operate in highly competitive environments regularly outperform the competition by a significant margin.

So if we can expect several more decades of rapid change, then we're going to have to learn how to make corporate culture something that isn't a change anchor but instead something that facilitates firms adapting to change. And what people have got to do is to understand more about what those cultures are like, and then work to produce them in their own organizations. I believe that what we are going to see in the twenty-first century is much more effort to try to create those cultures.

▶ *How would you characterize the new, more adaptive kind of corporate culture that will enable companies to compete successfully in the twenty-first century?*

It has many characteristics. But the two core elements are, first, that **the management group deeply, honestly, sincerely values the various players in the corporate drama**. And not just themselves. In other words, they highly value the basic constituencies that support their business, starting with customers—but not ending with customers—and going right through to suppliers, employees and stockholders. As a result, they look outward not inward. They really do care about customers. They really do care about their stockholders. They really do care about their employees. That single characteristic is enormously important in producing flexible and adaptive cultures. Cultures that tend to be anchors on change are cultures where what managers implicitly value most of all is managers. Where you have an inward focus and a lot of self-interest.

The second core characteristic of healthy cultures is that **initiative and leadership are truly valued and encouraged at every level in the organization**. Not just at the top, but at the middle and even lower levels too. In change-anchoring cultures, leadership tends to be valued not much at all. And if it is tolerated, it's tolerated only at the very top of the organization.

The combination of these two core characteristics—a deep concern for the basic constituencies outside of management that make up the enterprise, and leadership up and down the hierarchy—gives you an incredible capacity to be able to navigate in a turbulent environment. Why? Because people are not just turned inward, looking at themselves. They are focused outward, looking at the basic constituencies, starting with customers, where the real action is. Then, when they see problems or opportunities, which they will, it's not just up to one or two people to do something, as it is when the whole center of initiative for leadership is invested in one or two people. Instead, it's possible for hundreds or even thousands of people to initiate action to solve the problems or take advantage of the opportunities.

It's the combination of these two characteristics that can help you to adapt remarkably well in a rapidly changing environment and to outperform even financially stronger competitors by significant amounts. Because, first, you've got all the eyeballs facing outward, so you can spot things changing faster, and then you've got so many sources of initiative inside the organization to do something about it. And this makes it possible even for an aircraft carrier to be relatively manoeuverable in a very volatile environment.

Those are the two core characteristics, but there are lots of others that kind of group around the first two. Things like a relatively high sense of urgency on a continuous basis. A tendency towards teamwork up and down the organization. A willingness to delegate many of the management functions to lower levels in the organization, not just having senior-level management do them. A true belief in internal simplicity; in other words, keeping the inside of the organization as simple and as clean as possible, not having all kinds of policies and rules and gunk that build up over the years like barnacles on a ship, but having a continuous cleaning process to keep it simple inside. A minimum number of levels in the hierarchy. A minimal amount of bureaucracy in the hierarchy. All of this tends to be consistent with my first two core characteristics, and it all adds up to the kind of adaptive culture we're talking about.

Hewlett-Packard is a company that grew up in one set of businesses and has successfully made a huge transition into basically another set of businesses. It has gone from being only an instrument company to being mostly in the computer industry. And there are some very important differences between what it takes to be an old-fashioned great instrumentation company and what it takes to be a modern computer company.

The fact that it was able to make the change—not just somewhat successfully but fabulously successfully—is very much related to the fact that it has had, and tried to maintain and nurture, the kind of culture that I've just described. It was a very strong and deeply ingrained culture, and yet nevertheless that culture did not stop the company from making both the strategic and the organizational changes that it needed to make. On the contrary, the culture *facilitated* these changes. So Hewlett-Packard is a primary example of how corporate culture can work successfully.

➤ *Why is it, then, that most companies tend to develop a change-anchoring kind of culture?*

Often it's because they have been so very successful in the past. And that success has, ironically, poisoned their culture.

Usually, it all starts with a visionary entrepreneur. It's someone who creates and implements a very successful business strategy, and who then manages to get a relatively dominant position in some markets. That dominant position, in turn, leads to a great deal more success and growth over a period of years which, if you are not very, very careful, leads to a number of other things that ultimately create a change-reducing or a change-resisting culture.

One is that management begins to get more and more arrogant about its own 'wonderfulness'. They think, 'We're so successful, we must be geniuses.' So they stop listening. They tend to turn inward. Senior management becomes even more arrogant than middle management, and they tend to centralize things around themselves.

When you're growing like mad, there are often very few strategic decisions that need to be made, and very little change that is essential besides building more and more of the same. The big challenges are all internal—hiring people fast enough, building another plant fast enough—and it tends to be managerial expertise, with its capacity to keep things under control, that becomes valued. So it's people who seem to have that expertise who are promoted, and before long you discover that those guys are running the place. And they value management, not leadership. This then seeps into the culture which, in turn, becomes arrogant, inwardly focused and manager focused. That kind of a culture is a change anchor.

And the whole thing develops because you were so successful in the past.

That's what happened to Xerox, for example. It was unbelievably successful in the 1960s. Its 914 office copier became the most profitable product in the history of US business. And so the company went through a period of prolific growth. But it simultaneously went through a devastating cultural transformation. It became arrogant and insular. It centralized decision making. It discouraged experimentation and it showed little tolerance for initiative or leadership from the ranks. Then along came the Japanese competition in the 1970s and 1980s and that changed the whole nature of the copier business. Xerox watched somewhat helplessly as its worldwide share of copier revenues plummeted from 82 percent down to just under 40 percent in only six years. And it completely failed to exploit the opportunity for personal computers, which it more or less invented in its Palo Alto Research Center, while companies like Apple Computer were using some of the center's best ideas. In fact, if Xerox had not worked very hard to change its culture in a major way in the 1980s, some people believe that it would have gone bankrupt.

Steps to successful transformation

In *Leading Change* I list eight different steps in a successful transformation effort. It starts off with pushing the urgency rate up. What people have to do is to start focusing attention on performance data and on industry data. In other words, they've got to look objectively at how the organization is doing, and at where the industry is going, in the hope that by getting enough people looking at the real situation, those people will either become convinced that there is a crisis, or they will begin to see some major opportunities that they hadn't seen before. In either case the urgency rate goes up, and all of a sudden you've got an opportunity to get things going.

The next step is to form an appropriate guiding coalition, a group that has enough power to lead the change effort. Then you've got to develop a vision, and a strategy for achieving it, and you've got to communicate that vision effectively to the whole organization. You've got to empower people to change systems and structures that stand in the way of the vision. And you've got to create some short-term wins, so that employees can begin to see visible improvements, and they can be recognized and rewarded for their part in those improvements.

Next it's a question of consolidating the credibility from those short-term wins to produce even more change. And finally, you must ensure that it is all institutionalized into a new culture. This in its entirety is a complicated and difficult process. It takes a long time. But it is one that people are increasingly learning how to do.

Of course, the best way to handle culture is to never let it get broken in the first place—to interrupt the syndrome by never letting it get to the point where you end up with an arrogant, internally focused, centralized and bureaucratic culture. This is possible to do. Hewlett-Packard so far has managed to avoid that kind of culture. Some people at the top either intuitively or in some other way figured this culture thing out, and they have paid attention to it. They have looked for signs that norms or shared values are moving in a bad direction, and when they have seen those signs, they've taken action to try to stop it.

It's like anything else in life. The more that people are aware of what the potential problems are, the more they'll be on the lookout for those problems. Then, when they see any bad signs, they are in a good position to stop those problems before they really happen.

Twenty-first-century leadership

A typical CEO of a major firm might interact on a typical day with 20 out of, say, 50,000 employees. That being the reality, there is no way that such a person through personal contact—which is what happens in small firms—is going to be able to influence or lead all of the people in the organization directly. Most of the leadership has to come indirectly through the environment. And a very powerful element in the environment—the one that, if it's wrong, becomes a huge problem or, if it's right, becomes a very, very powerful influence—is culture. So, at least in the context of big firms, the CEO often has his or her biggest influence on results through the corporate culture.

The problem is that we have developed four or five generations of executives who know much more about management than they do about leadership. Happily, that is changing.

Today, if you watch succession discussions going on inside firms, there is much more sensitivity on average to whether these candidates know anything about how to lead—as opposed to just being good managers—than you would have seen ten years ago, and infinitely more than twenty years ago. So we are changing.

But still the reality is that we have a lot more people out there who know more about management than about leadership. And that's a big issue, because a good manager/poor leader tends not to be very good at dealing with questions of culture. Managers work through formal structures, systems, procedures, rules. Those are their influence tools. Culture isn't.

Leaders, on the other hand, usually understand culture at some gut level. Besides just the face-to-face influence that they have on people through their communications, they're almost always sensitive to cultural influences. They pay attention to creating the kind of culture that they think will be appropriate for whatever it is that they are trying to achieve.

So what we need for the future is to produce many more people who know something about leadership. Because if we have another generation of people running our big companies that are just managers, they will never produce the kind of cultures that are going to be necessary to adapt to a rapidly changing twenty-first century.

There are many role models around for this kind of leadership, although not a lot that are 'grand'. Let me give you some of the people I like to use as interesting role models when I'm out speaking.

Obviously, there's Jack Welch of General Electric. Then there's Konosuke Matsushita. Another one I like to talk about is Sir John Harvey-Jones of ICI. Then there's Mary Kay Ash, of Mary Kay Cosmetics in the United States. Another one is Mike Harper who ran ConAgra for a number of years, and who has now come out of retirement to run RJR Nabisco. Then there is Kazuo Inamori who founded Kyocera, the Japanese electronics company. These are the kind of people that I think are major role models.

What makes them so special is that they're damn good leaders. In a world that is still dominated by managers, they know something about leadership. They know something about challenging the status quo, about developing a vision that makes sense in the light of economic realities and about how to create strategies for achieving that vision. They're compulsive communicators. They know that they need to get people above them and below them, and outside the organization and all over the place, to understand and believe in those visions. They're compulsive empowerers. They realize that they have to let go and give people enough rope to be able to go out and energetically create and implement those visions.

Let's face it, that's still the exception out there. That's not the norm. It's not the norm in business, and it most certainly isn't the norm outside of business in the non-profit, the health, or the education world. Or the government world, which is even worse.

Creating a guiding coalition

Producing major change in an organization is not just about signing up one charismatic leader. You need a group—a team—to be able to drive the change. One person, even a terrific charismatic leader, is never strong enough to make all this happen.

Even more to the point, as I tried to spell out in *Corporate Culture and Performance*, the kind of cultures that we are talking about—that can survive and prosper in a rapidly changing environment—are ones that try to create and nurture lots of leadership up and down the hierarchy. Which means that you end up with multiple players in leadership roles. Now this doesn't mean 60 or 6000 people trying to be the CEO. It simply means that, **whatever their job is, people see their role as not just to be doing things the way they're designed today, but to figure out the way they ought to be done tomorrow**. To clarify a vision for their little function or their little department or their little office, and to get the relevant players on board to implement that vision. Then to create conditions that empower the people around them not only to produce good short-term results, but to produce the better future that they have envisioned.

As long as you have leadership at the top which provides an overall vision to which these people can connect their smaller visions, you can have many different people up and down the organization playing a leadership role, all in concert.

People who think of leaders as strongly independent individuals often can't imagine an organization full of leaders. They assume that all the leaders would be fighting each other all the time. Indeed, that can happen, if you don't have a strong team at the top that has this overarching vision and that is successful at getting the others to buy into that vision. If you've got weak managerial types at the top, and a bunch of strong independent leaders underneath them, what you'll end up with is a lot of fighting and some degree of chaos. But if you've got good leaders at the top, and they are successful at aligning the people below them, then you can get an enormous amount of leadership throughout the organization and it will all kind of flow in the same direction. Under these circumstances, you've got, not just one engine at the center, but hundreds or even thousands of little engines all over the place. That, in turn, means—if they're all working in tandem—that the power of the overall system is very, very strong.

▶ *How do you encourage these potential leaders to start actually behaving as leaders?*

The first thing you can do is to help clarify what leadership is, and why it's important to *them*, not just to the world and to the company. Then you put up a mirror to remind them that they haven't quite achieved their potential yet, and you give them some evidence that people can grow if they have potential.

All that will help to create the motivation for people to get off their butts, to start trying something and over time to learn whatever they need to learn in order to maximize their potential.

The other thing you have to do, of course, is to work with companies to stop them from being leadership-killing organizations. We created bureaucracies in the nineteenth and twentieth centuries that were very, very hard on leadership. They did nothing to encourage people to lead. They did nothing to nurture leadership. Quite the contrary. Whenever you put people into narrow jobs and micro-manage them, you are doing almost nothing to help them grow as leaders.

So it's a combination of reforming organizations to make them more leadership-incubating organisms, and working on individuals to help them to understand better what leadership is and why it is important, so that you can motivate them to start taking action and to cultivate whatever leadership potential they've got.

▶ *How does a leader go about creating a culture within which people from widely different nationalities and backgrounds can work together comfortably?*

It's very simple. You don't appeal to national cultures; you appeal to human nature. Remember, we've all got the same DNA. I don't care if you were raised in Beijing or Kuala Lumpur or Houston, it's all basically the same

DNA structure. And even though national cultures certainly do create groups that are different in some important ways, there is something human that we all share. To be able to bring together a highly diverse group of people, in terms of nationalities, I think you have to appeal to that common human element. And it's very possible to do. People are doing it today, although not often enough.

I mentioned Kazuo Inamori, the guy who built Kyocera. One US broadcasting station did a story on him and his company maybe a decade ago or more. I can still remember these five minutes of videotape where they visited his San Diego facility. It was fascinating. The workforce was a combination of Japanese, Filipinos, African Americans and white Americans. The plant manager was a Jewish American. And the whole thing was running beautifully. It ran well because there was some kind of an overarching vision about this enterprise and what it stood for. And there were appeals that were being made to people that had nothing to do with national culture. Instead, they had everything to do with what human beings are all about.

Inamori is a leader who, like Matsushita, has thought a great deal about the nature of enterprise, about the nature of people and about what constitutes an appropriate management philosophy. It's nothing 'Japanese'. In fact, the Japanese sometimes think he's an odd guy. The core of his philosophy appeals to something in human nature. And then he builds these ideas into the implicit psychological employment contract that he has with his people. And he ends up with this—at least on the surface—highly diverse group of people, all working together extremely well.

I'll give you another example. In the early 1980s, both British Airways and SAS—the former under Lord King and then Sir Colin Marshall, and the latter under Jan Carlzon—tried to change their corporate cultures to prepare themselves for a much more competitive globalized airline environment. One of the first things they did, which was unusual, is that they both spent a small fortune on some training programs. And the training programs were put together by a little Danish consulting firm called Time Manager International. Now, the seminar wasn't called 'Putting Customers First'. It was 'Putting People First'. So they went up a level, beyond the focus on national cultures, to something that they thought people could buy into, regardless of citizenship or business function. And remember, in the case of both SAS and British Airways, it's not as if all their employees are from one nation. British Airways obviously has a lot of Brits and SAS has a lot of Swedes, but both of them also employ many other nationalities because they operate around the world. What they figured out is that the way to try to hook into all of these people was not by putting customers first—even though that was really the message they were interested in—it was by putting *people* first, because they thought that everybody could relate to that at some deep psychological level. And it was to this that they attached messages that had more to do with the customer.

Corporate culture in the new organization

As organizations become increasingly 'boundaryless', distributed and networked with other companies, cultures will not happen quite as quickly and quite as easily as they have in the past. Cultures tend to develop a certain strength and thickness much more easily when you've got everybody in the same office together. When you spread them out over ten offices it happens more slowly and it doesn't necessarily get as thick. And so, if information and communication technology moves us increasingly towards not having people in the same office together, you would logically expect that cultures would not automatically develop as quickly and as thickly as we have been used to in the twentieth century.

But then you say: 'Is this good or bad?' And I think it's like most things: it's probably mixed. That is to say, it's not all good or all bad. I think the fact that cultures don't become strong so easily will mean that the syndrome we were talking about earlier will happen less easily too, and that's good.

If 50 percent of the people are outsourced, then instead of having 100,000 employees we'll have 50,000. And the 50,000 that will remain may be more dispersed than they are today, because some of them won't be working in the office all the time. But you're still going to have huge collections of people around, which means that the principles we've been discussing will still hold true. Culture for the mother ship—whether that mother ship has 50,000 or 100,000 people—will still be relevant in the sense that we've been talking about it.

In some ways you could argue, using that same logic, that it will be an improvement. Because, let's face it, if you've got a culture that holds you back, changing it is more difficult when you've got 100,000 employees than when you've got 50,000 employees, because mass just makes it harder. So by shrinking things down, in that sense, it's going to make it easier to change bad into good.

But, remember, all these little satellites that will be floating around the mother ship will have to have good leadership too. And leadership that is sensitive to the cultural issues, so that they can create adaptive cultures in their little satellites. Today, if you get one good strong person in charge of a big company who understands culture, he or she can get the ball rolling on creating more adaptive norms and values. **In the future, with a smaller mother ship and all these little satellites, one person isn't going to do it. Every one of those satellites is going to have to have somebody or some group of people in it that is sensitive to culture. So we're back to 'multiple leaders' again.**

➤ *What can leaders do right now to make sure that their own corporate culture will be a strategic asset, rather than a change anchor?*

I suppose the place to start is with a realistic assessment of what that culture currently is. And that's not a small deal. Because if you've lived and worked in a culture all your life, just sitting down with a pad of paper and writing down what you think it is, even if you are a very smart person, won't necessarily get you the answer. So you've got to find a more objective way to try to assess what the current culture is. That would be step one.

Step two, of course, is to look at it and ask yourself—given the way the environment seems to be progressing into the twenty-first century, especially if you agree that it's going to get even more turbulent—is this culture going to be an asset or an anchor in that environment? And if the answer is 'asset', then the name of the game becomes preserving it, not letting it slip away, not letting it slide down into that nasty syndrome. If the answer is 'anchor', or 'potential anchor', then the name of the game has to be: what actions can we take over time to turn our change-anchor culture into a more adaptive culture? What practices need to be altered? And then we're on to the eight-step transformation process that I talked about a little earlier, which is designed to help organizations change bad practices into good ones, and eventually settle into a new and different culture.

Creating an adaptive culture, if it doesn't exist, is never easy. But the alternative is to be pulverized by the increasingly turbulent business environment. **"**

John Kotter

John P Kotter is the Konosuke Matsushita Professor of Leadership at the Harvard Business School in Boston, Massachusetts. He is, without doubt, one of the world's foremost authorities on managerial behavior and business leadership. Professor Kotter is a graduate of MIT and Harvard, and was one of the youngest people in the history of Harvard University to be honored with a full professorship at the Business School. He is the author of seven bestselling business books and has received the prestigious McKinsey award for his articles in the Harvard Business Review, *as well as the Johnson, Smith & Knisely Award for new perspectives on executive leadership. Professor Kotter is a frequent speaker at top management meetings around the world.*

Recommended reading

Leading Change (1996) US: Harvard Business School Press.
The New Rules: How to succeed in today's post-corporate world (1995) US/UK: Free Press.
Corporate Culture and Performance (1992) John P Kotter & James L Heskett, US: Free Press/UK: Macmillan.
A Force for Change: How leadership differs from management (1990) US/UK: Free Press.
The Leadership Factor (1988) US: Free Press/UK: Collier Macmillan.
The General Managers (1982) US: Free Press.

Rethinking

MARKETS

Focused in a Fuzzy World

Al Ries & Jack Trout

Mapping the Future Marketplace

Philip Kotler

"You can't be too fuzzy... You've got to stay positioned cleanly in the mind."

FOCUSED IN A FUZZY WORLD

Al Ries & Jack Trout

“

RIES: THE KEY TREND affecting marketing strategy in the twenty-first century will be global trade. Because there's no question that the world is becoming a global economy and a global marketplace.

Look at the computer industry. Windows is just as much a standard in Europe as it is in South America or the Far East. Products and brands are moving around the world. Take razor blades. The Gillette Sensor was launched simultaneously in 19 countries.

TROUT: That means it's going to get a lot tougher. As competition spreads on a global scale, everybody is going to be after everybody else's business. **I think the twenty-first century will make the twentieth century look like a tea party.**

We just came back from a speaking tour of the Far East and that part of the world is sucking up as much marketing information as it can get. Countries like Indonesia, Malaysia, India, Singapore, even the Philippines. They are getting themselves ready to pursue business really aggressively in the new economy. And let me tell you, those are hard-working folks.

If you thought Japan, Taiwan or Korea were tough, we've now got a whole new cast of characters entering the marketplace in the southern part of the Pacific, and pretty soon they are going to be just as tough to compete with.

Companies over there have a big advantage because, basically, they have no encumbrances. It's not like many parts of the world where you have to sort of unravel the whole social apparatus if you're going to be competitive. They don't have labor unions to worry about. They don't have to undo all that bureaucracy and get people to agree with them. These new players can just set themselves up to be lean, mean competitive machines. So, in a way, they have a bit of a running start.

RIES: You'll see massive changes taking place in response to these global developments. For example, what happens to your marketing program as your market doubles, triples or quadruples in size? What happens when your market expands to encompass the globe, as opposed to just your individual country or your economic region?

Logic might tell you that you need a broader line to serve the world. You might say, 'Well, the Germans want our product to have this feature, the French want something different, the English want something else… so we've got to broaden our line.'

What should happen is exactly the opposite. **Conceptually, the bigger the market, the more specialized you have to become if you want to succeed.**

Let me give you an analogy. If you lived in a small town in America, out west someplace, in a community of a hundred people, there would be one store. The sign would say General Store. They'd pump gas out front, and inside they'd sell food, clothing, shoes, hunting knives, rifles, they'd sell everything.

Now, if you lived in New York City and you opened a general store like that, you'd go bankrupt. Because in a big city, you have gas stations, you have clothing stores, you have food stores etc. In other words, the larger the market the more specialized you have to become to be successful. That's true in retailing. That's true in every industry.

As marketing becomes more global in the twenty-first century, the Time Warners of this world, the Machine Bulls, the Olivettis, the General Electrics and all the other big, diversified companies are going to find themselves under incredible pressure.

Look at Europe, where you have a lot of companies like Siemens, Philips and Olivetti. As these companies go global, I think they are missing the principle of specialization, because I don't see any narrowing of their product lines. Take Olivetti. When your market is just Italy, with 58 million people, a broad line is all right. But when your market is global, a broad line is very dangerous.

➤ *So what are you suggesting that these big, diversified companies do?*

RIES: Become more focused before it's too late.

Take IBM, a company that's into everything. IBM is into personal computers, workstations, mid-range computers, mainframe computers, network software. They have made a major foray into the software business with the purchase of Lotus Development Corporation. They also, along with Sears, own Prodigy, a network service.

Should IBM break up into all these individual units in order to become more entrepreneurial? No. Decentralization doesn't work either.

What IBM should do is get rid of all the things that are outside its main line and focus on where its real future is.

If I ran IBM, I would focus on client-server, mission-critical, large-company computer systems. And I would get out of home computers, personal computers, software and all that other stuff.

Of course, there are advantages in having smaller, more flexible, more entrepreneurial types of units within organizations—ABB is a typical example. And maybe that type of organization will enable you to stay profitable for a decade or so.

But in the long term, an ABB-type organization is just another form of conglomerate. It's putting a Band Aid on the problem. Long term, those big wide conglomerates, even though they're lean and mean and efficient, are still going to be in trouble. That's why my latest book is called *Focus: The future of your company depends on it.*

As business becomes global, you've got to narrow your focus to a specific segment of the global market. And, carrying it one step further, you've got to try to own a single word in the mind.

TROUT: Exactly. You can't be too fuzzy. And that's what often happens. A lot of companies get themselves too confused. Too diversified. Too spread around. But you have to stand for something. You've got to stay positioned cleanly in the mind.

➤ *Why do companies tend to become so fuzzy in their positioning? Why do they often start out very well but later lose their focus?*

RIES: My example is a closet. It starts out neat and tidy, and over time it degenerates into a complete mess.

There's a law of nature called entropy. In the natural world, things move from order to disorder. And entropy in a corporation means the same thing: you can very easily go from order to disorder.

A company like Volvo can be narrowly focused on safety. But if somebody at the top isn't screaming 'safety, safety, safety' every single day for the next decade, in ten years you'll have a wide diversified manufacturer of everything that's automotive. In fact, that is exactly what is happening. Volvo has announced that, together with an English company, it is planning to spend $200 million to build sporty Volvos, based on coupés and convertibles.

It happens every day. Every company I know thinks in this direction. Instead of narrowing their focus and standing for something, they're thinking about broadening their focus to increase the size of their business. Like Volvo: 'If we can sell safe cars, maybe we can also sell unsafe cars.'

Rethinking positioning

TROUT: I recently completed a sequel to *Positioning*, entitled *The New Positioning*. Because, while many people use the word 'positioning', not many truly understand what we're talking about, even after all this time—the fact that **perceptions are really what make you and break you**. That you win or lose in the mind of your customer and prospect. And that getting into the mind is a tricky piece of work.

The point is that it's going to get even trickier. When the original *Positioning* was first written, we wrote about the overcommunicated society of the US market. Well, guess what? We were just warming up! There was so much in terms of communications that we didn't even envision back then—like the information superhighway and some of the communication technology that's now available.

We didn't envision, for example, the 500 channels of television they're talking about. Nor did we envision the incredible array of satellites which was going to span the globe. And how the rest of the world is now moving into an overcommunicated phase. So what we're beginning to see is that this whole overcommunications thing is spreading rapidly. We're becoming, not an overcommunicated society, but an overcommunicated world!

Change is also such a big factor now. We never wrote much about change in *Positioning*. Now that's creating a whole new challenge. Because what you really have to deal with in this game of change is something I call repositioning. That's going to become the big word in the years ahead.

The middle section of my book *The New Positioning* explains that repositioning is being played out in two directions in the US market. **The first direction is when a company goes back to its basic roots, and it's for those who've sort of drifted away from what they originally stood for.**

Many companies got into trouble in the past with too many brand extensions. Or they chased too many different businesses. You know, they wanted to be in this business and in that business, and it caused them enormous problems. Diversification was an absolute monster for many companies. So what you're now seeing is that people are shedding all of these other activities. They learned the lessons, and now they are consolidating and getting back to the basics. They are getting back to doing what they do best. In other words, they are repositioning themselves back to where they came from.

Take Marlboro. They became very messy at one point. But now they've come back to cowboys and simplicity. You don't see Marlboro Menthols out there anymore. Because real cowboys don't smoke menthols.

So that's the first direction that repositioning is taking, as brands go back to their fundamentals in order to survive. The other side of the coin is about moving forward. You see this especially in the technology world. **As the world changes, you've got to reposition yourself against the future.**

Take a company like Lotus Development Corporation. It was famous for the spreadsheet, an idea it invented. But now the spreadsheet market has become a very difficult, competitive world, with limited growth potential. It's flattened out. Lotus has enormous competition from Microsoft, Borland and a lot of other people. So it came to us a number of years ago and said: 'We want to grow. What we've got to do is move to another idea. In a way, we have a repositioning problem, because where do we go next?' This is tricky.

What we encouraged the company to do, which it has done very well, is to move to something called groupware. Groupware is software for networks of computers. Lotus had the credentials to do that because it had a product called Notes. Notes was the first successful piece of software designed for networks of computers or groups of computers.

So Lotus recognized groupware as the next big concept that was going to take it into the future. And it has used the concept to reposition itself for the next decade.

The point is, sometimes you just can't stay with what you are. You've got to move forward. Some companies need to reposition themselves from point A to point B in order to make it into the twenty-first century.

RIES: Groupware has been very successful at Lotus, but I told the company at the time we worked for it that the name Notes was bad. If I say Notes, what am I talking about? Musical notes? Post-it notes?

What it needed was a separate company name, so that it could focus on groupware as a company, not as a part of Lotus. Instead, it is having to transform the name Lotus from a spreadsheet company to a groupware company, which is a lot more difficult than if it had started with a new name. These days, of course, Lotus has another name involved—IBM—so that's going to confuse things even more.

Toyota used the right naming strategy when it came out with Lexus. And Honda used it when it introduced the Acura. These sound like company names. They don't sound like descriptive model names. Nobody calls these cars Toyota Lexuses or Honda Acuras. But they do call the groupware product Lotus Notes, because Notes isn't perceived as a company name.

So at Lotus, the strategy was right—and it's going to work because the company was there first—but it didn't execute the strategy well.

TROUT: What I think this illustrates is that repositioning yourself forward—going from A to B—is easier said than done. It's a brutal process sometimes. First, because you're trying to change people's perceptions, which is very difficult to do. Second, because, more often than not, you're dealing with big egos in the company itself. And that can be murderous. At Lotus it was a horror. Twelve vice-presidents actually quit! So it takes enormous focus and it takes visionary leadership to go for a niche like that. But it worked, to the tune of 3.5 billion dollars, which is what IBM payed for the company.

➤ *What happens when you are dealing with a huge multinational? Just how focused can a company like that become?*

RIES: When you get to a certain size, you can afford to think about multiple focuses instead of a single focus. But you should treat second brands, like Lexus at Toyota or Dockers at Levi's, as separate fully fledged brands.

Creating a separate brand is not a project for a smaller company. It requires the resources of a major company like one of the multinationals.

The secret to making a multiple-focus strategy work is tight coordination of the brands. General Motors once had a multiple-focus strategy with its five brands: Chevrolet, Pontiac, Oldsmobile, Buick and Cadillac. But as a corporation it still had a single focus on automobiles.

And, again, that's not enough. What does General Motors actually stand for today? Because it's not enough to just stand for making cars. You've got to stand for making safe cars, like Volvo. Or luxury cars like Mercedes. Or small, ugly, reliable, inexpensive cars like Volkswagen did with the Beetle. GM got fuzzy when it destroyed the identity of its brands, when it allowed each division to broaden its line.

Volkswagen is another example of a company that became unfocused. It stopped paying attention to the small town/big town principle I mentioned earlier. Volkswagen is the number one automobile brand in Europe, yet Volkswagen has been a disaster in recent years in the United States.

Why? Because it tried to market Volkswagens in the US exactly the way it markets them in Europe, as a full line of terrific cars.

On the other hand, the idea of bringing back the Beetle is absolutely terrific. That car is going to work in the US because it represents what VW still owns in the mind: small, ugly, reliable and inexpensive. And marketing is a battle that takes place inside the mind. As long as the company goes back to being what it owns in the mind, then it's going to work.

The good news is: if you own a strong position in the mind, you can milk that position forever. The bad news is: you can't easily change that position. Volkswagen tried to change its position to modern, good-looking, front-wheel drive, watercooled engines and so forth, and it wasn't very successful in the US market.

The significance of brands

TROUT: I'd say that brands will still be brands in the future. We did research on 20 product categories and found that the lead brands back in 1923 are essentially the same lead brands as they are today, with the exception of five. So in other words, 15 out of 20 are still in the number one place. Which means that, generally speaking, Gillette will still probably have the dominant razor blade brand for decades into the future.

We looked at this in *Marketing Warfare* when we said that lead brands own the 'top of the mountain' position. They play it smart up there. They block competitive moves. They attack themselves with new ideas.

In other words, the strong brands will continue to be the strong brands. Marlboro will ride into the twenty-first century and become bigger and better around the globe, until such time as the world stops smoking.

There are going to be two successful kinds of players. There will be the big powerful brands. The mega brands. The big companies who can really put the muscle in around the world. So the strong leaders.

And then there will be the specialists or the well-positioned niche brands. The small players. You might call them, to use our terminology, the 'guerrillas'.

The brands that are going to have the most trouble are the ones in the mushy middle. If you find yourself there, I think you are either going to have to go specialist, or split up into smaller niched players, or you're going to have to find a way to become the number one or two brand in your market.

Ries: It's not just a question of size—of big brands and small brands—although I still think that there is power in being big. It's really a question of a narrow focus. Power comes from being a specialist. Being a big specialist is even better than being a small specialist.

Marketing in the twenty-first century

Trout: I think marketers will get better and better as we progress into the twenty-first century. They're essentially honing in on improving everything they do, whether it's distribution or improving their relationships with customers or whatever.

For example, they're using computers to help them stay connected to customers who have bought from them in the past. I'm impressed with some of the car manufacturers. You buy a car now and you have a hard time getting these guys off your back!

You'll get phone calls saying, 'Well, you just had your car serviced. How did that work out? Were you satisfied with this, were you satisfied with that?' It's incredible.

What they're trying to say is, 'once we've got you, we want to keep you'.

Once you buy a BMW, they want to keep you as a BMW customer. They'll even send you a BMW magazine! It's impressive.

So we're going to be seeing more and more of these carefully targeted, service-driven relationship programs. They will use computers. They will use telemarketing. They will use a lot of follow-up. Now that's not going to attract new customers, but certainly what they've discovered is 'let's hang on to our old customers'.

➤ *What about advertising? What developments do you expect to see here in the future?*

Ries: The larger the community, the more narrowly focused—the more specialized—you have to be. The same is true in advertising.

What's the difference between today and twenty years ago? Today we have more media. We have more communications. We have more options for our advertising. So what should your advertising be today? More narrowly focused.

Twenty years ago, you might have run five campaigns, on five different aspects of the product, in five different markets. Today, you should run one. In other words, the more confusion there is out there, the simpler your advertising has to be. That's true of the message. That's also true of the media.

Creating a monopoly

Ries: Many companies believe that as the world becomes more complicated, the product lines they manufacture have to become more complicated.

It's the reverse. **As the world becomes more complicated, the product line that you manufacture has to become simpler.**

When you have a very simple line, preferably one product or brand, you can concentrate on the concept that works best in marketing today: creating a monopoly.

You don't really want to compete on a level playing field with your competitors around the world. You want to create a brand that has no real competition.

Take Heineken beer. A customer might like Beck's beer better than Heineken, but if the customer is in a bar in Buenos Aires, he is likely to ask for a Heineken because he knows it will be there.

Similarly, you might like Pepsi-Cola better than Coca-Cola, but in a restaurant you will probably ask the waiter for a Coke. Why? Because everybody carries Coca-Cola. Not everyone carries Pepsi.

Think about it from the point of view of the owner of the restaurant or bar. The owner says: 'I have room for only one brand of imported beer, so I'll stock Heineken because it's the most popular.' When you narrow the focus and own a word or a concept in the mind, you can become a powerful force in marketing. You can create your own monopoly. That's the ultimate objective of any marketing campaign.

In the twenty-first century, marketing strategy won't change a great deal from the twentieth century. It's like warfare. In warfare, the weapons have become more sophisticated. The tactics have changed. But the strategy has not.

The way to win a war today is to mass or concentrate your forces against a narrow target. As a matter of fact, that's exactly the strategy Stormin' Norman Schwarzkopf used in the Gulf War. Everybody thought he was going to attack on a broad front. He did not. He attacked on a narrow front. Of course, the Iraqi army wasn't much of a challenge.

The same is true of marketing. You win by massing or concentrating your forces. This is essentially the concept of focus. While the tactics of marketing (interactive advertising, direct mail, infomercials, Internet or whatever) might change, the strategy is not going to change.

➤ *What do you believe is the essence of good marketing strategy?*

RIES: There are two. Focus is one, but the other component of a good marketing strategy is predicting the future. When IBM came out with the desktop personal computer, it was betting a billion dollars on the direction of the computer business. When Lotus invested $500 million on Notes, it was betting that the computer software business would go 'network'.

Heineken went global. Why? Because it believed that there would be an opportunity to build a worldwide beer brand. And today Heineken is really the only worldwide beer brand. Brilliant move.

When you make a good marketing move, it tends to be based on a prediction of the future.

There are inherent dangers in predicting the future. The real tragedy right now is this concept called convergence. The driving force in management thinking today is the notion that entire industries are coming together. And many, many companies are betting on the future based on this idea. That's why the telephone companies are getting into cable. And the cable companies are getting into the telephone business. And the entertainment companies are getting television. And the computer companies are getting into communications.

This is such a tragedy because industries don't converge. They divide. It's the law of nature.

Take countries. Are they combining? Not that I know of. Czechoslovakia has broken up into two countries. The Soviet Union used to be one country; now it's eleven countries. And watch your clock. It's going to be twelve countries any minute now. Yugoslavia has become at least three countries.

Things break up, they divide. They don't combine. Take automobiles. An automobile used to be an automobile. In the United States you had a choice between a Chevrolet, a Ford or a Plymouth. Today, you've got small cars, large cars, compact cars, sports cars, four-wheel drive cars, sport-utility vehicles. In other words, the automotive market has divided into segments. And each segment develops its own leader. That's the fundamental reason companies have to specialize.

What undermines a company like IBM is thinking that it's in the 'computer' business. So instead of narrowing the focus, it is forced to stretch itself to encompass all the elements of the computer business. In the long run, as the computer industry divides, it's going to get pulled apart. It's like being on the rack!

Over time, what looks like one market becomes two markets, then three markets, then more. First we just had mainframe computers. Then we had minicomputers, and now we have desktop computers. The only company that makes all of them today is IBM, and it's under extreme pressure, particularly in desktop computers.

Marketing power is in specialization. The power is not in being all things to all people. As time goes on, things divide. And if you don't specialize—if you try to offer a full line—you're going to be in trouble.

That's why this convergence idea is so devastating. If you think computers and television are coming together, then you have to say, 'Hey, we've got to get into both businesses.' So you get into both businesses, and you're doing the opposite of what good strategy is all about.

You can put microchips into telephones and you can put modems into computers, but from a marketing point of view, a telephone is a telephone and a computer is a computer. And the brands that customers prefer are different. So are the outlets where you buy the products. You go to a telephone store to buy a telephone and you go to a computer store to buy a computer. These are totally different markets. And there's an opportunity for a different brand to dominate each market. Not one brand spread over two markets.

There are many combination products, but most of them are not succeeding. For example, Canon came out with a fax/phone/copier. It spent millions developing the product and millions promoting it. I made a speech the other day and said: 'How many people have a fax/phone/copier?' Two hundred people in the audience. Not one hand went up.

In the vast majority of businesses today, you have phones and you have fax machines and you have copiers in the office. Although combination products are on the market, not very many people have a combination fax/phone/copier.

The problem with a combination device is that it's not a very good fax, it's not a very good phone and it's not a very good copier. I'm not saying that nobody is going to buy one. A few people will. If you have a small office at home, perhaps you will. But it's not a mainstream product.

So a lot of companies are going to get into trouble by betting on convergence. They're basing their futures on everything coming together. I don't pretend to know what will happen in the future. But, based on studying the past, I would say that the future will tend to be the opposite of what they expect. **Markets will divide. They will not converge.**

Immutable laws of marketing

TROUT: In *The 22 Immutable Laws of Marketing* we said: 'Folks, as we move into the global economy, and into the twenty-first century, you've got to follow the laws out there or you'll get killed!'

We feel very strongly that as the world gets more competitive, marketing is going to get more difficult. Companies that make mistakes in this new twenty-first-century world are going to pay a terrific price. There are competitors just hanging there waiting, so when you stumble, they get your business.

For example, General Motors lost 11 share points in the last decade. Now a share point is over a billion dollars. That's 10 or 12 billion dollars in sales that are now gone. And its market share shrank from almost 50 down to the low 30s. The point is that if you stumble today, your business instantly goes to somebody else. And guess what? You don't get it back! In the old days you could figure on getting it back somehow. Now you don't get it back, because somebody else now has your business. General Motors has not increased its share, in fact it has lost more.

So in a way that's why we wrote the laws. Having studied 20 years of these kind of battles out there, we can say that most of the marketing mistakes companies have made, especially the big US companies, were essentially fundamental mistakes. They were violations of some fundamental laws that play out over and over again, and you've got to understand these laws because you can't afford to make mistakes today. As we said, violate them at your own risk!

RIES: You don't have to obey all of the laws. What you should look at is which law best applies to your situation.

Is it the 'Law of Leadership' or the 'Law of the Opposite'? The 'Law of Leadership' is for the leader, and the 'Law of the Opposite' is for the number two company. Not all of the laws apply to everybody.

The real trick in marketing is to know which law to apply. It's like the game of golf. You might have 22 clubs in your bag, but the difference between a professional and an amateur is that the professional knows which club to pick for a given shot, and how to use it. The laws themselves are kind of straightforward and easy to understand, but picking the law to apply and then applying it—in a sense taking the shot with the club—that's difficult.

The same holds true for our other book, *Marketing Warfare*. The real trick is learning how to make the transition from one form of warfare to another.

Most leaders—the defensive players—started out as guerrillas. Heineken started out as a guerrilla and is now a defender. Making the transition is the most difficult part.

We worked with Digital Equipment Corporation and we made a strong point with them: 'Look, your minicomputer is your flanking success. Now you have to defend your position; you have to shift to defensive warfare.' What is defensive warfare? You've got to block competitive moves. The company owned the small computer position, but it never blocked the attack by the personal computer. And we begged Ken Olsen to do just that:

launch a line of personal computers before IBM did. Its flanking with the minicomputer was very successful, but its blocking of the personal computer was a major disaster.

You need to know how to make the transition from one law—or one form of warfare—to another. Because your mindset has to change when you go from flanking to defensive, or from guerrilla to offensive, or from guerrilla to defensive. You have to know where the crossover points are.

➤ *What would be your basic message to today's corporations, as they rethink their marketing strategies for the twenty-first century?*

TROUT: I'll tell you what our advice is to corporations: **top management has got to get involved in the marketing process**.

In the old days, you had marketing managers. And the top managers said: 'OK, we'll let those guys figure it out'. Wrong! Marketing is too important to be left to the middle-level folks. The CEO has to take charge of the marketing. He's the only one who can get the stuff done. He has to put his reputation out there and get involved.

That means you have to get a CEO who understands the laws of marketing. Someone who's willing to figure out what the hell his 'Wow' is, if you want to use Tom Peters's term, or how he's going to differentiate his company. And then he's got to be willing to drive and lead that marketing vision through the organization.

What I would say to today's top management is: 'Stop hiding out in your ivory towers! Get down to the front and find out what the hell's going on. And then lead the charge. Think like General George S Patton.'

RIES: My basic message would be: 'Focus. Focus. Focus.' I would say the same thing to the CEO as I would say to the marketing manager. The word for the twenty-first century is 'focus'. Whatever you are doing today, do fewer things tomorrow. But do them better. 99

Al Ries & Jack Trout

Al Ries and Jack Trout are probably the world's best-known marketing strategists. For over two decades they have had a powerful influence on the thinking of marketing and advertising people alike, and their internationally bestselling books have become undisputed marketing classics. Their books, along with their articles and speeches, have been credited with making 'positioning' one of the most widely used concepts in the advertising and marketing field. For many years, Ries and Trout ran a successful consulting firm together in Greenwich, Connecticut, doing strategic work for IBM, Intel, Chase Manhattan, Xerox, Merck, AT&T, Procter & Gamble and other Fortune 500 companies. They have now chosen to work independently, and each has recently published a new book, Ries on Focus *and Trout on* The New Positioning.

Recommended reading

Focus: The future of your company depends on it (1996) Al Ries, US/UK: HarperCollins.

The New Positioning: The battle for your mind escalates (1995) Jack Trout & Steve Riukin, US/UK: McGraw-Hill.

Marketing Warfare (1986) Al Ries & Jack Trout, US/UK: McGraw-Hill.

Positioning: The battle for your mind (new edn 1987) Al Ries & Jack Trout, US: Warner Books/UK: McGraw-Hill.

"Marketers will move from focusing on large segments to targeting specific niches. In niches there are riches."

MAPPING THE FUTURE MARKETPLACE

Philip Kotler

"

OUR ONLY CERTAINTY is that things will change.

Back in the 1950s, who would have anticipated TV and Internet home shopping? Home banking? Thirty-day satisfaction guarantees on newly purchased automobiles? Customized bicycles? Factory-outlet shopping malls?

So we have to expect the unexpected. I'm sure we're going to see the marketplace go through some radical changes over the next few decades that will sound like science fiction.

Having said that, though, it is possible to anticipate certain developments in the future marketplace.

Consider the changing demographics. **I expect that more consumer marketing will start focusing on the needs of the older generation**, at least in the developed world. We're increasingly living in an ageing society. The dominant demographic force of the early twenty-first century will be the mature consumers—the 55-year-olds and older.

We've seen the marketing focus shift each decade since the post-war period: from babies to teenagers, from teenagers to young adults, from young marrieds to early middle-agers and now to the late middle-agers. As the 'baby boomers' reach their fifties and sixties, the focus will shift towards health products, retirement homes and less strenuous forms of recreation.

Today we think of healthcare as something needed when you're sick. But in the future, the mature consumer will want to be healthy forever. We're going to see healthcare facilities where mature consumers pay a fee to have regular diagnostic checks, almost like having your car serviced annually. And the medical people will present a complete recommendation on exercise, nutrition and stress management.

We will also witness a growing demand for light foods, low-calorie beverages, home exercise equipment, vitamins, beauty care and skin-care cosmetics—anything that will make you look and feel younger and healthier than your age suggests.

Mature consumers will have money to spend and they'll pay for luxuries like cosmetic surgery, personal exercise coaches, exotic travel destinations and continuing education courses.

In the past, mature consumers have typically been segmented into three groups; the 'go-gos', the 'go-slows' and the 'no-gos'. The emphasis is going to shift from the last group to the first group.

We used to view retirement as a time of inactivity, when you sat in a rocking chair on the porch with a pipe and a blanket. But that's all going to change. Tomorrow's 55-year-olds are probably going to have the attitudes and outlooks you would expect from a 35-year-old. They are going to think young. So they're going to love marketers who appeal to that youthfulness inside them.

At the other end of the age spectrum, children and teenagers will be more grown-up and sophisticated than in the past. The people at Ogilvy and Mather Trendsights refer to them as 'mini-adults'. They are going to master computers the way the previous generations mastered typewriters. They will have access to information over the Internet that was never before available. They will shop electronically. They will be smart consumers.

An entertainment explosion

I expect an explosion in entertainment. **People will want to be entertained whatever they're doing, whether they're working, shopping or consuming.**

Recently I saw a cyclist on an expensive bike, driving at a furious speed, all the way listening to music on his Walkman. I call this the multi-processing consumer who does two or three things at the same time, primarily because time is short and there is so much that we want to do.

I think entertainment will be a guiding principle and it will be factored into many situations. We will want our jobs, our shopping experiences and our consumption experiences to be entertaining. Smart retailers know this. Niketown is a three-storey shoe store that presents shoes and clothing in a highly entertaining way, with a basketball court next to the basketball shoe department, with pictures of sports heroes in every department and so on. Barnes and Noble bookstores are not only large, but they include a coffee bar, book signings and talks by well-known authors, and a library atmosphere for browsing. Restaurants and hotels build special atmospheres and surprises into their offerings.

Even museums, whose fundamental purpose is education, are beginning to use entertainment to attract visitors. They have to make their exhibits interesting. I have seen computers added to a fine arts show where the visitor could answer quiz questions about the artists and get a score on 'art knowledge'. Disney's EPCOT center shows what can be done to raise technology education to an entertaining level.

Similarly, symphony orchestras are going to have to figure out how to offer their audiences a more exciting experience. Some research that I'm doing suggests that symphony orchestras shouldn't be simply playing music; they should be creating events.

People will be drawn to a symphony orchestra performance because, on that evening, something very special will happen. It might be an extraordinary guest appearance, a background lecture, a pre-performance cocktail party or a special performance for contributors after the regular show.

High-income consumers

We're going to see the buying market segmented into high-income consumers and low-income consumers, while the middle class, our largest class currently, will continue to diminish in size. This is always a dangerous development because the middle class provides an anchor of social stability.

Many companies will continue to target the middle class. But a great opportunity exists for companies that clearly target their products and services at either the high-income or low-income class.

High-income consumers will demand high-quality products and personalized service. At the opposite end will be people who just want basic, no-frills products and services at the lowest possible price.

Each class can be further segmented by education, occupation and lifestyle variables.

If we look at the high-income consumers of the future, they will be different from previous generations. More of them will come from the overclass, as *Newsweek* magazine has dubbed it, namely high-achieving people with technical knowledge, not just those who have inherited wealth. The future belongs to knowledge workers, who will be highly paid for their knowledge.

Members of the overclass will be better educated, better traveled, better informed. They will be cosmopolitan. They will know what 'the good life' is.

Part of this is going to be reflected in the way people divide their time between leisure and work and consumption. Work will be meaningful to these people because they are applying special skills. But work will not be an end in itself. They will work to live, instead of living to work. They will want more quality time apart from work to enjoy leisure and other pursuits.

For time-starved, high-income people, the opportunity is to figure out how to make products and services available in a hassle-free way. Because the resistance to buying something may not be just the price. It's the time involved, the risk involved, the psychic costs.

There will be a great increase in home-based shopping. A growing number of people now order their clothes, appliances and so forth from catalogues. They don't want to fight traffic and hunt for parking space. They prefer home banking and home shopping, even for groceries.

Today we can get on a computer and use a software program called PeaPod to shop for groceries. A menu of food items comes up and we click on the food items that we want, indicate when we want delivery, and two hours later the groceries can be delivered to our home. With a charge, of course. But the total cost of shopping from home is really less than if we went to the store. Because we don't buy impulse goods. (The average shopper in a supermarket buys twice as many items as on their original shopping list.) There's no gasoline used or any time spent. It is also easier to notice those items that are price discounted.

So with regard to home-based activity, we are going to see the live experience being replaced more and more by a mediated experience. And of course, many homes in the future will have a giant screen. People will invite their friends to spend an evening watching a new movie release, complete with popcorn and drinks.

➤ *If we continue to map the marketplace of the future and we zoom in a level closer with an imaginary satellite camera, how many different demographic segments can we already identify?*

Today, the Claritis Corporation has developed a geoclustering approach called PRIZM, which classifies all US residential neighborhoods into 62 distinct lifestyle groupings called PRIZM clusters.

The groupings take into consideration 39 factors in five broad categories: education and affluence, family lifecycle, urbanization, race and ethnicity, and mobility. The neighborhoods are broken down by zip code, zip code plus four digits or sometimes even by block. The clusters are given descriptive titles which convey their essence, such as Blue Blood Estates, Young Influentials, Urban Gold Coast, Gray Power, Emergent Minorities, Shotguns and Pickups, and Towns and Gowns.

Each cluster is characterized by what products and brands the people in that cluster buy, the media that they use, the stores they prefer to shop at, and where they are concentrated geographically.

The result is that marketers can use PRIZM to answer such questions as: Which clusters produce our most valuable customers? Which media should carry our messages? How much can the cluster afford to pay for our products? Where would they probably shop for our products?

All segmentation is of course somewhat artificial. We use certain variables to group people into segments. And there are people who oscillate between segments, or who can't be totally described. Generally though, segment descriptions represent a compromise between viewing all buyers as similar versus all buyers as individually different.

The point is, customer targeting has become far more precise than it was in the past, when we aimed all our products at families with a working husband, a homemaking wife and two children. Today, this family type accounts for only 7 percent of the American public.

Marketers will move from focusing on large segments to searching for and targeting specific niches. In niches there are riches. Usually only one or two firms serve a niche and serve it well, and consequently earn a high margin.

New media

There is a constant search for new media. Chris Whittle, an American media entrepreneur, has invented new media to reach highly targeted markets. For example, he developed a unique health magazine for patients sitting in physicians' waiting rooms, and also placed TV sets in high school lunchrooms to carry programs and ads appealing to students.

Supermarkets are adding new media too. While shopping, consumers will be confronted by many advertising messages. You may see the name Coca-Cola on the floor tiles. You may pass food displays with talking messages. You may push a shopping cart with a video display and advertising. At the checkout counter, you'll watch TV commercials while waiting in line.

Cable television stations will provide advertisers with much more targeted audiences. There will be a station for those who like sports, another station for those who like science, still another for those who like to watch old movies.

Audience demographics will be known, and advertisers will be able to reach specific groups who would have a high interest in their product. This has already happened with US magazines, where over 4000 different audiences can be delivered to advertisers by special interest magazines.

➤ *Just how direct and personalized do you expect marketing to become in the twenty-first century?*

Marketing used to be alchemy, and now it is moving from a pseudo-science to a real science. **The key is response measurement.** Direct marketing is about sending messages to specific addressable consumers and learning which ones placed an order. It started with direct mail and moved to telemarketing. Today, we have added other direct marketing media, specifically infomercials, audio and videotape, CD-Roms, computer disks and fax-mail, e-mail and voice-mail.

Companies are rapidly building sophisticated customer databases from which they can draw the best prospects for an offer. For example, the Fingerhut company has about 1400 items of information about each customer, including demographics, lifestyles and past transactions. Fingerhut can tell whether each customer is a good or a poor credit risk and has classified its customers into several thousand groups. One group might be men who previously bought a blue shirt and a red tie: this gives Fingerhut ideas on what they might buy next if the right ad catches their eye.

Bank marketers are using their databases to send happy birthday cards to key customers on their birthdays, to advertise college loans to families with a child who is approaching age 18 and to send investment ads to families who just became 'empty nesters'. These messages can be customized to fit each customer's situation.

Products, too, will increasingly be customized. Today there are companies who will work with you to design your own bicycle (where you choose the size, the color, the features etc.), your own bathing suit, your own car and so on. This indicates that the buying process will become far more interactive, with the consumer co-designing the product.

The importance of brands

Brands will always be important, although today the importance of national brands is diminishing somewhat.

We used to have a clear idea as to brand hierarchies in many categories. In soft drinks, Coca-Cola was number one, Pepsi-Cola was number two and Royal Crown was number three. In auto rentals, Hertz was number one, Avis number two and National number three. Most of us preferred the number one.

Now the brand's rank order matters less. All three are similar and acceptable. Consumers are increasingly comparing the brands on price, and if one is on sale this week they will buy that brand, regardless of small differences in preference. No wonder much more money is pouring into sales promotion, a lot of it representing price incentives, and less into advertising. And with less money going into advertising, no wonder perceived brand differences are eroding.

The other problem facing national brands is that giant retailers are introducing strong private brands that are now almost as good, or just as good, as the national brands, but that cost less. A great example is the private brand called President's Choice, belonging to Loblaws, a Canadian supermarket chain. Its cookies, colas and other items are so popular with consumers that Loblaws's competitor wants to be licenced to carry them. But Loblaws has refused. However, it has licenced the brand to several noncompeting supermarket chains in various parts of the world. This is the first time that a store's private brand is achieving the status of a global brand.

In general, retail chains now prefer to carry one or two leading national brands, one or two of their own private brands and maybe a generic brand. They will drop the weaker national brands, some of whom will end up producing for the private brands. **The message is that if your brand is not number one or two, you may be kicked out of the market.**

This has a deeper implication, namely that companies producing many products would be better off putting their resources into making a few of them strong category leaders, in preference to marketing a host of weak brands.

Quality, pricing and service

If your company doesn't produce high quality, you are either going to have to sell to low-income groups or go out of business. High product quality will become a 'ticket of entry' to the marketplace. But just having high quality won't be enough to make the sale, because your competitors will also have high quality.

To win, companies will need to offer high quality for a lower price than their competitors.

A medical equipment company achieved a breakthrough—a new appliance with 20 percent higher performance. And the company wanted to price it 20 percent higher. Yet some of its managers advocated raising the price by only 10 percent, as a way to improve value to the customers. Some managers even suggested not raising the price at all, and simply advertising the product's improved performance. They did this and grabbed a large market share from their competitors.

The key to good pricing is to figure out to whom you want to sell the product, and what they think of the product—what they think it's worth—and then to design the product and its service bundle so that it can be priced that way. Every product should be designed with a specific group of customers—and a price they are willing to pay—in mind. The rest is to engineer down the costs in order to make the target profit. **This is called price-driven costing, rather than cost-driven pricing.**

Customers are becoming more discerning and more demanding. They'll be more astute in assessing the value of your offer. So you will need to justify your prices, using arguments with substance, rather than relying on image alone.

Service will grow increasingly important as a competitive tool, especially as products become more similar. Service augmentations and service quality can provide strong differentiation. **Companies will have a golden opportunity to build a more comprehensive offer around any product they sell.**

For example, an auto dealer should not only sell you the car, but every time you come in for a service they should wash your car for free, make maintenance suggestions and in general help you to enhance the use-value, which goes beyond the purchase-value.

There are a lot of ways to add service value. For example, the Savoy hotel in London offers to pick up guests at Heathrow airport and bring them back as part of staying at the Savoy for a week. The Ritz-Carlton hotel system remembers every wish of their guests, from wanting an extra pillow to wanting a fax in their room.

Cause-related marketing

I believe many companies can gain attention and differentiate themselves by seriously sponsoring high-consensus social causes. The Body Shop has attracted many loyal customers based on the company's support of social causes, such as environmental protection, helping the homeless, saving the whales and so on. The Nike company invites its customers to turn in old Nike shoes so that they can be distributed to the needy, or recycled into gymnasium pads or something else. Ben and Jerry's ice cream gives away 7 percent of its profit each year to good causes.

Building a civic character, not just a business character, can build interest, respect and loyalty.

Some companies carry out cause-related marketing for only a month—if you buy their product, they're going to give money to the cancer fund. But this doesn't make the corporation seem permanently dedicated to anything. I think Ben and Jerry's and The Body Shop are good examples of how it should be done, if it is done at all.

➤ *Another dynamic factor for the future is certain to be speed. How will companies cope with the need to continually increase their pace?*

Speed will be crucial. Competitors are moving fast. The windows of opportunity in the market are getting shorter. And consumers want things fast. No one is prepared to wait eight weeks to have purchased furniture delivered.

So companies must become turbo marketers. They must learn how to be faster in product development, in manufacturing, in distribution and in service. Each of these areas can present a competitive advantage.

Product development cycle times used to be far too long. Auto manufacturers today can bring new cars to the market in half the time that it used to take. Manufacturing and distribution times are also being reduced, through systems such as just-in-time delivery.

Decision making will have to be quicker, too. It will be aided by expert system software. There will be war gaming rooms in major companies, where executives meet every morning to observe what is going on in real time, and to make their decisions for the day. Military generals do this in the battlefield, using sophisticated intelligence equipment to assess the current situation. There is a meeting every morning at a major airline to do just that. And large clothing manufacturers, such as Levi's, know each evening what sizes and styles of jeans were sold the night before throughout the country. Levi's operates a continuous replenishment system by alerting its suppliers to ship exactly the goods needed each day to replace the stock that has been sold.

Other companies are using technology to speed up their service, whether they're developing photographs, delivering pizzas, handling your bank account or organizing your travel plans.

➤ *Will traditional salesforces become a thing of the past?*

Salesforces are one of the most expensive marketing tools, and companies have been exploring cost-effective alternatives.

One auto dealer recently released 12 of his salespeople. Then he lowered his price, and his business boomed. So a low price becomes a substitute for an expensive salesforce. His low price created so much value that nobody was needed to sell 'value'.

Field salesforces will be increasingly replaced or supplemented by telephone selling and computer shopping programs.

Of course, if a company is selling nuclear plants or jumbo jets, it will need a sales team. Except that it won't be a sales team, it will be a business team. In highly complex negotiations, selling must be conducted by high-level managers, as is the case when Proctor & Gamble negotiates with Wal-Mart.

Low-income markets

Low-income markets can also be served profitably. It's a matter of careful targeting, product development and cost efficiency.

Aldi is an example of a low-cost, low-price supermarket chain that is growing rapidly. Aldi stores carry only a limited number of brands, shoppers bring their own shopping bags, goods are shelved in their original cartons and stores are located in low-income, low-rent areas.

In the future, entrepreneurs will organize second-hand goods and 'used' goods markets. Low-income consumers can now buy at flea-markets, super discount stores, factory-outlet stores, garage sales etc. Goods will be recycled by entrepreneurs, rather than destroyed, and these goods will gravitate from high-income markets down to low-income markets.

New organizations will arise that will clean the clothes or fix the appliances and resell them. This is done today by the Salvation Army and some other organizations, and the practice is prominent in the informal markets found in poorer countries.

It may be that more people in the twenty-first century will choose to be poor. Work will be of little interest to them, even if it were available. Look at how many people today choose homelessness, even when offered a shelter.

According to Charles Handy and other observers, companies will employ fewer full-time workers and more part-time and temporary workers. So there may be more people who redefine the good life not in terms of money and material possessions, but in terms of contentments of other kinds.

Of course, this will be a challenge to marketers and to public authorities who must create job opportunities. An economy's health depends on jobs being created, and this in turn depends on demand being stimulated.

Outsourcing

All companies that want to be globally competitive must practice outsourcing. **Always buy the supplies you need from the source that can give you the best value for the money. If you buy from inefficient or high-cost suppliers, you are at a competitive disadvantage.**

I knew back in 1970 that America could not sustain its real income growth, because we were paying $16 an hour to steel and auto workers and could get more value for our money elsewhere. Protectionism is no answer; it can only make things worse.

Smart countries recognize and encourage a recycling of their industries. Japan has a policy on 'exit industries'. It encourages its weaker industries to move to lower-cost countries—originally it was Korea and Taiwan, and today it is Indonesia, Malaysia and China.

Any company would be smart to outsource from the place where it can get either the same quality at a lower price or higher quality for the same price. And in a global marketplace, that means shopping around from country to country.

It is precisely industrial overcapacity that is going to make competition fiercer than ever. Western economies must gird themselves for the competition that will come from China, India, Brazil and other developing countries.

The bottom line is that some US industries will lose and others will gain from the growing international competition. The worst thing the US might do is to try to protect the dying industries instead of supporting the high-opportunity industries.

We must remember that the emerging markets in lesser developed countries will offer US companies significant new marketing opportunities. These markets have never really been targeted before, but we are going to see some important investment opportunities in places like Asia, Eastern Europe, Latin America and Africa.

Tomorrow's winners will be those companies that lead their industry in targeting their markets carefully and producing the best value for money in those target markets.

To prepare for the twenty-first century, companies need to imagine alternative scenarios for the marketplace of the future, and use these scenarios to stimulate their thinking about possible contingencies and strategies.

My advice, therefore, is get busy building scenarios and determining what they imply in the way of strategic planning. Don't think 'business as usual'.

To quote Yogi Berra, 'the future ain't what it used to be'. **,,**

Philip Kotler

Dr Philip Kotler is the SC Johnson & Son Distinguished Professor of International Marketing at the Kellogg Graduate School of Management, Northwestern University in Illinois. One of the world's leading authorities on marketing, Kotler has been chairman of the College of Marketing of the Institute of Management Sciences (TIMS), a director of the American Marketing Association, a trustee of the Marketing Science Institute and a director of the Mac Group. Educated at the University of Chicago and MIT, he did his postdoctoral work at Harvard University, and has received several honorary degrees. During his distinguished career, Kotler has also received numerous prestigious awards for his contributions to marketing. He has been a consultant to many major companies on marketing strategy, and has published over 100 articles in leading business journals. He is the author of 15 books, including Marketing Management, *now in its ninth edition, which is the most widely used marketing textbook in graduate business schools worldwide.*

Recommended reading

Marketing Management: Analysis, Planning, Implementation and Control (9th edn 1996) US/UK: Prentice-Hall.

Principles of Marketing (1993) US/UK: Prentice-Hall.

Marketing Places: Attracting investment, industry and tourism to cities, states and nations (1993) US/UK: Free Press.

Marketing: An introduction (1992) US/UK: Prentice-Hall.

Strategic Marketing for Nonprofit Organizations: Cases and readings (1987) US/UK: Prentice-Hall.

Marketing for Health Care Organizations (1986) US/UK: Prentice-Hall.

Rethinking

THE WORLD

From Nation States to Networks

John Naisbitt

Changing the Nature of Capitalism

Lester Thurow

The New Biology of Business

Kevin Kelly

"My one-word message for the twenty-first century is 'Asia'."

FROM NATION STATES TO NETWORKS

John Naisbitt

" FOR MANY YEARS the mindset has been that the global economy will be dominated by huge multinational companies. And that's turned out not to be the case. In fact, we have to reexamine our vocabulary and our definition of what multinational means.

I have a company called Megatrends Ltd, and we have 57 joint ventures in 42 countries, and we have only four employees including myself. We outsource everything. Well, almost everything. So I'm a multinational company. I must be, obviously, because I'm in 42 countries. But I'm not big. I'm small.

In other words, the word multinational has a new meaning. And if we say that the global economy will be dominated by multinationals in the new sense, then there is some truth to it. But if we mean it in the old way, that these huge global companies will control everything, that couldn't be more wrong.

What I think is really important is that **there's a new kind of bigness. And that's big networks, rather than big mainframes**. This is the metaphor I use.

I remember being in my kitchen in Telluride, Colorado and watching CNN. It was when the G7 were meeting in Naples for the economic summit. And as I saw the leaders of these seven great industrial nations talking to each other, it struck me that this is a bunch of mainframes talking to each other in a PC world. It's part of the whole irrelevance of the G7, and by the twenty-first century I think it will be totally out the window—it just doesn't make sense any more.

We no longer live in a world of big mainframes. We live in a world where the real power is in big networks. By big networks, I mean a lot of individuals networked together. And, by definition, a network doesn't have any headquarters. **For a network to work, everyone has to feel that they are in the center. That's when it's really powerful.**

The only huge company that I know of that's really done this is Asea Brown Boveri. If you listen to Percy Barnevik, he says: 'We grow all the time, but we also shrink all the time.' The network gets larger but the nodes get smaller.

The power of small companies

The point is, you can now replicate quality anywhere in the world. So the competitive differentiation comes from swiftness to market and innovation. And, in that regard, small companies, right down to the individual, can beat big bureaucratic companies ten out of ten times. Therefore, unless the big companies reconstitute themselves as a collection of small companies, they will just continue to go out of business.

It's really quite remarkable that the *Fortune* 500 now constitutes only 10 percent of the US economy, down from 20 percent as recently as 1970. That's why it's such a distortion when you read about US companies, because you read mostly, if not exclusively, about the *Fortune* 500. You read that Sears is going to lay off 30,000 people in the next two years and General Data is going to lay off 25,000 people in the next three years. All of those stories are about only 10 percent of the economy. I think that, as we get into the next decade and into the next century, the *Fortune* 500 will be down to below 5 percent of the US economy.

It's the small companies who are creating the global economy, not the *Fortune* 500. And these days a small company can be as small as one person. In *Megatrends 2000* I gave the example of my neighbors. Maybe I can repeat it here.

Linde and Lito have a publishing company called Western Eye Press. It's just two people and they publish wonderful photographic books and guide books. They create them on Macintosh computers in their basement in Telluride. They print out the camera-ready pages on their own high-resolution laser printer. Then they Federal Express these pages to Seoul, Korea, and the printer there manufactures their books and then ships them to distributors all over the world.

Western Eye Press is a player in the global economy and it's just two people on this little mountain perch in Colorado.

➤ *But can we really build a global economy on solo players and on small to mid-sized organizations?*

It's not 'Can we?'. We are. Right now, 50 percent of US exports are created by companies with 19 or fewer employees. Only 7 percent are created by companies with 500 or more employees. And the United States is by far the largest exporter in the world. The figures are similar in Germany.

The global economy of the twenty-first century will be dominated by small and middle-sized players. Look at the biggest industry there is: tourism. It employs one out of nine people in the world. And it will get even bigger in the twenty-first century as the world becomes more and more affluent. But apart from a few big players like the airlines, who provide the infrastructure, tourism is made up of millions and millions of entrepreneurs.

The global economy is a reality. And as we move into the twenty-first century, with the Cold War over and other conditions becoming more favorable, we're going to see the global economy really take off. In 1994, world trade increased by 9 percent. That's the most it has increased in twenty years; double what it did the year before. Right now, every economy in the world is growing and it's the first time that has happened in my lifetime.

Appropriate scale

Small is beautiful, but what is really beautiful in this context is appropriate scale.

In other words, I know very well that I can't build a Boeing 747 in my garage. Of course we need big companies for these things. But it's all about finding the appropriate scale. Increasingly, appropriate scale is smaller and more powerful.

The increase in power comes from a presence that's out of proportion to size, as we used to think about it. The new technology extends your individual power.

Already this morning I have had calls from Vienna, Kuala Lumpur and Shanghai, here in my home. This is a basic change that has happened within my lifetime. When I was a kid, the only way you could contact Europe was through radio. And now you can do almost anything with telecommunications.

The revolution in telecommunications is simultaneously creating the huge, global, single-market economy, while making the parts smaller and more powerful.

When I say telecommunications, I think we can generally agree that it now includes consumer electronics and computers, because one of the things we're doing now is blending. By the time the twenty-first century comes, we will have blended technologies in who knows how many combinations. That's why I made the point in the conclusion of *Global Paradox* that it's thousands of alliances and thousands of entrepreneurs that will be putting all of these ideas and media together in thousands of combinations.

We know that the real revolution in telecommunications is upon us, but we don't know exactly what it will produce. These thousands and thousands of combinations will create things that are perhaps even unimaginable today. And I don't even mean that in the 'gee whizz' sort of way. It's actually quite straightforward. You've got all these entrepreneurs competing to come up with new products and services, so I'm sure we're going to get some wonderful stuff in the future.

Big companies in the twenty-first century

Unless big companies can reconfigure themselves into small, fast-moving units, I don't think they stand a chance of surviving in the twenty-first century. But the other side of technology is that it allows big companies to deconstruct, to decentralize radically, to push power and decision making down to the lowest point. So there's the great opportunity, and many companies are doing just that. They have to. Because big old bureaucratic institutions can't even begin to compete with fast-moving small players.

What you see happening everywhere now is that even the really huge companies are restyling themselves as networks of entrepreneurs. They're breaking up into confederations of small, autonomous companies and outsourcing, delayering, downsizing.

Again, Asea Brown Boveri is a good example. It is a giant company, actually the world's largest power-engineering group. But it has subdivided itself into 1300 companies and 5000 autonomous units.

Or look at GE. Jack Welch says: 'What we're trying relentlessly to do is to get that small company soul—and small company speed—inside our big company body.'

Paul Allaire, chairman of Xerox, is doing something similar. Then there's AT&T, Grand Metropolitan, Coca-Cola, Johnson & Johnson. The list goes on. So there's a lot of this going on all over the world, and it is widely understood. When AT&T announced that it was breaking up into three separate companies, the value of the stock increased by 10 billion dollars.

Whereas Louis Gerstner, the CEO of IBM, talks about incorporating small-company attributes but he seems to be doing the opposite of that. He's centralizing everything. I think it's totally out of sync with what's going on.

So is IBM going to last? I don't know. *Fortune* magazine quoted me as saying that Gerstner is very, very good at what doesn't work any more.

Every once in a while you see an announcement about IBM delaying the introduction of something or other. That's because the company is still full of bureaucracy. And it can't compete with the small, swift-moving companies.

Think locally, act globally

Something else that has happened is that the New Age mantra, 'think globally, act locally', is being turned on its head. Because, as the world becomes more global we tend to think more tribally. So now it's 'think locally', or tribally in fact, and 'act globally'.

A very good example is language. English is becoming the universal language of the world. The only other candidate, and it can happen in the twenty-first century, is Mandarin.

I say Mandarin not just because of China but because of China plus the overseas Chinese. There are 54 million overseas Chinese in Asia outside the mainland, and they're running the economies there. All the economies of Asia are run by overseas Chinese, except Japan and Korea. So Mandarin is a candidate.

But English is becoming the universal language, and the more English becomes people's second language, the more precious their first language, their mother tongue, becomes to them. Because that's what constitutes their identity.

In other words, the more you yield some of your identity through language, because of economic dependency and so forth, the more you hold on to what constitutes the rest of your identity.

That's why, even in the twenty-first century, there is not going to be a common currency in Europe. Because that's part of people's identity too. Their national heroes and icons are on their currency, and they're not going to give that up.

The more universal we become, the more tribal we act. The more we become dependent, economically dependent, on others, the more we hold on to what constitutes our core basic identity. Because none of us likes to lose hold on our identity, which, as I mentioned, is expressed in language, in cultural history and so forth. It's a very human thing.

In South Korea, there is a renaissance of interest in their 5000-year-old cultural history and in the Korean language. And new cultural museums are being put together all over the world.

If you think about it, it's psychologically quite superficial for an Asian to decide to wear a western business suit. Or to listen to some western music. What is really in our bones is our language, our history and our culture. Those things don't yield very easily at all.

But it's not as if people wake up one day and shout, 'Hey, we're losing our identity, we'd better hold on to it.' They don't articulate it that way. They just sort of feel it. So, almost without knowing it, they get more interested in their own language, they get more interested in their history, and their schools start to teach it more. Or they pass laws to protect their language. As they have done in Quebec, in Moscow, in the Ukraine, in Lithuania or Indonesia, for example. Or like France—but there it's too late.

Of course, on the other side you have the Japanese, who are so promiscuous about embracing everyone's language. They have all these German words and especially English words in Japanese, but that's another story.

New economies

The riddle of the early twenty-first century will be: what's going to become universal and what's going to remain tribal? And what has already become universal is market mechanisms for organizing our economic lives. These mechanisms have given rise to liberalization and privatization. And that's what has given rise to the new economies all over the world.

One very exciting new player is Malaysia. Malaysia has been growing at 8 or 9 percent for eight years. It is the largest exporter of computer chips in the world. The country has only 18 million people and they've been doing so well that they now have tremendous labor shortages, both professionally and in construction. Right now, they're building the tallest building in the world there. It has twin towers, taller than Sears tower in Chicago. I see it every time I go there, it has gone up several storeys already. But, because of the labor shortages, it's being built by 20,000 Indonesians. Round the clock. In three shifts.

Another player that people are starting to talk about is Vietnam. It has 73 million people and a 95 percent literacy rate. Its élite went to the best schools and the best universities in the world. BMW has started to assemble cars there, and Mercedes Benz, Ford and General Motors have announced that they, too, will be assembling cars in Vietnam. I think it's going to be a very interesting new player.

A number of people in Asia have said to me that they are going to prevail economically in the long run because they don't have any social security system. They don't have a welfare state. Indeed, it's a horrifying idea to Asian families, where family comes first, that the central government would have anything to do with your family.

Put that together with the signal from BMW and Mercedes Benz. Why are they going to Vietnam? Because back in Germany they pay $30 an hour for their workers, 50 percent of which goes to central government for the welfare state. In Vietnam, they are paying a dollar a day. Now that is going to go up, of course, but companies are not going to be burdened by these heavy social costs.

Something else the Asians say is that the welfare state has been corrupting self-reliance. Which is why we have all the problems in the US, for example children being born out of wedlock and divorce rates, and so many people homeless and on welfare. The Asians say it's because you pull the self-reliance rug out from under people.

Look at the Swedes. They're trying to cut back on the welfare state. In Sweden, if a couple has a child, either the father or the mother can take a year off work and get 80 percent of their pay. Now they are trying to cut that back to 75 percent and the Swedes are going nuts. They are saying, 'Why cut it back?'. So we're paying people for not working.

In Germany, you can almost get just as much money for not working as you can for working. Now that is crazy.

The end of politics

In government, I think we're moving towards a kind of direct democracy.

In the US, our version of representative democracy was invented 218 years ago, even before the Pony Express, not to mention computers and telephones and so on. In other words, back then, before we had these means of communication, we had to have someone go off and represent us and then come back and tell us what happened. But we don't need that kind of representation any more, because now we're all on line in real time. We know as much as everybody else does. And what is happening is that, all over the world, sitting governments are getting blown out of the water.

We're in a very transitional period. And in terms of political leadership, people don't know what the new leadership should be. They just know that what they've got is not what they want.

Some people in the media say, 'Where are the Charles de Gaulles these days?'. But I'm not sure those are the appropriate leaders for today, or especially for the twenty-first century. They were great for their time. They were totally appropriate for their time. But even if you really did have a Charles de Gaulle now, I'm not sure that would be appropriate.

So we're in a very interesting period for political leadership and we're just casting about to see what kind of a new leader we need.

Personally, I think that the new political leader will not be unlike the new leader in business. After all, business is often the harbinger of what happens in other sectors of our lives. **And the new leaders in business are facilitators. They sort out what's tribal and what's universal.** They facilitate the entrepreneurism and that's really important.

Economies are replaced and revitalized by entrepreneurs, bottom up. And one of the reasons I think Europe is going to be stuck in the mud for a long time is that the bureaucratic governments of Europe are not nourishing the entrepreneurs. In fact, they're downright hostile to entrepreneurs. It's really astonishing.

By contrast, and this is why I think the United States is in such great shape, in 1993 we created 880,000 new companies. That's almost a million new start-ups in the United States. This is very dramatic, because if you look back to the 1950s and 1960s, when the US was roaring along as this great industrial power, we only created about 50–60,000 new companies each year.

Then in the 1970s, when the whole basic nature of the economy was changing, which is always a great time for entrepreneurs, we started to create 100,000, 200,000, 300–400,000, and in the 1990s, 880,000 new companies.

But aside from these basic changes in the nature of the economy, one of the reasons mechanically that the United States is so nurturing and supportive of entrepreneurs is that, unlike in Europe, you don't have to register your company with any central government. You register it locally. Or you register it in the state. And you can do that within an hour. So in the United States you can start a company within a hour.

What has happened is that the states themselves are competing with each other to get companies to come and start a business in their state. They offer all these incentives, like they'll forgive taxes for the first three years or whatever. So, over the decades, this has resulted in an incredibly supportive environment for entrepreneurs in all of the United States.

Megatrends Asia

By far the most important thing that is going on in the world today is the modernization of Asia, not only for Asians but for the whole world. It's going to change everything.

In *Megatrends Asia*, there are eight chapters about eight major shifts in Asia. And the first one is the **shift from nation states to networks**. Of course, the notion that we are moving away from nation states has occurred to everyone, but what is important is that Asia is shifting from a region that was dominated by Japan to a region that is driven by the overseas Chinese network. It's a network of 57 million Chinese who live outside the mainland, 54 million of them in Asia, and they're autonomous entrepreneurs and entrepreneurial families. Each family is a network of companies and enterprises and in turn those networks are all networked together. They do a lot with each other as part of the network but at the same time they function as individuals and as very efficient units.

I said in *Global Paradox* that the bigger the system the more efficient the parts must be, and the most efficient parts are autonomous. It's like the Internet. On the Internet there are about 30,000 networks and they are all linked together in a network of networks, but the reason that the Internet can get so big is that it's totally decentralized right down to the individual. It's actually 50 million autonomous parts and on the way to becoming a billion autonomous parts. It is only accessed by the individual. Similarly, the overseas Chinese network is made up of autonomous entrepreneurial families. Just like the Internet, it's a network of networks but it's also totally decentralized.

So the point is, it's not the nation state of China that will dominate Asia, but the overseas Chinese network. And it's not about who is going to join China, whether Taiwan, Hong Kong, Macao or whatever, but about which entrepreneurs, which pieces of China, are joining that overseas Chinese network. Because, for several years now, the overseas Chinese network has been joined by entrepreneurs on the mainland.

The overseas Chinese network is the first of the huge global economic networks—right now it's probably about the third largest economy in the world. And we will see more of these new networks emerging. We'll probably also have an Indian network, for example. We'll have all kinds of networks, as networks replace the idea of the nation state.

The second of the Asian megatrends is the **shift from export-led to consumer-driven**. Up until recently, the economies of Asia have been built on exports. But in the process of building an export-led economy, you raise the standard of living to a point where the people in your country start to become consumers. And then you add to the export-led economy the drive or the impetus of consumer activity, which means that the whole economy starts to feed on itself, and then it can really roar. Now, because the standard of living has been raised all over Asia in the process of building these export-led dynamic economies, we're moving into a period where those economies are really starting to be driven by consumer activity within the countries. In fact, the explosion of intra-Asian trade is remarkable.

What the West doesn't have a clue about is that the West now needs the East a lot more than the East needs the West.

The next megatrend I talk about in the book is the move **from western influence to the Asian way**. Asia is a region where most of the countries have a kind of predestination about things, where things have always been quite fixed due to traditions and so forth. But this explosion of economic activities has led to people being conscious that they have options about things. About the kind of government they're going to have, about consumer spending, even about religion. And it's just opening up the whole region from this sort of predestination and tradition to what I call 'multiple options'.

The fourth Asian megatrend is **from government-controlled to market-driven**. This is happening all over the world, of course. And it's happening with a vengeance in Asia. Except for Japan, Asia has been so open to foreign investments and foreign participation, and this has been a very, very important aspect in the growth of their economies.

What has happened is that the dynamic economies of Asia are no longer government controlled. They are market driven. All across the region, government control is over, and it's yielding to market mechanisms . Even places like Burma are yielding to market mechanisms. Vietnam started several years ago. In Vietnam, the private sector is now generating about 70 or 80 percent of the economy, even though it is nominally a communist country, 'nominally' being the operative word here.

Then there's the fifth big shift—**from villages to supercities**—which is this whole phenomenon of rural to urban that is just sweeping across Asia. The region is rapidly moving from labor-intensive agriculture to manufacturing and service. Especially service. And I think that, in the future, all the big cities of the world are going to be in Asia.

Number six is **from labor-intensive to high technology**. What this is about is that we are increasingly squeezing out the labor content of all manufacturing products, so Asia's previous advantage of cheap labor is really out the window. Asia realized this before the West did, and the countries of Asia are moving very fast to become high-technology countries.

Malaysia is the great example. As I mentioned earlier, it is the world's largest exporter of computer chips. Who would have thought that years ago? So, in the area of high technology, Asia is really moving as fast as the West. Actually it's moving faster than the West and will soon catch up.

Another very interesting development is the trend **from male dominance to the emergence of women**. Like most of the world throughout history, Asia has been dominated by males. But one of the great phenomena in Asia today is the emergence of the young woman entrepreneur.

And it's happening all over Asia. Right across the board, women are emerging in leadership roles. This is something that I've been tracking for a while, and it represents quite a remarkable shift in the role of women in Asia.

The last of the eight Asian megatrends is **from West to East**, which is about the shift back to the East as the center of the world. In the fifteenth century, Asia was definitely the center of the world. Then we had 400 to 500 years in which the West dominated, and in which we called the world 'the western world'.

But now the center of the world is moving back to Asia—economically, politically and culturally—and in the twenty-first century it will become the dominant region again.

I say 'region' because, for all the time we can remember, the nations of Asia have functioned as independent, autonomous, very nationalistic countries, but now for the first time they're cooperating and coming together again. And this is constituting a whole new commonwealth of Asian countries based on economic symbiosis.

What we are seeing is the rise of a kind of Asian conscience. A real sense of Asia. I call it the Asianization of Asia.

Let me give you a little example of what I mean. You remember back at the beginning of the 1960s, when a lot of young people in Europe—young English people, or French people or Germans—started saying that they were Europeans. They were way ahead of the curve, as it were. And now the same thing is happening in Asia. Young people are saying that they're Asians. Formerly, a young Malaysian traveling in Europe or the United States, when asked 'Where are you from?', would almost always say 'Malaysia'. But now he or she is more likely to say 'Asia'.

So, all in all, what is happening in Asia is by far the most important thing that is happening on the planet. It's a kind of Asian renaissance. And, to me, nothing else comes close.

It will all be clear to us 50 years from now, and it's clear to a lot of Asians already, but it's not clear to people in the West that the modernization of Asia is going to reshape the whole world.

➤ *How accurate do you think we can be when we try to predict the future?*

I don't think anybody can really know in detail what is going to happen five years from now or six years from now. Because it depends so much on what happens today, and what happens next year and the year after. It's all shaped by millions and billions of variables. So I think we can only anticipate a little bit out in front of us.

My formulation on this is that the things we expect to happen always happen more slowly, and it's the surprises that overtake us. Except for the large shifts. And that's what I try to focus on.

➤ *What would be your message to individuals, to entrepreneurs, to companies—as well as to whole countries and their governments? What should they be doing right now to capitalize on these new realities?*

I think my one-word message for the twenty-first century is 'Asia'.

The center of economic, political and cultural gravity has shifted to Asia, and it will be the most important part of the world in all of those categories in the twenty-first century.

So if I were 22 years old, I would move to Asia and learn Mandarin, for sure. And I would advise anybody else to do that.

Apart from that, the avenues of opportunity to look at for the twenty-first century are entrepreneurism, joint ventures, partnerships, alliances, global networks. Things like these.

All of these are where the opportunities lie. Anywhere in the world. But especially in Asia.

Think local, act global. That's the new motto! „„

John Naisbitt

John Naisbitt is arguably the world's leading trend forecaster. Since the early 1980s, Naisbitt's bestselling books have been providing an accurate preview of the major changes that will affect our world. Formerly an executive with IBM and Eastman Kodak, he has been a visiting fellow at Harvard, a visiting professor at Moscow State University, and is distinguished international fellow of the Institute of Strategic and International Studies (ISIS), Malaysia. He is also on the faculty at Nanjing University in China and holds 12 doctorates in the humanities and sciences. Naisbitt is a renowned international speaker and adviser to many of the world's leading corporations and heads of state, and he annually addresses thousands of business leaders and opinion makers in the Americas, Europe and Asia. Today, he divides his time between Cambridge, Massachusetts; Kuala Lumpur, Malaysia; Telluride, Colorado; and global travel. His books have sold over eight million copies worldwide.

Recommended reading

Megatrends Asia: Eight Asian megatrends that are reshaping our world (1996) US: Simon & Schuster/UK: Nicholas Brealey.

Global Paradox: The bigger the world economy, the more powerful its smallest players (1995) US: Avon Books/UK: Nicholas Brealey.

Megatrends for Women: From liberation to leadership (1993) Patricia Aburdene and John Naisbitt, US: Fawcett Books.

Megatrends 2000: Ten new directions for the 1990s (1991) US: Avon Books.

Megatrends (1988) US: Warner Books.

Photo by Mark Ostour

"The dominant competitive weapon of the twenty-first century will be the education and skills of the workforce."

CHANGING THE NATURE OF CAPITALISM

Lester Thurow

" WE HAVE ENTERED a new phase of worldwide economic competition and this has come about because of two principal reasons. One is that the post-Second World War capitalist system has come to a natural stopping point. Its goal was to help the rest of the industrial world—or at least as much of it as possible—to catch up with the United States in terms of per capita GNP. And that has now happened, which changes the nature of the world's economics. The US has gone from having about 75 percent of the world's industrial production to having about 23 or 24 percent of the world's industrial production.

The second reason, of course, is the implosion of Communism. One third of humanity used to be outside of the capitalist system, playing in the Communist world economy. Now that one-third of humanity—representing 1.9 billion people—has decided to join the capitalist world. And this is going to change us as well as them. You can't digest something that big without some impact.

A good example would be the oil business. Five or ten years ago we used to say that Saudi Arabia was the largest producer of oil. This was never true. The Soviet Union was always the world's largest producer of oil, but it didn't matter to us and we didn't count it because not very much of that oil came to the capitalistic world. Now, if you say, 'Where is the largest pool of oil?', it's no longer under the Persian Gulf, it's under the Caspian Sea. So if you are in the oil business, this is a radically different world to the one we had before the Soviet Union collapsed.

➤ *In what ways have these economic developments changed the rules of the game?*

What has changed is the game itself. The new rules have not yet been written. To a large extent we are still trying to play by the old rules, and this is no longer sufficient.

Immediately after the war, the US did not have to worry about its economic position. The basic rules of the game were that Europe and Japan were supposed to recover, and the US would worry about military and political matters on a geo-world scale—*vis-à-vis* Communism. The thought was that the US economy is so big and so powerful that the people in Washington don't have to worry about it. And therefore we can be an open market. We don't have to worry about reciprocity with the Japanese and we don't have to do a whole set of things that you have to do if you are in a really competitive world.

So we created a set of rules for a unipolar world. But look what happened: Europe and Japan did recover; they became very strong economic powers in their own right, to the extent that they now rival the US for economic supremacy. Which means that we have essentially gone from a unipolar situation to a tripolar or three-way economic game. And the unipolar rules no longer apply. The trading system that governed world economics in the past will not be the system that governs it in the future.

We now have the development of a huge global economy, and the race is on between Japan, Europe and the US to gain dominance of that economy. In a sense, it's a race against the clock. One of the three will pull ahead and is likely to stay ahead. And the winner will force the losers to play by the winner's rules. **So this new phase of competition—the new game between these three economic superpowers—will determine who is going to own the twenty-first century.**

I also think, realistically, that we are moving towards regional economies before we move to a global economy. We have two things going on at once. First, there is this splintering of countries that we see everywhere. We see it in the Soviet Union. We see it in Yugoslavia. We see it in Canada. We see it in Spain. We also see it in France, where the Corsicans and the Bretons want some independence. And in Britain, the Labour Party is planning to give more independence to the Welsh and the Scots if they are elected. So you have a splintering going on at a local level, but at the same time you have everybody wanting to join these regional trading blocs. If you go to the Czech Republic and to Slovakia, you will find that they don't want to live with each other but they both want to join the European Union.

Therefore, I think that we won't just make one giant leap to a global economy, but rather we will make these relatively smaller steps first towards regionalism—in other words, free trade within regions and managed trade between regions.

I think some index of world trade would show you that free trade within regions over the next ten or twelve years will go up. And we already see a lot more management between regions.

Head-to-head competition

In the future, historians will look back on the twentieth century as a century of niche competition and the twenty-first century as a century of head-to-head competition. Let me explain what I mean.

If you go back to the old-fashioned idea of comparative advantage, it depended on two things: natural resource endowment and factory proportions. So if you had oil, you did oil. If you had farmland, you did farm products. And if you were a capital-rich land, you did capital-intensive products. So everybody had kind of a natural place in the world economy. They had their own niche, as it were.

But today we see a very different kind of competition emerging. If you really believe that we're now in an era of 'brainpower' industries—new materials, semiconductor chips, computers, software, those things—then there is no natural home for these industries. They can be anywhere on the face of the globe. Which means that anybody can potentially compete for them, if they can organize the necessary brainpower to do so.

If you go to any industrial country in the world at the moment and you say, 'List for me the seven industries in which you'd most love to have some strong players in your country', everybody will give you the same list. They wouldn't have done that a hundred years ago.

A common list would include microelectronics, biotechnology, the new materials-science industries, telecommunications, civil aviation, robotics and machine tools, and of course computer hardware and software. These are, in fact, what the Japanese have listed as the seven key industries for the early part of the twenty-first century.

But everybody wants them. And this is what I mean by the shift to head-to-head competition. Japan, the European Union and the US are now relatively equal contenders. And all three are competing for the same set of industries, to insure that their citizens get a world-class standard of living in the first half of the twenty-first century.

When we compare this to the economic battles of the past, the essential difference is the fact that comparative advantage is now manmade. Natural resources have dropped out of the competitive equation. In fact, a lack of natural resources may even be an advantage. Because the industries we are competing for—the industries of the future—are all based on brainpower.

If you think about who is the world's largest producer of copper, the answer is Chile. And if you ask 'Why?', the answer is that it has the world's best deposits of copper. If you say, 'Does the Netherlands produce any copper?', the answer is 'no', because there is no copper to be produced.

On the other hand, you can do computer software in the Netherlands or you can do it in Bangalore in India. The fact is, Bangalore is one of the computer software centers of the world. So, in that case, you've got an underdeveloped country competing with developed countries in a high-tech industry, something that was just not possible even 30 years ago.

The peculiar phenomenon we have at the moment, which fits in with this, is that, particularly in the US, in a large fraction of the population real wages are falling. And it's basically because in this global economy they have to compete against skilled people in the third world who get paid a lot less. The point is, there were always a few skilled people in the third world but it never used to make any difference, because they couldn't effectively compete against someone in the US. But now, with modern communications and transportation, they can.

If you are an economist, you have to believe in some kind of factor price equalization in the long run. In a global economy, either people move to the places where wages are high and drive them down, or production moves to places where wages are low and drives them up. But the problem is that it takes a long time to do that kind of equalization if you are talking about billions of people, which is what we are talking about now.

A zero-sum game

With classical comparative advantage, it was a positive-sum game. Niche competition is win–win. Everybody has their own niche where they can excel, so nobody goes out of business. But the new head-to-head competition is win–lose. It's a situation where everybody wants the same key industries, because these are the places that generate the high profits and the high wages. And some people are going to capture these industries, the rest are not. So you bring this element of a zero sum to the game.

If Microsoft dominates the computer software industry, for example, that means that a Japanese firm can't do it. They get 'frozen out'. If I have copper and you have copper, both of us can produce copper, but in industries where it really depends on getting a dominant position and moving very fast from generation to generation, you can be squeezed out. You can get into a position where you're not getting anything out of these new industries at all.

Not everybody is following exactly the same strategy to compete for these industries, but all the players certainly have the same bottom line as to what industries they would like to have and how they think they can get them. In a lot of cases there seems to be kind of a natural way to go at it. Of course, it varies from industry to industry. **But basically the dominant competitive weapon of the twenty-first century will be the education and skills of the workforce.**

So if you take biotechnology, the strategy has to be: are you producing very substantial numbers of PhDs in biotechnology? Because PhDs in biology are the equivalent of production workers in other industries. And there isn't any way around that problem. But you also need an environment which is accepting to these technologies. For example, the Germans have made it very hard to do biotechnology in their own country because they seem to think that somebody is going to create a Frankenstein monster in a bottle and it's going to get out! The only thing this has done is to make the German chemical firms like Hoechst and Bayer do their biotechnology research in the United States. It doesn't stop them from doing their work. It just stops them from hiring Germans to do the work.

What we are also seeing is that the emphasis is shifting from new product technologies to new process technologies. With reverse engineering it's relatively simple today for a skilled engineer to tear a new product apart and quickly learn how it's made. But it isn't as simple to figure out how to run the necessary manufacturing processes and to do a thousand things right. You can't just buy things like that. That's why the skills of the workforce will be such a powerful competitive weapon in the future. It's not enough to have the brainpower to create new products. Because those who can manufacture those products more cheaply can take them away from their inventors. Like the video camera and video recorder. Those were invented by Americans but they became Japanese products. Why? Because the Japanese had superior process technologies.

Thus one of the starting points for future competition will be having the skilled labor to master low-cost, high-tech processes. The fact is, in the future, both high-tech and even low-tech products will be made with high-tech processes. **Therefore, my basic argument is that, ultimately, product innovation won't do you much good if you don't have the processes to become the cheapest producer.** You've got to have some kind of a production advantage as opposed to just having invented the product. So, in a sense, you need both.

Take Intel in microprocessors. It has the product technologies as well as the process technologies. Which means that it can always keep one jump ahead. It has this phenomenal profit margin, and how does it earn it? The answer is that it is producing chip 'n + 1' while everybody else is still back on 'n'. And as long as Intel can keep '+ 1' ahead, it can make phenomenal profits. If it ever slips to being 'n – 1', it will make nothing.

▶ *In your latest book,* The Future of Capitalism, *you put forward the notion that the very foundations of capitalism are being shaken. What evidence would you point to to show that this is actually happening?*

The evidence is quite clear. Take Europe, which in terms of people is by far the largest economy, with 50 percent more people than the United States. How would you explain the fact that in the last 22 years Europe has created no net new jobs? Europe now has unemployment approaching 12 percent, and in some European countries it's even 20 percent. Now, that's Great Depression-type stuff!

If you look at the United States there's a difference of course, because we've had more than a one-third increase in our per capita GDP over the last 20 years. We created 38 million net new jobs while Europe created zero. But at the same time 80 percent of wages have fallen, once you correct for inflation. So, my question is, how can the tide go up and 80 percent of the boats sink?

Another example is Mexico, where they really did do everything right: they balanced their budget; they privatized their state companies; they deregulated—they did everything that an economist would tell you to do and the place still collapsed.

So I think we see many anomalies, and in *The Future of Capitalism* I argue that these are basically the equivalent of economic earthquakes and economic volcanoes. In other words, these are merely the surface manifestations of some far deeper and more fundamental changes in the underlying structure of our economic world.

The surface manifestations may differ quite substantially between economies, as they do between Europe and the United States. In Europe it shows up as rising unemployment and in the United States it shows up as falling wages. But the same fundamental forces are changing everybody's economies, and if we are going to understand the economic earthquakes and volcanoes, we are going to have to look at these forces that are causing them.

In my book I point to five forces. I call them economic plates, which is based on a concept from geology, where earthquakes and volcanoes are caused by the movement of huge continental plates—called tectonic plates—that float on the earth's molten core. What I am saying is that the movement of five economic tectonic plates is driving all these changes and fundamentally remaking the economic surface of the earth.

The first plate is **the end of Communism**. As I said earlier, one-third of humanity used to live in the Communist world. These people are going to join the capitalist world, and that's a very big meal to digest.

Second, **we're moving from natural resource-based industries to manmade brainpower industries**, which represents a very different industrial environment.

Third, if you look at demographics, three things are going on. **The world population is growing. It's also moving. And it's getting older.** By 2025, in every major industrial democracy in the world, we'll have a voting majority of people over the age of 65. That's going to change sociology, psychology, business, government budgets, everything. No society in human history has ever been dominated by the elderly. We're going to be the first.

At the same time, we're the first society in human history that will have **a genuinely global economy**, where you can produce anything anywhere on the face of the earth and sell it everywhere else on the face of the earth. This is the fourth tectonic plate.

Fifth and finally, for the first time in 200 years **we won't have a unipolar world with one dominant economic, political or military power**, like the British Empire in the nineteenth century or the Americans in the twentieth century. Someone that can basically dictate the way we play the game—that can say, 'I'm the jury, I'm the policeman, you're going to play it my way'. And if you have a global economic game where nobody is playing that role, it becomes a very different game.

In geology, the continental plates are moving because they float on the molten magma of the earth's inner core. In economics, the plates are driven by powerful currents in technology and ideology. **It is these currents that are shaking the foundations of twenty-first-century capitalism, because technology and ideology are in fact moving apart.**

There are many ways to illustrate this. Look at one example. Technology is making human skills and knowledge the only sources of sustainable competitive advantage. Therefore, as a firm, you ought to worry a lot about how you can attach those human skills to your organization. But, at the same time, we're downsizing. We're telling employees not to have any corporate loyalty, to think 'have gun will travel'. So the technology is moving one way, telling us we should attach people to the firm. The ideology is moving in the opposite direction. What I am arguing primarily is that this is an era where we are going to need a lot of social investments in things like infrastructure, R&D and education. But the ideology is telling us to get the government out of those kind of things. It's very much a kind of 'survival of the fittest' form of capitalism—based on the individual—as opposed to an ideology that says: 'Hey, we need some communitarian investments to make capitalism work.'

And we don't know where all this is going to lead us. Because we've created what biologists call a period of punctuated equilibrium, where the environment suddenly changes and the previously dominant species dies out and is replaced by another. I use the example in *The Future of Capitalism* of the dinosaurs and the mammals. We know what's going into the period of punctuated equilibrium, but nobody could have predicted that the mammals would have come out the other side.

In other words, we know the forces that are going to determine the future of capitalism. But what we don't know is the exact shape of the future, because that's not determined by the stars; it's determined by what we do.

That's the reason I use the metaphor from geology, because you can't predict the earthquakes and the volcanoes but you can understand plate tectonics. And if you understand plate tectonics, you can at least begin to understand what it takes to be the mammal coming out the other side, as opposed to the dinosaur who doesn't come out the other side.

At the moment, we don't know precisely what's going to work. It's still going to be capitalism, but it's going to be a very different form of capitalism. Nobody knows exactly what works in a world dominated by brainpower as opposed to being dominated by the steam engine. Nobody knows exactly what works in a world where you can have instant global communications.

How do you, for example, organize a business firm? Where do you put the offices? Where do you put the factories? Who reports to whom? If you look at most of our forms of business organizations, they're very much determined by the things invented by the nineteenth-century railways: orders down, information up; corporate headquarters; do what you're told; timetable; stopwatch. But the world has changed since the invention of the nineteenth-century railroad. And in the future, corporate organizations are going to be radically different.

Modern technology gives us new ways of organizing a business. Just look at the office building. At the moment, if you walk into most office buildings in the world at, say, 10.35 in the morning, you'll find that 25–30 percent of the chairs are empty. The people who are supposed to sit in them are away doing something else—they are selling; they are at office meetings; wherever they are, they're not in their chairs. With modern technology you don't have to have all that idle space and all those unused computers and telephones. Instead, you could run an office building like a hotel. You walk in and there's an electronic board that says room 1021 is empty. You go to 1021. You have your own personal telephone number. You call up your computer code. You press a button and your family picture is up on the flat-screen TV set on the wall. And that's your office for as long as you're there. The minute you leave, it ceases to be your office. We know why we don't do that at the moment; human beings like to have a cave. But the first company that figures out how to make this work will save 25 percent on office space, 25 percent on telephones, 25 percent on computers. **These will be the low-cost producers, and low-cost producers will inherit the earth.**

So we know that the way we do things in the future is not going to be the same as it is as at the moment. But nobody knows for sure exactly how it will be.

New threats to capitalism

The latest threat to capitalism is not some other 'ism': it is a kind of disintegration at the edges which sooner or later gets to the core. Look at economic disintegration: I mentioned Catalonia, the Basque country, the Bretons. And, of course, you see the same thing happening in the United States. If you look at the 'Contract with America', it's basically a proposal for setting up 50 different economies. Just giving everything back to the states except national defense. So we are going to have some poor economies and some wealthy economies. We're not going to have an American economy. We're going to have a New York economy or a Californian economy or whatever. I don't think it will work in the long run, but it's a phenomenon that we see worldwide.

The other thing we see everywhere in the world is that economic uncertainty leads to religious fundamentalism. If you are an economic failure and somebody can't tell you how to be a success, you tend to retreat into religious fundamentalism. Take these Freemen in Jordan, Montana who receive a lot of newspaper press around the world and certainly in the United States. Those people all went broke. Their ranches were being taken in foreclosure proceedings. That's why they have this incredible anti-government attitude: 'You can't take my ranch!' They overlay it with a little Christian fundamentalism and away they go. Now they think they have the right to shoot at government officials and secede from the United States.

Global cooperation

Competition in the future will be a little like competitive team sports, which are simultaneously competitive and cooperative. You can go to a game and yell for your team and still be friends after the game. And of course you have to do some cooperative things—hire the referee, arrange for a stadium, agree on the rules. So the sporting analogy is pretty good, because there is clearly a highly competitive part to it, but there is an absolutely vital cooperative part to it. In other words, one can remain friends but still want to win.

In tomorrow's global economy, there will be very tough economic competition, but the common environment will require global cooperation. Because if we are going to mutually prosper, we are going to have to cooperate to create a global economy that works. We will need rules—new systems for managing trade—because the old economic arrangements are not going to work any more. And we will have to force each other to adjust to these new rules.

Cooperation will be vital because we are going to have multinationals that play around the world, so it's not going to be so simple anymore to tell what is a Swiss firm and what's an American firm. There are also things that government has to do: long-tailed investments and things like research and development which are communitarian.

In addition, we're going to have to do cooperative things in terms of macroeconomics, otherwise the macroeconomic problems could destroy us all. So it's a question of how you put those things together. You have to put them together as an individual country, but you also have to put them together as a world.

The fact is, everyone wants to win. But we have to recognize that cooperation is necessary if the game is to be played at all.

➤ *What progress do you think we can expect to see on global environmental issues in the future?*

We are all beginning to understand that there is no point in having a global economy if you don't have a global environment that lets you survive and enjoy what you produce. And we recognize that there are some major problems that require cooperative action on a worldwide basis. The trouble is, how do you get cooperation when the problem isn't very evident? By the time the problem does become evident it's too late for the cooperation to work.

Take the issue of global warming—and let's just assume for the moment that it's true. You're not going to see the oceans rising very rapidly. It happens very slowly. And by the time the oceans are flooding our coastal cities, it will be much too late to do anything about it. The issue there is: how do you mobilize what would have to be a large-scale effort when the disastrous consequences are not very visible and come very slowly? Are you really going to be willing to pay a lot of taxes to prevent something that isn't going to happen until 2075?

On the other hand, there are some things that happen rather rapidly. The rainforest problem is one of these, and to an extent global warming is an extension of that problem. Now, that's something where it's reasonably easy to take some cooperative action. We would need to get together on a worldwide basis and ask ourselves: how can we make it more profitable for the Brazilians to plant trees than to cut them down? If you think about it logically, the tropical rainforests generate the atmosphere that we all need for survival. What could be more valuable than that? We pay for fresh water. Why shouldn't we pay for fresh air? And for an atmosphere that let's us go outside without getting skin cancer? So if the wealthy industrial world designs a system in which we pay rent for the rainforests, the Brazilians may find themselves in possession of something which is worth more than all the oil fields in the world.

As I say, that's a problem that we can deal with. There are some others that are much harder to find solutions for, because the costs are high and the effects occur very slowly, and they only occur in the distant future. But that doesn't mean that we should resign ourselves to whatever fate is in store for us. It's not like a Greek tragedy where the outcome is predetermined regardless of our actions. I believe that we really can turn these situations around, if we just have the will to do so. And that's why we need to get together on these issues. We need to create solutions in which we can all cooperate globally.

Japan

Japan is a society that has some very strong fundamental attributes. It saves a lot. It invests a lot. It's a society that is highly educated and obviously technologically sophisticated. But it has two principal failures. One is that it's a society that finds it very hard to turn a corner. The problem is that the Japanese economy was very carefully built to work in this post-Second World War world. But now we've got a brand new world, and the Japanese are finding it very hard to rebuild their economy. So they are not very quick at adapting to a new environment, and I think that's their biggest problem at the moment.

The other big handicap is that they have traditionally been very good at taking somebody else's invention and making it cheaper. But they have been very bad in coming up with their own brand new products. And this is the danger of having great process technologies without having the new product technologies. If you look at consumer electronics in Japan at the moment, it's in a disastrous state. Because they've been so good at producing the stuff that they've driven everybody else out of the consumer electronics business. And that means that nobody is inventing new products for them to produce more cheaply. They haven't been able to come up with any new products of their own either.

The question is: can they add a dash of individuality to their very good communitarian economy? Because that's part of the problem in inventing new products. If you are highly communitarian, it's very hard to invent new products, because the people who invent new products tend to be the oddballs who are not the best team players.

Over the last four or five years, if you look at Japanese corporations as a whole, they probably haven't made any money at all. A few corporations have made money, others corporations have lost a lot of money. So corporate profits in the aggregate are close to zero, if they did the accounting the way the Americans would do the accounting.

They also can't seem to get a grip on some of the important industries. Whereas in consumer electronics they are dominant, in computers they have a very weak position. They're having real problems in computer hardware, and of course they are absolutely nowhere in software. If you take software in Japan, most of it is run in English, because you can program a computer to do Japanese characters but it's so complicated that it's easier to learn English. So computers and computer software are an industry where they haven't been able to gain a strong competitive position.

On the other hand, I think in the long run that the Japanese will get themselves straightened out, because they do have certain fundamentals— they are well educated, they are technically sophisticated, they invest a lot—

which will make the difference over the long term, even if they have a problem getting organized in the short term.

We have to remember that, in the past, Japan's companies have been almost impossible to beat in a head-to-head competition. And of course nobody has been investing more in their future. So Japan will continue to be a very formidable opponent, even if they now look less formidable than they did five years ago.

What may happen in the twenty-first century is that the rest of the world will start to play Japan's rules back on them. For decades they have been very good at keeping others out of their market, and that's still true. But if the rest of the world began to play by the same rules, by instituting overt restrictions on Japanese imports, then Japan would obviously be in a great deal of trouble. Because their whole success has been based on an export-led economy. What this would do is to force Japan to open its market. If America and Europe start to play hardball, I think you'll see that, to some degree, the Japanese will have to play softball.

The United States

In the last four or five years, the US economy has probably been the best performer in the industrial world. And we are clearly becoming more cognitive of the fact that we have to start worrying about economics. But I still don't think we really have a clear strategy yet for how we are going to deal with it.

America has two big weaknesses. One big weakness is that we don't save and invest enough. And the other is that our education system is unbalanced. We have an education system for about 30 percent of the population which is very, very good, maybe the world's best. And then we have an education system for the bottom 30 percent of the population that in terms of the industrial world may be the world's worst. So we're producing a first-world economy and a third-world economy that live side by side in one country.

On the other hand, if you take inventiveness or innovation, coming up with new products, dominating new industries, nobody does it better. Microsoft is a good example, as is Intel, as is Hewlett-Packard. None of those companies was big 35 years ago, and they're all big companies today that sometimes dominate their industries.

The other positive thing is that many companies in the US have gotten their act together in the last five years, and now they are much better players in the world economic game. If you take the automobile companies, for example, they've had a remarkable turnaround. They're getting market share back from the Japanese automobile companies. They've gone from big losses in the 1980s to big profits in the 1990s and they look like much more formidable competitors today than they looked back in 1985.

Europe

I think Europe is likely to write the new rules for international trade in the twenty-first century. Not in the sense of sitting down with a piece of paper and saying, 'These are the rules boys, play by them', but almost in the same way that you set standards in a competitive industry. In fact, we already see that. Look at the ISO9000 standard. That's a European standard. Thirty years ago, if we had had a quality standard for the manufacturing industry, it would have been an American standard.

Take another example. Would NAFTA exist if the European Union didn't exist? The answer is clearly 'no'. If the European Union didn't exist and NAFTA didn't exist, would the people in the Pacific Rim be talking about a regional trading group? Again, the answer has got to be 'no'.

The other reason that Europe is going to write the rules is because it's the biggest economy and because it's in the rule-writing business. I mean, there are people in Brussels just sitting there writing rules. Whereas nobody in the United States is writing rules for world trade. Therefore, if we are going to get new rules for international trade in the twenty-first century, I think the world is going to look to the guy who is already in the business of writing rules—as opposed to somebody else. And if Europe gets to write the rules, they are obviously going to favor those who play the game the European way.

If you look at the last five years, obviously there have been some disappointments in European economic performance. But there have been huge American and Japanese disappointments too. On the whole though, the basic thing is moving forward. Maastricht ended up being signed. Three of the four countries that voted on joining the European Union voted 'yes'.

Nobody knows exactly what Europe is going to do about a common currency, but somehow there's a feeling that you've got to do something. And, of course, if you did have a common currency, even if it was just started between France and Germany, everybody else would eventually have to join. Even the British would join. Because if they didn't join, the financial capital of Europe would move from London to somewhere on the Continent. And Britain can't afford to let that happen. So Britain can kick and scream and say that it doesn't want a common currency, but if this actually starts to happen it's like joining the European Union; Britain will simply have to join.

➤ *What are Europe's chances of capturing some of the key industries we have been talking about?*

If you go through those seven industries which the Japanese outlined, you'll find that the Europeans have some very good positions—or potential positions—in several of them. Aerospace is not a race between the Americans and the Japanese; it's a race between the Americans and the Europeans—it's about Airbus and all that. The European companies have also been very good in chemicals, and you've got these big industries coming along in new materials. So it's not at all obvious that European companies aren't going to play a big role in the new materials business.

The point about Europe is: imagine if the House of Europe expanded further east. What would happen if you combined the high-tech science capabilities of the former Soviet Union with the world-class production capabilities of the Germans? And with natural gas supplied by the new Commonwealth, Europe could even be energy self-sufficient. It wouldn't have to depend anymore on oil from the Persian Gulf. Then imagine you combined all this with the design flair of Italy and France and the world-class capital market in London. If you succeeded in bringing everything together in a kind of self-contained House of Europe, you would be creating an economic region that could definitely pull ahead of the rest.

I'm not saying that Europe will win. But I'm saying that Europe still holds the best strategic position on the world's economic chessboard. It's like a chess 'endgame', where white can win in, say, five moves, regardless of what black does. **If Europe can make the right moves, I believe that it really does have the potential to own the twenty-first century, economically speaking, regardless of what Japan and America do.** But first Europe has to find those moves. And then make them. Which is not going to be easy.

Asia

The first thing to remember about the global economy is that to be successful you have to be the equivalent of an economic marathon runner. Can you put decade after decade after decade of success together? It took Japan 130 years to catch up with the United States. You don't do it in 20 years or even 30 years. And so one of the questions is: are the countries of Asia going to be able to sustain the momentum that they've clearly had for the last 15 years?

The other issue is that the People's Republic of China is starting from the level of a per capita GNP of $400. The developed world has a per capita GNP of somewhere between $25,000 and $30,000. Just sit down with your calculator and put in whatever you think is the highest rate of growth that China can sustain on average over the next 100 years. Put in whatever you think Germany and Japan or the United States are going to do over the next 100 years and you'll still have China with a per capita GNP of half to two-thirds that of the developed world.

Now that doesn't mean that China isn't going to be important. China is already important today. After the United States, it's probably the second military superpower in the world. I'm actually a China optimist, but at the same time I think you have to be realistic. I mean, China is 1 percent of the world's GNP. Japan is about 15 percent of the world's GNP and the US is about 24 percent. So what I'm saying is that it's a very long and tough process, and maybe they'll make it, but it won't be in your lifetime or mine.

Asia is certainly an exciting place to be right now, because it's been growing economically somewhere between 8 and 10 percent a year. And 1.2 billion people are envisioned. That's almost a quarter of humanity, and it sounds like a pretty nice market. But on the other hand, a 10 percent growth rate in China represents $30 billion. One half of 1 percent growth rate in the US is $30 billion.

Asia is very peculiar because parts of it are doing very well and other parts are doing very badly. Of course, one of the problems you have in Asia is that Japan has 15 percent of the world's GDP, and the rest of East Asia has only 3 percent. So a −1 percent growth rate in Japan is the equivalent of +5 percent growth in the rest of the world. Since Japan has been negative and you've got these big countries like the Philippines that have more people than Singapore, Hong Kong, Taiwan and Korea combined, the net growth of all of East Asia is essentially zero. Some countries are growing economically, some countries are shrinking, but the biggest country is not growing. So this is a very mixed picture.

I think the idea that all of East Asia is booming and that it is going to inherit the earth is a little premature, to say the least. If there is to be a Chinese century, it will be the twenty-second century, not the twenty-first.

The emerging South-east Asian players have gotten to the point where they have to make a kind of a transition. For a long time they could compete as low-wage economies. But now they've got to go upscale in technology, because there are places out there with lower-wage economies. Their wages have now gone up to a level where there are no longer huge wage gaps between, say, Singapore and the Netherlands. Wages are still higher in the Netherlands, but they are not radically different. So they've got to make this transition, and some of those countries will make it more successfully than others.

The other big question is: will the South-east Asian countries get market access somewhere in the industrial world? Traditionally people have always relied on getting market access to the United States. But that's something nobody can rely on any more. This means they are going to have a problem, because they've never been able to sell in Japan, and they've never sold very much in Europe. So I think the market access problem is going to be critical for those countries.

➤ *What should we be doing right now as individuals, as countries and as corporations if we want to be winners in the global economy of the twenty-first century?*

It's very clear what individuals should be doing. If you want to be a successful worker/earner in the twenty-first century, you are going to have to have a lot more skills and education than you had to have in the nineteenth or the twentieth century. And where that becomes particularly important is the bottom 60 percent of the workforce. If you look at that part of the workforce in the United States, their wages have fallen about 20 percent from where they were 20 years ago, and they're going to continue to fall as long as that part of the workforce has the education and work skills that it currently has.

So as societies we have to decide whether we are going to invest in the education and skills of our workforce, and whether we are going to create an environment where a skill and training program can pay off. In both Europe and the United States, we're so busy fighting inflation and keeping growth rates low that you couldn't make an education program pay off even if it was the right education program. In the United States, wages are falling for males at all education levels, including people with PhDs. There is no education you can give a person that will put him or her on an 'up escalator'. And if you put them on the escalator that is going down, you just knock somebody off the bottom of it a little bit faster, which means that you haven't done any net good to society.

These are not problems that are solved with magic silver bullets. They are solved by doing a series of things that have to be done in concert in order to reestablish 'up escalators' for most of the workforce. But that is something governments have to do. And they're so wrapped up taking care of the elderly that they have no time or money to worry about anybody else.

If you believe that we're entering an era of 'brainpower' industries, then there are two things which countries have to focus on. One: **Are you building your skill base?** And by skill base I mean everything from PhDs down to skilled production workers. And two: **Are you making the right investments in research and development?** So that you're building your knowledge base, in order to compete in some of these key future industries.

Korea is a country whose per capita GNP is somewhere between 30 and 40 percent that of the Netherlands, but it's putting more money into research and development—as a percentage of its GNP—than is the Netherlands. So the Koreans are committed to making the investment in both skills and knowledge, whereas some European countries are and some aren't. If you take a country like Spain, which is about the same size as South Korea in terms of people, it invests just a very small fraction of what the Koreans are investing in R&D.

Corporations, of course, have a different mindset. They are clearly becoming global much faster than any governments are. If I'm a corporation, I'm not going to worry about the UK. If the UK doesn't give me what I want, I just move. I'm not going to put my time and energy into changing it. I've got better things in life to do and if there's a better educated worker in China than there is in Sussex then I'll go to China. Let Sussex worry about its own education system.

One of the places to start is with international benchmarking, where you basically have to say, 'Let's honestly look at ourselves and determine what we do well and what we do badly. And where we do things badly, let's figure out what the world standard is, and then find some way to commit to reaching that standard.' That's very easy to say but it's very tough to do. **"**

Lester Thurow

Lester C Thurow is a leading world expert on economic issues and an important shaping voice in US economic policy. He is professor of management and economics at Massachusetts Institute of Technology and a former dean of MIT's Sloan School of Management. A graduate of Williams College, Thurow received his PhD at Harvard University, and taught there in the 1960s after a term as staff economist on President Lyndon Johnson's Council of Economic Advisers. He is the author of several bestselling books on global economic issues, and has served on the editorial board of the New York Times, *as a contributing editor for* Newsweek *and as a member of* Time *magazine's board of economists. He also appears regularly on television on the* Nightly Business Report.

Recommended reading

The Future of Capitalism: How today's economic forces will shape tomorrow's world (1996) US: William Morrow/UK: Nicholas Brealey.
Head to Head: The coming economic battle among Japan, Europe and America (1994) US: William Morrow/UK: Nicholas Brealey.

"Corporations are starting to take on the complexity of biological systems. And at that point, they become out of our control."

THE NEW BIOLOGY OF BUSINESS

Kevin Kelly

"   FOR A LONG time, people have talked about institutions and organizations as if they were biological, as if they were a living organism. So the notion of the biological metaphor itself is not new. What is new is the exactness with which we can now fill in that metaphor, which at one time was just poetry. We now have some very exact and very advanced sciences that make the biological metaphor a lot more useful to us. And a lot more profitable.

An example of how we can better understand our organizations as biological organisms is by looking at the way very distributed systems work in nature. I refer in my book *Out of Control* to something I call 'hive mind', which is shorthand for the larger dynamic that can emerge from a whole mess of very small dynamics, like the bees in a hive, without the bees even being aware of a larger dynamic occurring.

Adam Smith's whole notion of the invisible hand is another example of that. What changes Adam Smith's understanding into one that is more biological is some of the research that scientists are now doing into very complex systems in computer software. They can see, for example, how the elements in these systems, which often appear to be very free and *laissez faire*, actually have very different properties than we would imagine, and when given enough room and time, they begin to congeal into something that from all appearances resembles a living organism.

So in understanding a business or a corporation as a living entity, the kind of things we want to ask ourselves are: How does an organization adapt over time? And how can we bring in some of the specific things that scientists know about adaptation in the living world and apply them to a business?

The exciting thing that we discover is that there is a great fit between what happens in the natural world and what happens in complex organizational relationships. We begin to see how some of the principles of ecology, for instance the interactions between, say, a dragonfly and a frog and duckweed, can be very, very powerful when we bring them into the world of business.

What this is telling us is that, rather than understanding businesses using a sort of industrial model—as little production lines, as self-contained entities that are mechanical in their operation—we will have to start understanding them more like an ecology of organisms.

The old models don't work any more, because of the increasing complexity of our human-made artifacts. And by artifacts I mean the things that we produce, like appliances and gadgets as well as institutions and processes. These are all things that humans make. And all of these things are becoming increasingly complex. From VCRs to accounting and tax systems, to institutions and corporations, these are all becoming so complex that they are starting to take on the complexity of biological systems. And at that point, they take on the kind of complexity that is basically ungovernable and unmanageable by a mechanical mindset. It's just too complex to control in a linear way.

What happens is that the increasing complexity allows these institutions and these artifacts to acquire some of their own inertia or agenda. So they become a little bit out of our control. Yet that 'out-of-controlness' is something that we can use, because in fact what we often want from the things we make is that they can run on their own, and that we don't have to babysit them so much. In a certain sense, we want to have houses and cars and even factories that in some ways can run themselves and repair themselves and maintain themselves, without us having to think about controlling them at every single step.

So it is inevitable that, as we make things more and more complex, they will become increasingly out of our control. And this 'out of controlness' has two sides. On the one side, it is something that is quite scary for us. Something we need to be careful about. But on the other side, it is something that we can use.

Resolving complexity into simplicity

Right now, technology is our culture. I define technology as anything that humans make, which is very abstract. Even a system like double-entry bookkeeping is a kind of technology; it's like a software program developed by the monks of Europe. Anything that we make is basically technology. And more and more of the world is being remade or made by humans. In other words, what we are moving to is a world in which the things that we make resemble biological entities, and at the same time we're using technology more and more to try to engineer the biological entities that we know about. So the two are converging, and things in general are drifting toward the biological state and towards complexity. Technology is something that is continuing to shape us, just as we shape the technology. It goes both ways.

The curious thing about technology is the way it resolves complexity into simplicity. Let's take a tomato. A tomato is in a very abstract sense a kind of technology—not in the sense of my vocabulary which defines technology as being human made; it's not human made at the moment, although it is increasingly becoming so because we are fiddling with its genes—but in the sense that a tomato is made up of very complex processes that are all integrated and which work very well. So it's something very parallel to technology. Yet when we look at a tomato, it seems very simple to us. It's easy to pick. We can hold it in our hand. It has a very bounded identity. But, obviously, if we tried to invent a tomato from scratch, it would be impossibly complex. So most of the things that we think of as simple are actually not very simple behind the scenes. They are very complex. But biological 'technology', for all its complexity, makes things appear to be simple.

What I would say about human-made technology is that there has been this reaction against it as being dreadful and very inhuman. To a certain extent that criticism is correct, because the technology of the 1950s, say up until the 1960s or 1970s, was in fact very stupid, very brutal, very industrial. In a sense it was still mechanical. It was not really fitted to the human scale.

But the prospect of having a 'biologicalized' technology is that we allow technology to be smarter, more lifelike, more fitted to our human scale and habits. And when it does that, it appears to us to be simple. It appears to fit us. So we are relieved of all that unnecessary complexity, although, in fact, behind the scenes, it is very, very complex indeed. It is more complex than ever. But it fits and adapts to the way we are. And that is the great promise of technology.

Right now, industrial technology is not very friendly to humans. But it doesn't have to be that way. **We can actually make technology much more friendly, but the way we do that is by giving it biological complexity.**

For example, technology makes it possible for us to put more complex information and more intelligence into our products. This not only increases their value but it also makes them a lot friendlier to use. Technology also enables us to put more complexity and more intelligence into the design and the manufacturing process, allowing adaptation to happen, which means that we get customized and personalized products. So in a sense, this is a new frontier. And it's raising both product design and process design to far higher levels, as we strive to put biological complexity into the things we make.

Organizational networks

The natural organizing metaphor for complexity is something that resembles a network. It is certainly the generic model for biology. So the new metaphor is to assemble organizations in a biological manner which means to use networks. The idea is that there are hierarchies of dependence and hierarchies of interaction and that's one of the attributes of biological models.

The trouble with the whole networking thing is that it's a little fuzzy. Just defining networks is tough. An old-boy network isn't the same kind of network as a network of neurons. There aren't even any real mathematical models of networks. So as a metaphor, it's certainly a very useful thing for trying to understand structures and interrelationships, but it's difficult to define what networks actually are.

Essentially a network is a decentralized organism that has no hard boundaries, that has no center. There's no head. There's nothing essentially in charge. And the causes of things are not linear, since it's very hard to tell what causes what.

In the old Greek, classical industrial model, A causes B causes C causes D. So the task for philosophers and for others was to determine what the prime cause was in that chain. For example, you can figure that out for a clock. But you can't figure that out for a meadow, or for most networked things like intelligence or living organisms. Because there, what you have is A causes B causes C causes D, but then D causes A. So you have this circular causality—a sort of self-causation—or what I call the field of causes, rather than a linear cause. **And that's why, when you have a network, you have this sense of not being in control. You have a sense of uncertainty, a sense of interdependency, a sense even of relativity.** It's something that is increasingly permeating our entire culture.

In a way, it parallels Alvin Toffler's 'Third Wave'. First, we went through the agricultural phase, which had a kind of traditional wisdom that was more case based: if you see this, then do this; if A then B. Then there was the industrial age, which had the Greek logic of looking at causality and observation and experiment. Things could be reduced to a very logical line. But what we are moving into now is a sort of ecological era, in which things are arranged in networks. And a neo-biological civilization, in which you have a field of causality, a circle of causality. You have things like the uncertainty principle, which is based on relativity. You have things like hypertext, which is basically another type of network—it's literature in a network, where you navigate through a text of your own choice. You assemble your own meaning.

➤ *What effect is this producing in business corporations?*

The business landscape is going through some important changes. The main point to understand is that we are moving away from monolithic, vertical, homogenized institutions, to extremely decentralized, extremely distributed, heterogeneous and flattened organizations. Networks, in other words. Specifically this would mean organizations that are spread out very wide, geographically. Organizations that have a different kind of bigness, meaning that they may be global in impact—and maybe even global in revenue scale—but maybe not employing as many people as an industrial-sized corporation would. And it means organizations that are bound together, not by geography, but by information; by very intense and very fast flows of information that flood through this web of distributed parts.

In this new kind of organization, there is an increased blurriness and an increased uncertainty about who is actually part of the corporation, and who is not. In other words, there are lots of consultants. Lots of subcontractors. Lots of part-time people. Even the customers may at times feel that they are part of the company. There is kind of a blurring between the customers and the employees.

At *Wired* magazine, for instance, we have subscriptions—and, of course, most traditional magazines have subscriptions, at least in the United States. So for *Wired's* staff, that means that subscriptions have to be kept and maintained, the data has to be entered, and then mailing labels are sent out by a very large corporation in the Midwest that all magazines use for that task. It's very expensive. It's cumbersome and awkward. And it's not a very efficient process. So what *Wired* is trying to do is to have the subscribers run the subscription department themselves. They access *Wired* electronically, on line, on the Web or whatever, and they type in their address, because they know their address best, and they have a lot more practice in typing it in than we do, so they get it right. And they maintain their own subscription. They fill it out. They renew it. They pay for it. At that point, the question is: are the subscribers working for *Wired*? Because they are now doing what *Wired* used to pay people to do.

Similarly, when you go on to the Federal Express Web and you start tracking your own package, you are now doing what Federal Express used to do, what they paid people to do. So there is almost a kind of biological messiness or fuzziness that we are beginning to see in organizations. And we'll see that fuzziness extend throughout the entire organism so that it becomes more like an ecology—where things don't have such definite borders. The corporation will become a web, a network of nodes, of people who come and go, maybe assemble for a project and then go on. People who have different contracts and relationships. So it will be a society of little work centers, little nodes that act as the distributed cores of the organization. And, on a grander scale, it will be one big web that extends out to include everybody with whom the company interacts in the market: employees, suppliers, dealers, customers. They all become part of the company's collective being. In a sense, they *are* the company.

Hive mind

As organizations become more distributed and more decentralized, there has to be much more reliance on a bottom-up kind of control—emergent control—like you have in a flock of birds, or a swarm of bees.

I was interviewing Steve Jobs, who, of course, was the main architect of the Apple Macintosh computer and who created the Next computer, which is probably still the best desktop computer ever made. We were talking about the recipes for making a superb organization that can generate ideas and wealth in the new economy. And he was basically saying that you hire people who are 20 times better than anyone else around, and you gather them and you let them do what they want. So, in that sense, there is much more of letting the bottom control things than we had in the industrial model.

But there are several things that need to be said about that. Anyone who knows Steve Jobs knows that there is also a tremendous leadership role that he is playing. Therefore, what I am not saying is that, in these new corporations, you just let the bottom decide what to do, with no leadership at all. Because we want organizations to be more than just beehives, going wherever they want to and doing whatever they want to. We want organizations to do certain things. To go in certain directions. So there is still a role for leadership. But it's a different kind of leadership. **It's not a leadership that is controlling things. It's a leadership that is suggesting or pointing to a particular destination. It is envisioning or trying to anticipate the future.**

So rather than trying to steer the organization, it is actually trying to look ahead and describe the view coming down, and then trying to articulate that so that the bottom understands it, and then the bottom can steer towards it.

We see that happening in computer models of very complex systems that can adapt. One of the main functions that they evolve very quickly is this look-ahead capability. So if we apply that principle to the new kind of business organization which has to be highly adaptive, what it means is that the higher level of the organization has to try to anticipate the future. The bottom can steer, but only if it has a clear vision of where it wants to go.

Network economics

I also talk in my book about network economics, which is a very simple idea. Basically, computers are over. All of the effects that our society can expect from stand-alone computing machines have already happened. Even desktop computers are over. There will be no more significant consequences from them, even if they got really small.

It's like the motor. Back in the early years of the twentieth century, people talked about 'home motors' and they had advertisements for home motors. Their vision was that we would have these great big motors at home, and that was part of the industrial revolution. But what actually happened is that motors became ubiquitous. They just dissolved into our environment. We now have motors in our wrist watches. We have motors in our cameras. We have motors everywhere, and we don't even know it.

Something similar will happen with computing. It will become ubiquitous. It will be everywhere. The real change—the thing that is reshaping the economy—and the revolution that we really find ourselves in, is not a computer revolution, but a communications revolution. We're talking about connecting everything in the world to everything else. That means that every artifact that we make will be embedded with some chip, some little sliver of dim intelligence, maybe only as smart as a bee or an ant. But all those pieces, some of them moving around and some stationary, will be connected, and will be communicating with each other. So the graph of the number of things that we make, and the graph of the numbers of things that are connected, will in the near future converge and meet, and everything we make will be connected to everything else. And that is the network. That is the Net, in the large sense that we talk about.

When I talk about the Net, I'm not talking about a lot of people sitting at their computers typing, although it includes that. I'm talking about every cash register in the world, every camcorder, every little sensor in the earth or on a farm, everything that is collecting data and sending data and throwing it into this membrane around the earth that is the Net. And that creates an entirely new environment, a sea of information and connection. And that web—that Net—is shifting our economics. Because it affects everything we do.

The foremost effect is what economists call 'the law of increasing returns'. I call it 'the fax effect'. It says very simply that if you have one telephone it is worth nothing. If you have a second telephone, the first phone is worth a little more. And with each further telephone, the value of my telephone increases. To such an extent that I become an evangelist for telephones; I want everyone to get a phone because that increases the value of my own phone. We saw the same thing with faxes. People went around saying, 'You should get a fax.' Why were they saying that? Because it increased the value of their own fax. The same is true of e-mail.

So we have a curious reverse of classical economics, which told us that the more there is of a particular thing, the less valuable that thing becomes. Like gold or diamonds, where scarcity increases value. **What we have now is that plenitude increases value, which is a complete turnaround.** And it's just one indication of the ways in which this new economy is very different from the industrial economy.

If plenitude increases value, then the way to wealth may actually be to give things away. In fact, we see this with Netscape, which is an on-line network-based product for the Web. The company gave away four million copies, and it is making a bundle. The way it makes money is that it gives away the client browser and it sells the server browser. It's like giving phones away, but selling the telephone switching network or the services. And this idea is very common. We see that with Shareware—people giving away software, and then selling the support for it, or the manuals.

So there are many very counter-intuitive things that just wouldn't work in an industrial economy. Imagine a corporation board meeting, somewhere in 1950, and a guy raises his hand and says: 'I have an idea. Let's just give away the first four million units of our product.' They would have kicked him out of the place.

Another important thing about the Net is that it's a planetary-sized copying machine, and anything you put on it will be copied. Trying to stop copying on the Net is impossible. You can't do it. So what you have to do is to let the copies flow, but then have other ways of getting paid for them. You have to separate the flow of revenue from the flow of copies. And that's going to be a big step.

In fact the music industry has some experience in that. For decades companies have been giving away copies of their music to radio stations. The more copies the better. And then the radio stations pay the authors or artists royalties on a kind of statistical basis. So that's an example of how to divorce the flow of revenue from the flow of copies.

In other words, the network economy is reshaping and revolutionizing every sector of business. Not just the way we distribute software—movies, music, books, magazines—but also things like financial services—instant cash, instant credit. It's everything. And the effect of the network economy is that it's allowing us to reconfigure the world to our specifications. So we get personal newspapers, video on demand, tailor-made music albums. The focus is on the individual.

▶ *How will the network economy affect the speed at which we do business?*

If you are not doing business in real time, you'll be dead. The network economy speeds up the whole velocity of money and information. Electronic money can be paid and deducted and billed in real time, and also in fractions of a penny—in units that are much smaller than we deal with right now. And information about customer purchases will also tend towards real time. All the big clothing manufacturers have electronic networks that link the cash registers in their chain stores around the world. As customers purchase items, the bar-code information is directed right back to the factory floor, so that the items are essentially reordered. They also have very complex networks that alert suppliers to the fact that they will be needing more jersey yarn to make the kind of sweaters that are being purchased at this very moment. This works in conjunction with things like electronic bidding for supplies from vendors, and sophisticated systems for warehousing, shipping and tracking the clothes. So it's essentially, like many other things, about information flow. And the faster that information can flow through the network, the better the customer is served.

Again, it goes back to the premise that in this new environment, competitive advantage is towards the nimble. And the ultimate extrapolation of that is when everything you do is in real time.

Virtual corporations

Virtual corporations are organizations in which, when you go to examine them, you find there is nobody home. There is just a skeletal shell of processes, and most of the work is being outsourced to other companies, who in turn often outsource some of that work to others. So if you tried to actually draw an organization chart it would be very hard, because it's not at all clear who is actually doing the work or owning the work. And there are numerous examples.

In my book, I give the example of a hypothetical car company that is basically outsourced the whole way. So there is this core group of 8 to 10 people who are overseeing a process, and they are outsourcing everything else: the accounting, the clerical work, of course the manufacturing of the car, the distribution and what not. And it turns out that there are actually a number of companies like that already. But the fact that they are virtual is sort of invisible. Even the Apple computer itself was originally made that way. Apple, when it first began, didn't make anything. It just designed the computer and everything else was hired out.

What allows this to happen at such a large scale today is the increased complexity of information processing and the low transactional cost of having information available from a distance. Things like better videoconferencing are going to lower the costs even further. And there are many other kinds of technologies that are facilitating this: accounting technologies, scheduling technologies, groupware. All of these are going to dismember or decentralize the work. They make it possible for people to work from a distance, and also to work for more than one company at a time. So organizations are going to become very distributed.

It's very hard to say how big these new kinds of corporations will be. It is certain that large companies, generating large revenues and employing significant numbers of employees, will continue to play a powerful role in the global economy. But it's also true that very small companies, with less than 100 people, or even less than 10 people, will have an equally global presence, and will also generate immense amounts of money.

What we are going to see is a global economy—a network economy—in which there will be a variety of large players and a variety of small players. And, again, this will depend on how you define the size of a company, because it's going to be very hard to tell where one organization actually ends and the next one begins.

I also think that there is a natural coalescing of a work team at around eight to a dozen people. Studies have shown from other groups—in expeditions, in the military and in start-ups—that that's somehow the essential number. We call it a 'strange attractor'. It's a number that works best. And it's one that allows communication to require very little overhead. I can see that as the limit beyond which people aren't as effective. Beyond that number you start to have overhead costs—which have been reduced, of course, and will continue to be reduced by the communication technology.

But I can imagine a world of cellular nodes of a dozen people, working on a project often on an ad hoc or temporary basis, and then reassembling in some time frame to become another node. So there is this web of very small teams.

Obviously there are limits to this, depending on the project you are working on, but a number of companies are trying to do this. Where we see it most, right now, is in Hollywood. Many people argue, and I tend to believe them, that **Hollywood acts as a model for tomorrow's huge corporations**. Because the big thing now is having project-based work. And in Hollywood, people come in for the project, or the film, and they assemble in teams, and they probably won't even have a permanent headquarters. They may actually be distributed in buildings throughout Burbank or wherever. They set up temporary offices of some sort and they make the film, which may last a couple of years, depending on their part in it. In fact, their part may only last a year. And then they disperse again to work on the next film, under a completely different arrangement. These are all professional people. And we're seeing more and more of that, even in high-tech industries. There's a multimedia project, or a chip project, for which people are assembled in that way, without permanent office space and without a permanent overseeing structure.

➤ *As organizations increasingly become networked with other organizations, do you think we are going to see the development of large business groups or guilds—rather like the Japanese Keiretsu, with their preferred suppliers and customers?*

I think we may see some groups developing. In fact, I looked into this at one time, because I wanted to see if there was a biological metaphor for what we see happening, and I looked for current literature on guilds in biology. There was a time when they thought there were guilds, but actually we don't see them very much in ecology. What I think we will see in the new economy will be more alliances and trading blocs. And I think there's even going to be a change in attitude to monopolies—like the whole fuss about Microsoft. Because I think a monopoly is just something that occurs very naturally. It may actually have a quicker lifecycle. And I think we are going to find that monopolies are sort of beneficial in some fashion or another.

In other words, all these things are going to be present. And this movement towards groupings—these trans-level groupings—is all part of what I call a different kind of bigness. It's a bigness that is very flat and wide, rather than vertical and monolithic.

In the old days, when we had a very static environment, you could go vertical and you could control the whole chain of value. The competitive advantage was in optimization, which is what industrial processes did. They optimized the daylights out of whatever they discovered that worked, and that's how they made wealth and that was their advantage. But when you have an environment like we do now, and like we'll increasingly have in the future—where things are changing and turning over very rapidly—the competitive advantage goes to those who are nimble, those who can adapt. And the structure for adaptation is invariably a network, because it is the least form-specific of forms. Adaptation requires this sort of distributed being.

There is an ecology of things. Gardeners know this. Any single organism is dependent on symbiotic things—little bacteria, or even parasites, at times which are preying on it, which often indirectly provide something that the organism needs. So it becomes almost impossible to isolate the organism from its environment. You can't even tell in an abstract sense where one begins and another one ends. Of course, there are boundaries. If it's a vegetable or a flower, you can hold the thing. But you can't have a bounded existence. You certainly can't thrive alone like that for very long.

So we look out of the window, and we see grasses and flowers and birds and bees, and they are all interconnected. They're all thriving off each other. And it's very unclear exactly who is supporting whom, or who is working for whom. In fact, you might say they are all working together.

The same is true today of corporations. What we are seeing is networks of strategic alliances and symbiotic partnerships, even symbiotic competitors working together. The borders between many industries are disappearing, and all we see instead is this kind of indefinite web of related organizations.

It's also a real principle of economics. The curious thing about open systems—called vivisystems—is that every additional new business that comes along actually creates the environment for another business to come. So rather than being a zero-sum game—where every new business causes some other old business to die—it's quite the opposite. The more businesses there are around, the more room there is for new businesses.

Again, this is very much like life, and nature, and biology. Every new bit of life actually creates a niche for yet more life. So this is another biological principle that we can apply to business: **you actually want more and more businesses, because that's better for business**.

Industrial ecology

In nature there is no waste. Nothing is thrown away. There's no such thing as garbage. The waste from one organism becomes the raw material for another. So if we could take that kind of ecological approach to industry, we could essentially eliminate problems like pollution, because the waste that is created by one process could be seen as raw material for another process.

Again, information technology allows the intelligent movement of this material, which has been the main bottleneck so far, because one process may have been creating some material that would be useful for another, but nobody knew about it. Then there's always been the economics of transporting it. But information and technology are now solving those problems.

In Denmark they are experimenting with a kind of embryonic industrial ecosystem. There's a networked community of different industries. including a cement factory, a gypsum board manufacturer, some greenhouses producing flowers, a waste-treatment plant and a steam-generating plant that provides the heat for the village. What happens is that most of the materials flow within that one little area. So the waste from the cement factory goes to the gypsum board manufacturer, and the excess heat from the manufacturing process is used to heat the greenhouses, and the waste from the village is treated and used for fertilizing the greenhouses. What you end up with is a very closed network, a closed circuit of different materials and energy flowing through this community. And from the outside, it looks like there's no waste. Because there is nothing coming out that has to be dumped or buried. So it's all very intelligent.

There's a similar kind of process going on in a metal-plating plant in Massachusetts, where they are adding intelligence to their processes by cleaning their own water after they use it. In the past, the water would flow into the factory from the rivers and they would use it and then let it flow out into the rivers again, or into the sea, with some heavy metals in it. Now, after the industrial process, they remove the impurities from the water, so that they have clean water to use again. This actually makes it purer than the water they were getting from the rivers, so apart from eventually saving money by using their own water, they are actually making a higher-quality product as well. And the heavy metals are not just extracted from the water, but really reclaimed, because they now use these materials again in some way. So there's no pollution. No waste.

This notion of recapturing all your materials and energy is called closed-loop manufacturing, because nothing comes outside the greater web of connections that you've made. It's now being used as a model for a lot of other processes, from steel, to chemicals, to all kinds of things. 3M has a big corporate project that is aimed at doing this within its own manufacturing factories. And it's entirely sensible. One wonders why this never happened before. But, in part, what is allowing this to happen now is that we have the technology to be able to measure things, to be able to move small quantities and to make it economically feasible by allowing these things to be matched with people who need those waste products.

> *Are you confident that industry can learn to work together with nature?*

I've been spending a lot of time thinking specifically about that question since I wrote *Out of Control*. I have a hunch that it can. And I've been trying out some of my reasoning, but the proof has yet to be seen, so I don't have it at my fingertips. It's just something that I intuitively feel is a real possibility.

There's a fundamental rift right now in our society between those who believe that nature and industry are enemies, and those who believe that the two can be compatible. I think that's an assumption that we as a people really haven't examined in the light of new technologies. We haven't considered that it might be possible to build a type of technology that would lead to a high standard of living—maybe even close to what the West enjoys now—for all people of the world, without further degrading natural habitats or natural species. It seems to be very difficult for many people to imagine how that could happen, but I don't see anything inherent in technology that would prevent it. Maybe it will be difficult to get from here to there, but it's not impossible.

One of the things that we are seeing with technology is that the more biological we make the processes, the safer they are for humans and for the environment. There is a tendency in general to make manufacturing processes less dangerous and less toxic. So there's the hope that as manufacturing becomes more intelligent—using less energy, less water and generating less toxic materials—it will be better for our habitat.

But that's just one part of the problem of nature and industry co-existing. There is a larger problem, which is the interface between natural habitats and civilization itself. Because what is not clear is the effects of our cities, and the towns and the roads that we build, which right now cut into the places where animals and plants live.

I think that, ultimately, industry will inevitably adopt a biological mindset, and essentially biological ways of doing things. Because nature teaches us how to manage our increasingly complex inventions, our organizations and processes. It teaches us how to do a better job by using fewer materials. And it teaches us that we cannot just push the natural world aside to make room for our industries and our civilization, without facing some tragic consequences down the line.

➤ *What thought would you want to leave with businesspeople as they rethink their organizations for the twenty-first century?*

Most organizations and most organisms are built to increase and optimize fitness: to find out what they do well, and then to do it better. But in this new economy—this new landscape that's very rapidly changing—the most important thing is not to optimize what you do, but to find out and decide what you should be doing. In other words, to explore this landscape, to find out where you should really be and to make sure that you are climbing the tallest peak, not just a false summit, to use the jargon of biologists.

What this means is that you're always pushing up and up, and you have the apparatus that's optimizing everything you do, but if you get stuck on a small mountain, you get to the top and look around and you find you're on the wrong mountain. A mile away is a mountain that's twice as tall.

This presents us with two major challenges. One is to learn how to search the landscape very widely, and to make sure we find the tallest mountain to climb—that we find the right thing to do. And having done that, if we find ourselves on top of a false summit, which we are probably going to do more often, we have to understand, as institutions and as corporations, how to devolve, how to go down. In other words, we've got to go down the mountain, and cross that desert, and come up on the tallest peak. And that's called letting go. That's called killing a product at its peak.

That's basically taking mainframes and ditching them right at the point when they are most profitable, and getting into PCs. That's taking the decision, when your revenue stream is entirely silver-based film, to let go and do things digitally. So it's doing all kinds of unthinkable things. But that's the landscape we are talking about.

Those, then, are the two messages: exploring widely and finding out the right thing to do, rather than just doing things right; and second, being able to let go of success at the peak, and reverse engines and devolve. These are very, very tough steps to undertake, because they go against the grain for almost any organization. They are dangerous; they are hard. But as a biological model, this can be a great help to us in understanding how to deal with the new business landscape. And that understanding is going to make all the difference between success and failure in the twenty-first century. **99**

Kevin Kelly

Kevin Kelly is the executive editor of Wired *magazine, and a member of the* Global Business Network. *Formerly publisher and editor of the influential West Coast journal* Whole Earth Review (WER), *Kelly has helped to launch a number of pioneering ideas for weaving technology into our culture. These include the Hackers' Conference, the virtual reality Cyberthon, and the WELL, an on-line community used as a model for the expanding Internet population. His book* Out of Control *is about the dawn of a new technological era in which humanmade systems (including corporations) are reaching the complexity of living entities, and where biology becomes the best metaphor for understanding how to control our world.*

Recommended reading

Out of Control: The new biology of machines, social systems and the economic world (1995) US: Addison-Wesley/UK: Fourth Estate.

INDEX